O'RYAN'S LAW

A Novel by

MICHAEL PATRICK MURRAY

1stBooks - rev. 11/05/01

Love objects are not frequently come by nor
easily put aside.

Distance is only a formality. The mind takes
no real notice of it.

Saul Bellow

Prologue

Lake O'Neill had a special enchantment that warm September night in 1964. Chrissy Long had just become engaged to David Hall, a Naval R.O.T.C. midshipman. David was winding up a summer cruise as a Marine Corps option candidate at Camp Pendleton, California, a sprawling Marine base housing some thirty five thousand Marines. The base seemed far removed from the deadly training for war that was served daily over terrain covering almost twenty miles north and south a few miles above San Diego, and some twenty miles east and west at its widest point stretching from the greatest beaches in California to the boundaries of the Cleveland National Forest.

For Chrissy Long Camp Pendleton wasn't just a Marine base that special night. It was the most romantic spot on earth. David had asked Chrissy to be his wife over dinner at the Del Mar Officer's club two hours earlier. Lake O'Neill added to the romance with moonlight spreading a magic aura across the path they walked hand and hand as the warm breeze gently rippled the water along the banks of the lake. Chrissy rejoiced in the feeling that she and David were alone in their own, wonderful world of love far removed from the violence inherent in Marine Corps training which emphasized that a Marine's primary combat mission is to close with the enemy and destroy him. David Hall wanted to be a Marine Officer and Chrissy shared his pride in the Corps.

I will be a good Marine wife, she thought smiling. Her mind's role lasted but a brief moment.

******

"Hey squid. Where'd 'ya get the pussy?"

"What did you say?"

"David what's the matter?"

"What 'ya doing with a fuckin' squid, pretty little lady?"

"Knock it off," David admonished, addressing three Marines who were sitting off the path on a sloping bank leading to the water's edge.

"Fuck you, pelican," the closest Marine retorted. "Come and sit with us, blondie, and we'll show you what real men are all about. Probably have no idea hanging around with a fag sailor."

"That's enough," David interjected. "I want all three of you to stand up and hand over your I.D. cards. You are on report."

They stood as directed. And then killed David Hall with kicks and blows.

Then they each raped Chrissy Long. After they finished, they ran away leaving her battered and bleeding on the ground where she had walked so happily a short time before.

CHAPTER 1

Saturday, September 5, 1964

The main bar in the Los Angeles *Ambassador Hotel* had three things worth noting that summer afternoon. Sean Fitzpatrick O'Ryan, a hard charging lawyer specializing in criminal law; his best friend, Ed Tabor, a handsome Marine Sergeant Major who could pose for Greek statutes, and a challenging concoction of Wild Turkey and Southern Comfort which the bartender swears was invented right there. This particular version of legalized white lightning had been recommended by the barkeep, which was the only reason Sean an Ed gave it a try. Two swallows were enough to convince them they would be switching to beer on the second round.

Ed made a survey of the bar and said casually to Sean, "Don't look now, but I think the redhead on the other side is undressing you with her eyes." It was Ed's way of setting the scene and setting up Sean at the same time because Ed was interested in the brunette with the redhead and was subtly staking a claim. The lovely pair were exceptional even for Los Angeles which is famous for its attractive women.

They had slipped away from a wedding reception in the ballroom looking for some diversion in the bar. Being labor day weekend the bar was empty except for Ed and Sean, and the bartender, a skinny, little guy with a Hitler mustache.

Sean knew Ed was schmoozing, but the redhead was truly smashing, and if Ed wanted the brunette, then what the hell. After sending over a couple of drinks, Sean followed in his usual, never shy fashion and introduced himself.

"Hi, my name's Sean. That's *Sean* as in *Shawn*, which is the way the Irish pronounce names they spell differently. It's an old Gaelic tradition. That handsome guy over there is Ed." Ed waved, but didn't come over, and wasn't going to until Sean had completed the preliminary maneuvers. That's how you get to be a Sergeant Major, you carefully assess the terrain and situation before you launch your attack.

"Hi, Sean," the redhead said displaying a set of beautifully capped white teeth. "I'm Joy and this is Gerry."

Gerry flashed a similar display of even white teeth. No doubt a couple of dentists were enjoying a holiday in Las Vegas with the money they had earned on these smiles.

"If I had to guess, I'd say you are actresses," Sean said with a big grin revealing his own fine smile.

"Aspiring at this point, Sean, but still hopeful," Joy responded.

"Well, I don't know how good you can act, but I'll stipulate you can, and it appears you are half way there with your looks. I guess that's the first step in opening the door unless your father is a big star or owns the studio."

"I wish it were that easy," Gerry said with good humor. "We do get in a lot of doors. It's getting out that's the problem most of the time. It's the test before the reading that causes most of the headaches, if you know what I mean."

"I've heard the rumors but I thought the casting couch was out by this time. Apparently not. But I'm happy to report that neither Ed nor I are in the movie business and we won't make any promises to get you into pictures. On the other hand if you're going to be around for a while, we could get better acquainted. Ed and I are meeting an old friend in a minute and we have some serious talking to do, but I thought if you were still here when we get done, we could catch dinner or something."

"Well, yes and no, Sean. We're supposed to be at the wedding reception in the ballroom, but it's pretty dull. How much schmaltz can you handle after a while?" Joy replied. "But I'll tell you what, we'll pop back in after a bit and maybe you guys will be done with your business and we can see what happens."

"Sounds good. Look forward to seeing you later then," Sean said with an air of sincerity which he hoped disguised his lusty interest.

"Before you go, Sean, what's the rest of your wild Irish name in case we have to page you?" Joy asked.

"O'Ryan. Sean Fitzpatrick O'Ryan. The Fitzpatrick is from my Mother's maiden name. And you can page me anytime," Sean added with a smile as he moved back to the other side of the bar.

Just then Harry Dixon walked in and presented a striking picture against the richly appointed wood and brass that made the *Ambassador* bar a warm and inviting place. Harry was six feet one, the same height as Sean, but weighed some thirty pounds heavier than Sean's one hundred eighty five. Not that Harry was overweight; on the contrary he was solid like Ed. They both exuded an aura of strength and power, although for powerfully built men, deep down they were a surprisingly gentle breed.

The only difference between Ed and Harry wasn't in their good looks, but rather their color. Ed was tanned by the sun from days in the field as the Sergeant Major of a Marine infantry regiment. Harry was tanned from birth, with ancestral roots proudly running back to his African heritage. His great-great grandfather was born to a slave sold by renegade blacks to the Dutch and then to American traders after being unceremoniously captured from a village in what is now Southwest Africa. Harry's family history illustrates how so much good is often fashioned from outrage.

Ed and Sean greeted Harry with genuine affection. He was their friend and a man to whom Sean owed a couple of lives for the times he put his own on the line for him in Korea in 1950. "Good to see you, Marine. How ya doing?" Sean said giving Harry a hug and a handshake.

"Up 'till yesterday, all right, Sean. And seeing you guys lifts the weight a bit," Harry replied trying to smile through obvious concern over the reason why he had called late night and asked if they could get together this afternoon.

"Well, whatever it is, we'll take care of it, so no sweat. What will you have to drink? We are trying a real gut buster. Not sure I could recommend it, however. I don't know what they call it. I hear that it makes Janis Joplin happy mixing Southern Comfort with Wild Turkey, but either way it couldn't help her singing. And I use the word singing loosely."

"Holy, shit. You really drinking that stuff. I'll stick with beer, thanks anyway," Harry said looking dubious about even smelling the mixture Sean extended to him.

"I think you're right Harry, we'll both join you in a switch to Michelob. Let's sit down at a table and get to the heart of the matter so we can have a visit afterwards. May as well attack the problem head on and get it out of the way so we can have a pleasant reunion," Sean stated with confidence as he steered Ed and Harry to a table fairly removed from the bar area for privacy.

Ed went back to pick up the beers. Harry started to sound out the problem the minute they sat down. "My sister Esther has a son in the Corps. Name's Lee Johnson, a Corporal stationed at Camp Pendleton. Used to be with the 1st Division but got transferred to the Base to play basketball. He's a damn fine athlete, but kind of a hard case. We thought the Corps could help him with an attitude problem he's had since his father died five years ago, but it doesn't look like it turned out as we hoped."

"He must have been doing all right, Harry, if he made Corporal. We don't give away NCO stripes, as you well know, not even at that level," Ed remarked.

"Well, that's right, Ed, at least I thought maybe he was working it out. The Corps was sort of a father figure to him, and he chose the Marines because of me. I convinced him that a colored kid could make it in the Corps as good as any of the services, particularly if he was willing to be a hard charger," Harry replied.

"So what happened?" Sean asked. "Obviously something went wrong."

"Wrong is the word. Terribly wrong," Harry noted sadly. "Esther got a call from him yesterday and he said he was locked up in the Brig at Camp Pendleton charged with rape and murder, but he couldn't give her any details." Harry's voice was filled with anxiety. "Esther was damn near hysterical when she called me. I contacted the Brig but the duty warden couldn't tell me any more than Lee had told his Mother. He was apprehended late Thursday night and confined for rape and murder. That's all any of us know and naturally Esther is worried to death and I am worried and pissed off."

"What can Ed and I do to help?"

3

"I appreciate the offer, Sean, and frankly that's why I asked you to meet me. I know Ed can find out a lot on the side, but the Base is buttoned up until Tuesday since Monday is Labor Day. I also need your help as a lawyer. I don't know any other criminal lawyers and I'm aware of the reputation you are building working with Jake Rogers who everybody says is the best there is. So I need your legal skills for my nephew. Esther is my only sister and she is hurting. I've got to get help."

"Hell, you got it; you know that," Sean replied reassuringly.

"The problem is I don't have much savings," Harry added, "and I know Jake's firm is big time and it's gonna cost a bundle, but I'll take care of your fee if it takes forever."

"Listen, old friend, legal fees are the last thing I am concerned about. Christ, you're not only my friend, I also can't ever forget that you saved my life twice. How am I supposed to put a price on that? Neither of us will be worrying about fees, you got that Marine?"

"I read you, Sean, and I'm damn grateful. But the money issue is only on hold. We'll work something out, okay?"

"Okay, but don't sweat it. Now tell me. What's Lee's serial number, if you know, and his unit.

"I've got it here, Sean. His serial number is E27851473, and his unit is Headquarters and Service Company, Headquarters Battalion, Marine Corps Base, Camp Pendleton. He's a Corporal as I said, and the only Lee Johnson in the brig as of yesterday according to the duty warden."

"It's as good as done, old buddy, and since you don't know anymore than we do, there's nothing any of us can do until Tuesday. You know he can't have visitors except immediate family and his counsel. Since I am not his lawyer until he accepts me, I couldn't see him until Tuesday at the earliest. Also there is no bail in the military system, so the only place your nephew can be is in the brig right now."

Sean then added, "Even if there were a system of bail, you can bet he wouldn't get any because of the gravity of the charges. In any event I will call a friend of mine at Pendleton before Tuesday morning and see what I can find out. I'm sure Ed can make some discreet inquiries as well and will keep us up to speed."

"Damn, I appreciate this you guys. You haven't changed a bit since we were freezing our asses off at Chosin. I knew you'd come through. You always did. No wonder Ed's a Sergeant Major and still keeping the Corps on an even keel. And you, Sean, hell I remember when you were a brand new second lieutenant, scared as shit and more scared that someone would find out. Now you are a Major in the Marine Corps Reserve and fighting the good fight in the criminal courts instead of the bloody trails of Korea," Harry said with genuine pride.

Sean suggested they put the business of Harry's nephew on the back burner for the time being and catch up on the old days when they were all together in Korea. But he assured Harry that he and Ed would do everything they could to take care of his nephew. Joy and Gerry came back a couple of times, but gave up hope that three Marines swapping war stories were ever going to wind it up, so Joy scribbled a note on a bar napkin that said maybe some other time, if interested. She added her phone number. Sean excused himself briefly and walked over to Joy to let her know that he and Ed were definitely interested and promised to call real soon.

Ed was pleased they had salvaged contact with two new faces, although he already had a number of women in his stable. Sean also had a book full of numbers, including a special one, Susan Sullivan, with whom he was substantially involved. Nevertheless, it was good to have opportunities and neither he nor Ed were dedicated to monogamy. AIDS hadn't been heard of, and maybe not even invented by nature at that time, so safe sex meant avoiding VD and pregnancy, both of which were curable. Monogamous relationships did not appear to be a major necessity in 1964.

Sean convinced Harry to have dinner with him and Ed so they could enjoy a long over due reunion of three warriors who had survived over a year of combat in Harry Truman's police action in '50 and '51. They drove to *Lowry's* and, over a lingering dinner, reminisced about Korea and how they came to know each other.

CHAPTER 2

Seated in a comfortable booth at *Lowry's*, Harry noted how different the ambiance was from the last time the three of them had shared a meal in the cold of Korea. That meal, consisting of uncooked C-rations, left a lot to be desired.

"I often wondered if we were going to make it out," Harry mused, "much less be back together some thirteen years later in fancy digs like this."

"I did too, along with a lot of other doubts," Sean replied. "But it's a funny thing, I didn't worry about getting killed so much as I did being maimed. Just didn't want to come back all fucked up, especially in the sex department. I could see myself holding a grenade to my chest before I would let the docs cut off my arms or legs. And especially my balls."

"Amen, brother," Harry said and then added, "I remember how the three of us met, but Sean, I don't recall you ever mentioning how you decided on the Marine Corps rather than the other services."

"Actually the decision was easy once I decided to drop out of college for a while," Sean answered. "If I was going into the military I wanted the challenge I perceived the Marine Corps to offer. My Dad had been in the Army in World War II, but it didn't seem as glamorous as the Corps, at least that's the impression I got from reading a lot of gung ho Marine Corps history. I enlisted in the summer of 1949 when I found myself falling below the poverty level after my second year at UCLA.

Being restless and in need of a change from the deprived life style I was living since my arrival in Los Angeles fresh out of Chicago in 1947, in June of '49 I enlisted in a Marine officer program available to men who had at least two years of college. The Marine Corps made me a second lieutenant after ten weeks at Quantico. Then they kept me and the rest of my class hidden away for another nine months in The Basic School, way off in the hinterlands of Quantico to make us real officers and gentlemen. By the spring of 1950, I was ready to launch as an infantry platoon commander at my new duty station at Camp Pendleton."

Sean paused for a moment and then related those early days as a young officer fresh out of training in May 1950. He had stopped in Chicago on leave to attend his sister Margaret's wedding. Margaret was three years older but light years wiser. They had fought as kids, mostly over forgotten things, but Sean never lost his respect for her nor his genuine admiration of her strength and character. When she married a fine Irishman one spring morning in Saint Bridgets Catholic Church, Sean felt confident that her marriage would survive even in those changing times. Margaret was an Irish rock in the true tradition of Celtic women.

Sean told Ed and Harry about his first real love named Jessica McGuire, who he had called while he was home, and how pleased he was that she had consented

6

to a kind of date. She had insisted it could only be for lunch since Sean had treated her not too kindly when they broke up three years earlier before he left for California. Jessica was his genuine love, but she was sixteen and he seventeen when he went away, so there wasn't any hope at that point.

Jessica chose the *Palmer House* rather than an old favorite, the *Blackhawk Restaurant*, where she and Sean had a fight over dinner their last night together.

"You look handsome in your uniform," Jessica said. "It looks good with your light brown hair and blue eyes. I think you will be gray very young Sean, like most Irishmen, but it'll look distinguished on you."

"Thanks, Jessica, just what I needed. I'm twenty years old and you are turning me gray."

"Turnabout may be fair play. You gave me gray hair when I was only sixteen," Jessica laughed.

"What the hell, you know why I had to leave, and it had nothing to do with you."

"I know Sean, you had to chase your dreams. And while this may be a blow to your ego, in time I got over you. Well...sort of got over you. I guess I'll always love you but I couldn't wait forever. I'm engaged you know."

"Engaged? No I didn't know. When? And more importantly, why?"

"Because it's time, and if I waited for you we'd both be old and gray," Jessica said with deliberate mischief.

"What the hell am I supposed to say?" Sean demanded.

"Nothing, just be happy for me, and stop looking like somebody ran off with your girl. I'm not your girl. I wanted to be, but that was a long time ago when we were much too young and you weren't anymore ready for commitment than you are now. I think they wrote the song for you about loving the girl you're near when you're not near the girl you love."

"Jessica, how can you say that?" Sean protested, but without conviction.

"It's true, Sean, and you know it. But I'll tell you what, commit to me right now, and take me with you and marry me and I'll give up this other guy."

Jessica knew how to get to Sean. Irish girls are not reluctant to speak directly. She knew that marriage was the last thing he was thinking about and commitment to one woman was a concept he wasn't ready to embrace, and maybe never would. There wasn't anything left to say.

"I think you know I can't do that," Sean responded wistfully. "You win and I'm grudgingly happy for you."

"Thank you, Sean. Now let's talk about anything else while we enjoy this beautiful dining room." And they did, for a couple of hours recalling all the dopey things they did in high school, but not letting themselves slip into a *what might have been* maudlin mood.

After a long, lingering lunch, Sean dropped Jessica off at her home, and he wondered if he would ever see her again. He remembered when he had left for

California the first time back in '47, the day after their argument at the *Blackhawk*. He hadn't thought she would come to Union Station to say goodbye as he prepared to leave on the Santa Fe *El Capitan* for Los Angeles. But he believed he had caught a brief glimpse of her standing back in the shadows at the end of the platform as the train moved slowly away from all of their yesterdays.

Three years later, he had to leave again, once more without Jessica. After another tearful goodbye with his saintly Irish mother, he flew out to San Diego and then bussed up to Camp Pendleton to take up his duties with an infantry platoon.

"I see you had a little of the good life being stationed at Pendleton," Harry said with a big grin, "a grunt in the daytime and a stud at night."

"You got that right, Harry, and I'll admit that my brief stay in Southern California was delightful, particularly liberty in Laguna Beach. But the good life came to an end on June 25, 1950, that big day when ninety thousand North Korean troops crossed the 38th parallel into South Korea. 6500 of us jarheads became part of Brigadier General Eddie Craig's Regimental Combat Team. We later called it the 1st Provisional Marine Brigade. This was not just a rumor of war, but a bona fide call to arms, and most of us were pretty much unprepared. But like Marines have been doing since 1775, we did what we were told. This meant going to Korea."

Sean recounted how the Brigade had landed in early August 1950, and immediately took up a position in a sector which was part of the Pusan perimeter. Earlier the North Koreans had been kicking everybody's ass and pushed through most of South Korea which was in grave danger of collapsing completely.

"I want to tell you," Sean emphasized, "things had really turned to shit in those days. The fucking peacetime U.S. Army had been thrown into Korea after living high on the hog in Japan and got clobbered royally up to the time we arrived. But I've got to give those bastards credit, they made some truly heroic stands, although they had to keep pulling back in a long retreat after suffering terrible losses. The North Korean People's Army (the NKPA) dominated most of the South, and it had come close to winning the war in less than two months."

"I often wondered what it was like to be a green second lieutenant in charge of the lives of forty-one men the first time out of the box," Harry said.

"I can tell you, Harry, it's nothing like you think it's going to be. I mean the training at Quantico and Pendleton was terrific, but the real thing is something else. Like everyone else, I was excited and scared, but inexperienced enough to think I was invulnerable. At first it seemed like the other side was shooting at a crowd, but as you and Ed can attest, it doesn't take long to get disabused of that notion. I realized rather quickly that they were shooting at me, and war became decidedly personal when I understood it was my breathing habits the NKPA had designs on."

"How well I remember," Harry interjected. "How about you, Ed? What did you feel when you first got shot at?"

"Well, I'm a tad older than you guys. Mine came in World War II when we made the landing on Guam. I think of a lot of things, but mostly I have to agree with what you once told me Sean. That was about being young and inexperienced with an insatiable zest for living. You said something to the effect that when you realized you might be killed, you began to regret all the things you hadn't done in life. And you swore that if you made it out of that war alive, the next time you had to go to war, the only things you would regret would be those you couldn't do again."

"That's right," Sean replied softly. "And I assure you, the next time I do go to war, it will be just that way. Only this time I hope I know more about the reason why I am there. I didn't know much about Korea, but I was aware of Harry Truman's hard line against communism, so I figured if communism was what we were fighting, then it was a worthy mission. But at the time I didn't know anything about Truman sticking it to Chaing Kai-Shek and the Chinese Nationalist Army which is what I believe ultimately resulted in the loss of China to the Reds."

"I was always a typical lifer," Ed replied. "Never gave any thought to politics in relation to why I was wherever the Marine Corps sent me."

"I can understand that Ed," Sean replied, "I wasn't political in those days either. If I thought about Harry Truman at all, it was only that he had appointed Louis Johnson as Secretary of Defense following the suicide of James Forrestal, and it tuned out that Johnson was not qualified to fill that office. But incompetent or not, he carried out Truman's fiscally conservative policies. And as I recall Johnson did nothing when Truman kissed Red China's ass and turned his back on Formosa. All of which was contrary to the advice of the military services, which several historians have suggested was due to near sighted Harry's view of military officers who came out of the service academies because Truman had been rejected by both West Point and Annapolis due to poor eyesight."

"I never knew about that," Harry confided. "Hell I was just a kid when I enlisted. I didn't give a damn about politics."

"Well you're not alone, Harry, but ironically it was Truman who took us to Korea in the summer of '50, sorely unprepared for the invasion of the NKPA. I am convinced that he did this in spite of his experience in the trenches in World War I. Ironically, Korea was exactly that kind of war. Notwithstanding great air operations and naval support, as you found out when you were there, it was basically trench warfare."

"What outfit were you with in the Brigade when you first got to Korea?" Harry asked.

"I really lucked out there. I was fortunate to be assigned to the Fifth Marine Regiment commanded by Lieutenant Colonel Ray Murray, who had been a battalion commander of the old Sixth Marines on Guadalcanal, Tarawa and Saipan. His World War II Navy Cross and other decorations attested to his brilliance and bravery as a troop commander. Later he earned his second Navy Cross at the Chosin, but you know that since all three of us were with him through those terrible days."

"I remember Ray Murray very well," Harry advised. "But I didn't get into the war until we landed at Inchon in September of '50. What happened with you guys early in the war?"

"Well, Harry, we had our hands full night and day. The Fifth Marines formed a part of Task Force Kean assigned to launch an offensive to stop the North Korean 4th and 6th Divisions. Our counterpart in Task Force Kean, an Army Regimental Combat Team, got clobbered on the south road while we were having fairly easy time - if war is ever easy - along the coast road. So we had to cover the Army's butt with an attack to the rear as the force mission got all fucked up."

What Sean didn't add was that he had been in the land of the morning calm for only a few hours in that fateful August of 1950, before Korea turned ugly and violent. His primary concern became not only personal survival but the lives of the forty some men in his platoon who looked to him for life and death decisions. Charged with that responsibility, Sean knew he had to present an appearance of confidence and somehow overcome the natural instinct to run every time all hell broke loose.

There is nothing pleasant about combat unless you are a looney toon who gets his kicks from risking his life while wasting people, but there is an exhilaration one feels when you survive in battle. You don't think much about the fact that you took another man's life, and you try not to dwell on the awesome truth that this was a human being who most likely had loved ones and, at least someone would view his death as a tragic loss. After a while it becomes easier to rationalize the killing by realizing that the ones you killed were trying to kill you. Sean understood this and sensed that the reason American troops called the other side *gooks* was so they wouldn't have to think about the enemy's humanity. By debasing them it was easier to accept killing them.

Sean commented about the madness of war, and how, just when he thought he had a handle on the madness, he discovered how wrong he was. Reality set in one summer morning when his platoon got into an extended fire- fight with an NKPA patrol. The platoon chased them to a nameless village and filled that village with bullets and grenades until all return fire stopped. Then they moved in to check on the success of the mission. Not one casualty in the platoon, compared to twenty-four dead Koreans in the village.

But there was no joy in no name village. Only eight of the dead were North Korean soldiers. The other sixteen were South Korean women and children. Some without recognizable features. Some only in pieces. The gods of war are cynically indifferent. At times it seems the God of Abraham is too. One of the Marines exclaimed, "Holy fuck, Lieutenant!"

Another, "What the fuck happened?"

A third, "Shit, I'm gonna puke. Holy sweet, Jesus."

As the litany continued, every man in the platoon seemed to share the same revulsion. These weren't the enemy they called gooks. These were children, women, people, humans. Some only infants.

A tiny arm lay among the slaughter as if it had fallen off a doll. Sean thought of his three year old sister, Catherine, who he loved more than anyone. It looked like one of her little arms that had clung to him before she could walk. *Catherine dearest, how did your arm get here? Where is the rest of you?* Sean asked silently.

And then he saw her. But she didn't have a face. Only a terrible, red and purple, oozing gaping hole where her beautiful face used to be. The face he had kissed athousand times. *Catherine, Catherine, what have I done to you?* He turned away and vomited.

"What the fuck are you going to do, Lieutenant?" Staff Sergeant Gonzales asked. "Hey-fucking-soos, Lieutenant, what are you going to do?"

Sean looked at Gonzales ready to tear his head off, but remained quiet for a moment asking himself, *Why is it always the personal you when there's been a fuck up, instead of the editorial we?* But the question was rhetorical. Sean knew that rank has its privileges but also its responsibilities, including having to bite the bullet when things fall apart on your watch.

"What I'm going to do, Sergeant, is to get a whole lot sicker, and then I'm going to do what's necessary," Sean snapped.

"What's that, Sir?"

"I don't know, but I've got to report what happened. It's my responsibility."

"Fuck, Lieutenant, you don't have to tell 'em about the civilians. Just report the military types and fuck the rest of these gooks."

"What the fuck's the matter with you Sergeant? I always said you could turn a phrase, but your observations in this instance are outrageous," Sean answered angrily. "We didn't know about the civilians. We were just doing our job. If that puts my ass on the line, that's what they pay me for. These gold bars may not seem like much, but it makes me the man on the dime when the shit hits the fan. I'll do what I have to do."

If that conviction needed reinforcement, it was provided when Sean noticed for the first time an infant lying under its dead mother. An M-1 Ball Armor piercing bullet had torn through the mother's neck as she sheltered her baby. It exited in an angry fury of metal, bone, blood and flesh, and entered the child's head just over the brow taking everything above it and the helpless innocent into eternity.

Sean reported the nightmare he can never forget. It was investigated, but nothing came of it. Incidental casualties of a lawful act of war. The matter was closed, except in his soul.

CHAPTER 3

August - November 1950

No name village was relegated to painful memory as Sean's personal war continued, but it was never far from mind. His regiment had regrouped by August 17th and re-deployed to what was known as the Naktong Bulge with seven Army battalions to launch an all out assault on the NKPA 4th Division. As they say in the Corps, they kicked ass and took names. The North Korean division was defeated and never recovered. At the same time plans were under way for Doug MacArthur's famous Inchon landing to be spearheaded by the First Marine Division. Sean wanted to be a part of it, but his regiment was still in the Pusan perimeter and they were being called on again to help the Army.

On September 3rd, Marines and soldiers attacked the NKPA 9th Division, inflicting a slaughter greater than they had on the NKPA 4th. In two days they had killed some five thousand enemy and destroyed the NKPA 9th. But the enormity of the carnage was sprouting seed in the fields of their emotions. If they awarded purple hearts for emotional wounds, they would quickly run out. No one ever comes out of combat whole, no matter how glorious the tradition.

Ironically, while Marines were covering the Corps with glory, myopic Harry Truman refused to enlarge the Corps and wrote to a congressman, "For your information, the Marine Corps is the Navy's Police Force, and as long as I am the President, that is what it will remain. They have a propaganda machine that is almost equal to Stalin's." Clearly old Harry never forgave the admirals and generals for keeping him out of the service academies.

Finally it was decided to pull Marines from the Pusan perimeter to join the Inchon landing, but Sean's regiment almost didn't make it because they were needed to provide urgent support for the Army, which was hanging on valiantly in the face of over eighteen thousand casualties. General Walker, the commander of the United States Eighth Army, was convinced Marines were necessary to continue to shore up his defensive lines, but General MacArthur was not going to be dissuaded from his plan for a landing at Inchon to relieve the pressure on the Eighth Army from above. Thus Sean's regiment was finally pulled out on September 12th, and joined the 1st Marine Division at sea off Inchon. On September 15th, the invasion plans were put into effect and Marines stormed the sea walls at Inchon after extended naval gun fire and Marine and Naval aviation close air support.

Sean's company was in the battalion assigned to take Wolmi Island. They landed at 0633 hours. By noon, they had killed or captured 400 NKPA defenders. No Marines were killed and only seventeen wounded. As killing became an acceptable and commonplace event, Sean wondered if this was the best way to carry on his personal crusade against injustice. It seemed necessary, nonetheless, and he concluded that right or wrong there didn't seem to be any other alternative.

Two other battalions of the Fifth Marines went over the seawalls north of Wolmi Island. Three additional battalions of the Third Marines, commanded by the legendary, Chesty Puller, landed at Blue Beach to the south. In two days the combined forces mopped up Inchon and captured the vital Kimpo airfield.

The U.S. Army joined the invasion after the Marines had taken Inchon, and they pushed on jointly to Seoul. On September 25th, although the Army was wishfully claiming that Seoul had been recaptured from the NKPA, the city was still under enemy control and it took three Marine regiments to dig out the NKPA building by building. It wasn't until September 28th that Seoul was finally secure. The overall U.S. casualties to that time were over 27,0000, with 6000 killed.

By the time South Korea was cleared and General Walker's Eighth Army fully liberated, thousands of NKPA troops had escaped back to North Korea. Truman approved crossing the 38th Parallel to finish them off and to depose the North Korean Government. No one had to persuade Doug MacArthur on this point, and he promised all U.S. forces would accomplished the goals and be home by Christmas. It wasn't the first time that old Mac was dead wrong. Weather and the Chinese came storming into play.

After saddling up and landing on the eastern side of the peninsula, Marines were moving well on the way to the Yalu River with little resistance. At a couple of rest points Sean had seen a number of young Korean women, but he never got close to socializing, sexually or otherwise. He kept worrying about the mortality of his otherwise immortal soul in the tradition of fire and brimstone that had been drilled into him by the nuns and priests. He also was concerned about going into more battles without the luxury of confession. Which meant he might have to confess something he didn't feel needed confessing in the first place. Sean used to laugh at the idea that if he enjoyed sex with a woman, he would have to confess it. But it didn't make sense to him that he was supposed to feel contrite about a man-woman relationship, the most natural of all relationships, but when he killed people in combat, he didn't have to confess anything. Such are the ways of war and religion.

The technique of persuasion labeled, brainwashing, would merge into the national conscious as a result of the Korean War, but actually the papacy had perfected it centuries earlier. Not that Rome had a corner on pressure and scare tactics, since most main line religions, and even fringe cults, employ them to one degree or another. But no matter how sincere they claim to be, they all have their hypocrite ministers and preachers who pontificate on damnation for doing what comes naturally, while, with some frequency, redoing it themselves - in the closet

- with both sexes. Having been brainwashed over the years, it was out of theological and illogical fear that Sean remained celibate as his regiment advanced above the 38th parallel.

By November the reports of Chinese sightings were becoming more frequent, however, and the hard fact that China had entered the war was brought home in a devastating fashion well above the 38th parallel. Through it all, U.S. Army units would take a beating and the Marines might have done no better except for the fact that the lst Marine Division commanding general, O.P. Smith, had ordered Marines to stockpile ammunition, gas, and other supplies along the long route to the Chosin Reservoir. He also ordered holding the high ground in the more dangerous passes and to prepare an airstrip for the evacuation of dead and wounded when needed. He was right. They were desperately needed. Without these preparations, the *famous Marine attack in another direction* would have been stopped dead. "Retreat Hell" was the key phrase and the eventual withdrawal of the entire lst Marine Division is respected as the most successful retrograde in the history of the American military. All of this came after Sean's unit had arrived at the Chosin. It was on their way there that they kept running into and killing smaller pockets of Chinese troops without seeing any more North Korean soldiers.

Towards the end of November it was clear that the Chinese had arrived in force. It was a time when the word cold was an understatement and the battle for survival against the elements became as deadly as hostile fire. Temperatures were falling to twenty below zero; the chill factor with the wind made it about seventy below. After some U.S. Army units were badly hit, the 5th and 7th Marine Regiments were ordered to attack over severe terrain in blinding snow and subzero weather. But in sixteen hours of battle they were able to move only 1500 yards. By November 27th, at least thirty Chinese divisions had gone on the offensive and attacked relentlessly.

The physical and mental horrors of Chosin will remain frozen in Sean's personal time lock, but it had an upside. It was at Chosin that he first met Ed Tabor, the finest Marine he had ever known. Sean had lost the senior noncommissioned officer of his platoon, Staff Sergeant Gonzales, a few days earlier. Gonzales died as he lived, a tough, street kid from the Bronx, up front and direct. Sean regretted snapping at him in no name village as he looked back on the valor Gonzalez displayed on his last day. In a major attack he held his ground, and in spite of multiple wounds, he kept firing his M-1 rifle, cutting down the enemy, until death won the final charge.

Notwithstanding the horror of those terrible days and nights, their memory held a special meaning for Sean, which was the arrival of Ed Tabor. Fourteen years later, Sean and Ed and Harry sat at the table in *Lowry's* recalling those fateful days. Ed spoke softly, "I remember all of it only too well. The cold was the worst I have ever known, and I wasn't happy about changing platoons, but it worked out better than I had hoped."

Ed was a Staff Sergeant then. After Sergeant Gonzalez was killed, Harry Dixon filled in as acting sergeant until Ed joined the platoon. It was the night before Ed arrived that Harry saved Sean's life for the first time. Sean had been hit in a firefight and Harry didn't know how badly because Sean was down. Harry left his hole and ran over to Sean drawing more fire than either of them wanted, but he was able to drag Sean back to a makeshift bunker before he took any more hits. Fortunately the wound was such that the company corpsman was able to patch Sean up until he saw a field surgeon a week later. Nobody dared mention evacuation. Sean still carries a mean scar on his left leg from that night.

Ed had been sent to fill in as platoon sergeant and he came well recommended. Korea was his second war; his first started at Guam in July 1944, as a green kid so scared he says he "pissed in his pants" when he hit the beach in the first wave. The troops genuinely respected Ed. He was an instinctive leader, and his strong body added a dimension of solid reliability. The scars he carried from wounds received in his last war were referred to as badges of honor, and the men gave him unquestioned loyalty and devotion. He deserved it because he was one of them and they knew it. And yet Ed was something special and different in a way that could not be fully defined.

Sean never told Ed about the troops' feelings for him, but everyone in the platoon recognized that Ed was an old hand at staying alive and seemed blessed with a magic that would keep the rest of them alive as well. There is no way to explain that feeling. Maybe it's intuition; maybe blind hope. But Ed had the magic and they relied on it. At times Sean would catch Ed in deep reflection that lent a haunting look to his handsome face. Sean often wondered what memories caused this but Ed didn't talk about his private life during those troubled days and Sean respected his privacy.

Second Lieutenant platoon leaders have a short life expectancy, and while Sean realized he was respected, he was fully aware that he was expendable. But to the men, Ed was indispensable. It has always been this way with Marines. The staff noncommissioned officer is the backbone of the Corps. As a result one thing dominated in the hearts of the troops, which was the conviction that if they followed Ed's lead, they were once again invulnerable. Because he sensed how they felt, it was a terrible burden, and the magic didn't always work. Some of the *lads*, as he called them, took their hits. They bled. They died. And yet the survivors felt that if they believed, they would make it. And most did, even though they were thrown into some of the bloodiest battles of the war.

Sean's unit was in a defensive position that fateful November 27th at the Chosin Reservoir when the word filtered down that massive numbers of Chinese Communist troops were preparing for a night attack. As darkness arrived in sub-zero weather, the bloody confrontation began between thousands of living, breathing souls seeking to kill each other like gladiators fighting in an arena of ice with no more purpose than to brutally destroy the most precious of all God's gifts. Sean never liked the expression *gook* but when you are scared, cold, and angry, you call the executioner a lot of things. And gook was the least of the epithets that night. The use of the term for the most part simply was not intended to be a racial slur, but rather a normal response to an enemy who was trying to kill you. Civility is not a consideration in such moments.

The Marines were hit by overwhelming numbers of Chicoms who attacked blowing their bugles, screaming and shooting flares. As the Marines would cut down one Chinese formation, a fresh one would climb over the corpses and continue the assault. It was as if dying was not to be feared but rather accepted as a necessary adjunct to their battle tactics; something akin to the archaic war manuals of Eighteenth Century British and French.

The Chinese kept coming and charged again and again. The shrill sounds of the bugles and the shouting filled the spaces between the frightening noises of their burp guns. The terror increased with mortars and light artillery and grenades. The Marines' return fire was devastating and the madness exacerbated as the Chinese bodies piled up in wave after wave. And still they came, climbing over the dead and wounded as the night turned into day with the light of exploding ordnance, gunfire, and flares. It was terrifying. Sean couldn't get enough earth in front of him to feel safe. Two feet of hole aren't much anytime. They were a hundred feet too little at that moment. The pressure was unremitting, but the platoon had to hold the line. It was Sean's responsibility to see that they did, but he felt he contributed little compared to Ed. The discipline of training diminishes quickly if the troops aren't led by example. With Ed they were. At the fiercest moment of the attack, the instant when every instinct cries out to throw down your weapon and run, Ed stood up and walked the line in his commanding way, firing his M-1 and shouting encouragement. With anyone else you would have thought he was insane or faking macho. But not with Ed. There was no Hollywood grandstanding.

It was just, "Lads, we're all here together. We won't break."

The line held through five days and six nights of fanatical attacks. Sean could only marvel on how any of them survived the racking physical and mental torture. The kill ratio was twenty-three to one in favor of the Marines. Those who were still alive were filled with the euphoria that follows the stark terror of combat when you realize somehow you made it. Ed felt other emotions as he mourned the loss of their comrades who died. Sean was convinced that deep down Ed mourned for the dead on the other side too.

Sean picked up his second purple heart the sixth night at Chosin with wounds to his left arm that did little more than annoy him. There was no serious debilitation and he was grateful it wasn't worse. Three of his men had been cut off in a forward listening post. He'll never be able to explain why he reacted as he did, but he told Ed to stay with the platoon and to give him as much covering fire as he could. Against Ed's wise protest, Sean ran forward of the line and headed for a Chicom machine gun emplacement that had pinned down the Marines in the listening post and was bent on killing them.

Only God will ever know what made him leave the comparative safety of his hole, spare as it was, and expose himself to imminent destruction. Combat produces strange responses. Sean simply reacted without sufficient reflection on the potential consequences and immediately drew fire. He was hit before he'd gotten fifty yards, but adrenalin and stubbornness kept him going. More angry than hurt when he got hit, and in spite of his recklessness, Sean managed to get close enough to throw several grenades into the open makeshift bunker. Then he charged and found only one out of five Chinese soldiers alive. If you can call it living to be sitting in a pool of blood, snow and dirt with most of the lower half of your body missing.

Sean had seen too much death along the way and was sick over what had become incessant madness. He looked at this horribly broken human being and searched in vain to see the extent of the Chinese soldier's wounds. It looked like he may have lost his genitalia. The grossly mutilated soldier was stuck fast in the mire of his life ebbing blood turning the ground into a gruesome pit of death. Sean was sickened by the thought that he had turned the soldier into a half man, half freak.

The Chicom looked at Sean and made no effort to reach for a weapon, if any could be had. His eyes were deep holes of indescribable torment as he tried to speak, but he and Sean were strangers in a foreign land and no words could pass. And yet Sean understood the eyes as they silently cried, "Please."

Without hesitation he walked over and placed his 45-pistol against the soldier's head. The eyes pleaded once more and thanked Sean at the same time as they burned into his soul. Sean fired once and the man was at peace.

According to the laws of war and the Geneva Conventions, Sean had committed a war crime. He had killed a wounded enemy who had been rendered *hors de combat* - without an ability to fight. In that classic context he had murdered one of God's tragic creatures and deprived him of perhaps a few minutes more of hideous pain. He could not have survived longer. No one, except Ed, knew what Sean had done, and Sean never spoke of it, not even in confession. A year later he was given a medal for killing people. It was shaped like a cross.

Numbed by the experience of relentless attacks, the Marines were able to keep from going mad and they continued to fight with grim determination as they beat back the Chicoms through the long withdrawal to the sea. They broke out of the ice at Chosin and rescued remnants of an Army unit that had been split and decimated by the Chinese. They brought back all of their dead and wounded and the Army's too. Over four thousand were evacuated at the airstrip at Hagaru and the rest clawed and fought their way back through Koto-ri and Chinhung to Hungnam and relief. Statistics reflect that one hundred and five thousand troops were evacuated at Hungnam, along with ninety-one thousand refugees. They didn't win a total victory but the Marines looked back with justifiable pride. They had killed thirty-eight thousand Chinese Communist, and many times that number of other casualties were inflicted on the enemy as a result of Chosin. They held their heads high, and became ever referred to as the *frozen chosen*.

The war would last for another two and one-half years, but MacArthur was relieved for arrogantly advocating taking the war to the Chinese mainland. He was right, of course, but Truman was not going to let MacArthur defy him. He thought the old soldier should just fade away. General Ridgeway took over and more battles were fought. Maybe it was all worth it. Maybe it made the difference in turning back the communists' ambitions. Maybe not. One ridge taken by the Army later in the fray might say it best. It was called "Heartbreak."

Following Chosin, Ed and Sean spent close to another year in Korea and saw more action, but made it through. When their turn came to rotate back home, rather than return right away, they wrangled orders for a tour in Japan at Camp Fugi with the 3d Marine Division. It was enjoyable to spend time with Orientals who weren't trying to kill them.

Occasionally they drank too much to forget the emotional wounds and took delicious delight in committing sins of the flesh with a variety of women. Sean was still apprehensive about hell and damnation, but he didn't feel guilty. Old superstitions die hard even without guilt. A particular Japanese lady named Chieko became a special favorite of Sean, but he made no promises and Chieko understood she was not going to be another *Cio-Cio-San* which Pucini so beautifully and poignantly portrayed in *Madama Butterfly*. Nonetheless he thinks of her often and the memory is sweet.

CHAPTER 4

September 1964

They stayed at *Lowry's* until ten, at which time Harry had to get on home and see what he could do for his sister, at least to give her some moral support. As they said goodnight Sean and Ed each gave Harry a strong embrace and Sean again assured Harry that he and Ed would get on top of Lee Johnson's case as soon as Camp Pendleton unbuttoned from the long weekend. Ed was spending the holiday and when they arrived at Sean's apartment at the Marina, it was still early enough to call Major John Crandall an old friend who was currently assigned to Base Legal at Camp Pendleton. John was a first rate trial lawyer and an incurable night person. Sean felt confident calling him at midnight knowing John would still be up doing what he did best late at night, either reading or arguing some obscure philosophical point with whomever he could find. Since John was the senior prosecutor at Base Legal he would have substantial information on the Johnson matter even though it only happened two nights ago.

"John? Sean O'Ryan. How 'ya doing?"

"Hey, Sean-san. Good to hear your voice. You close by? I'll be right over, and while you're waiting, order me a Chevas Regal."

"Wish I could old buddy, but I haven't recovered from the last time we worked together. I'm sure neither one of us will forget the pair of falsely accused jarheads we represented in the supply officer case. Remember the supply type turkey who claimed he was working late and two alleged masked men broke into his office and made him open the safe and then relieved him of some eighty thousand bucks. Would have been all right, I guess, even with his self-inflicted hit on the head, if he hadn't used a confederate to buy him a new car and home with cash that equaled three years pay. Fortunately our clients were acquitted, but Jack Coleman made us work for our money."

"What do you mean, our money? You're the only one who could take a fee. I work for God and country," John fired back.

"Just look at it as doing your all for mom and apple pie, John. Our clients got tabbed for the robbery because they happened to be in the area and were deliberately misidentified by the alleged victim. They would still be in jail if it weren't for you uncovering the confederate scam."

"I'll accept the praise, Sean, but anytime you want to split the fee, I'll accept that too."

"Jeez, John, I spent it all on your scotch the week we closed the *Miramar* bar every night. Don't you ever get tired?"

"Hell, I thought you grunt types could drink anyone under the table. You've gotten soft since you went to law school," John chuckled. "But enough of this chit chat my boy, why are you calling me in the middle of the night? I hope it's to tell me Katie Dolan moved back to Southern California. How, and why, did you ever let her get away?"

"I don't know, John, just stupid I guess. She really is terrific, but unfortunately she moved to San Francisco and I only see her now and then. But I can tell you the memories will always be warm. Anyway, the reason I called is to talk about a rape and murder that supposedly occurred two nights ago on the base. I need to know what you know, because I've been asked to represent one of the suspects. Can you give me a leg up on this?"

"How did you hear about this? The General is trying to keep it low profile," John asked reflecting serious concern.

"Not likely he'll succeed," Sean suggested. "But no sweat as far as keeping it quiet. I got it from the kid's family, not any news source. I'll keep whatever you tell me on close hold."

"Okay. I'm counting on that. There are four Marines currently in the brig accused of raping a young woman and killing her date in a fight. Three of the Marines are white and the fourth is a Negro. It happened around 2230 hours or thereabouts last Thursday at Lake O'Neill, which you know swings by the Naval Hospital. What's your guy's name?"

"Lee Johnson. He'd be the Negro."

"As best I can recall, that's affirmative, Sean. The odd man out in this instance is named Lee Johnson, a Corporal from Headquarters Battalion. He was recently assigned to the Base from the 1st Division. An athlete as I understand it. Has an infantry MOS and average conduct and proficiency marks, so he has been keeping his nose pretty clean. Let's see what else is here."

John then added, "Your client has no prior courts, but one Article 15 for two hours unauthorized absence. No bust awarded but he got seven days extra duty, so he's had one goof but otherwise he has a fairly decent record."

"Just curious, but what color were the rape and murder victims?" Sean asked.

"White," John replied. "I think your client's in deep kimshi."

"Thanks, I could have gone all night without that bit of pessimism."

"Only call 'em like I see 'em, Marine," John laughed.

"Charges been sworn yet?" Sean asked.

"Probably not until Tuesday, and then counsel will be officially appointed, but off the record the Colonel tells me he is thinking about giving Jack Coleman to Johnson as his appointed counsel because he has a couple of strikes already being colored when the other participants are all white."

"Well, that's good news for a change. Jack's a fist rate litigator and I'll enjoy working with him for a change instead of against him. I understand he can stay in the case even though Johnson retains me as individual counsel. Am I right?"

"That's affirmative. If Jack gets in, he stays in even though you hired guns from L.A. show up on retainer. Only wish I were going to be around to let you buy me some more scotch, but I'll be in Okinawa on a murder case. The Colonel loaned me to the 3d Division for a couple of months so I won't get to see you in action this time."

"Really sorry to hear that. I'll miss your smiling face. Please note I didn't say ugly mug for a change, and I sure as hell will miss the chance to pick your brain."

"You'll have Jack with you, and he's a damn good substitute," John replied. "By the way, I'm not leaving 'till next weekend, so I presume I'll be seeing you before I go."

"Roger that. Plan to drive down on Tuesday. I'll check with you before I come to make sure Jack's been appointed and then set up a time to meet with him. In the meanwhile, thanks for all your help. Look forward to seeing you in a couple of days."

"Me too, old friend. Have a nice Labor Day if you can with all this on your mind," John said cheerfully. They disconnected and Sean turned to Ed who could read the concern on his face.

"This one looks like a ball buster, Sergeant Major, and I will need you to call in a few favors to help me get this case to court. Be nice if the kid is innocent, makes it a greater challenge and you know I love this kind of fight."

"Only too well. Only too well," Ed said smiling.

****

On Sunday, Ed and Sean went to a Dodger game. After the game Sean called Susan Sullivan and confirmed that on Monday he and Ed would be at her annual backyard bar-b-que which she hosts every Labor Day. Actually the call was a subterfuge in case Susan's fiancé, Stan Lerner, was at her place. Susan and Stan had been an item for sometime, and Sean suspected they were getting close to setting a wedding date. Stan and Sean had been classmates at UCLA Law School, and while Stan was a bit of a stuffed shirt, Anglophile, he was perceived by most who knew him as a nice enough guy. Sean thought Susan would be making a mistake marrying Stan, however, and he told her what he thought one night a few months ago when Stan was out of town on business.

Like many times with many women Sean's motives were not entirely honorable, but he rationalized his lack of grace in this instance by convincing himself that Susan was too good for Stan. And besides, Sean seriously lusted after her. He wasn't thinking of marriage, of course, at least not the ceremony part, but the idea of consummation had definite appeal. Not that marriage to

Susan was an unattractive thought; it was just that Sean wasn't thinking about marriage at that time. He did want to know Susan fully, however, because he found her to be intellectually interesting as well as sexually attractive. Sean had an undeniable weakness for good-looking, bright women.

Susan Sullivan wasn't her original name and she wasn't perfect. Sean knew this, but being admittedly biased he thought she was beautiful. She issued from fine Celtic European lineage, which blessed her with five feet seven inches of wonderfully proportioned body, and a lovely face with high cheek bones and deep green eyes. Her jaw was strong and her wide smile contrasted nicely with her small, sculptured nose.

Susan's Mother, then a widow, remarried when Susan was six and her adoptive father presented her with his name and a vicarious Irish heritage. Not that it mattered that this made her neo-Irish since Susan could be an immutable object when she chose every bit as if she had been born in County Dublin. Susan's substantial wealth was inherited from her surrogate grandfather who founded Sullivan Industries early in the century. Her personal fortune continued to grow through Susan's position as a director and officer of that successful company at the young age of twenty-six. Substantial wealth this early in life accounted for her aura of self-confidence. What she liked about being rich was not a desire to flaunt her status but, rather, the pleasure of telling the assholes who injected themselves into her life to drop dead when they bugged her.

In the middle of the afternoon on Labor Day, Ed and Sean arrived at Susan's mansion in the Pacific Palisades, which she had inherited. The backyard part of the bar-b-que roughly resembled three football fields, side by side, accessorized with a massive spit and grill located on an imported Italian patio. Directly off the patio was a garden that would rival Versailles. Before you descended the steps to the splendor of lush trees, shrubs, flowers and plants of a million colors, you had to traverse the patio which enjoys dimensions akin to Saint Peter's Square in the Vatican. A portable bar that seemed about a block long had been set up and was manned by a host of union hall bartenders and waiters.

"Some backyard bar-b-que," Ed muttered as they eased into a crowd that could have filled one of the end zones in the Los Angeles Memorial Coliseum, and headed for their friends, Sam Mann and his wife, Midge, as well as Bobby Stein, all of whom were among the *in-crowd* invited along with Ed and Sean. Bobby brought his latest lady in waiting named Cindy. It was a little hard keeping up with Bobby's stable. Sam and Bobby were also law classmates of Sean at UCLA and they had become close friends. Stan, on the other hand, never achieved the same close status even though he had been part of their study group over three years of law school. He and Sean did socialize somewhat following graduation, but Sean regularly reminded himself that he wouldn't jump on a hand grenade for Stan like he would for Ed, Sam or Bobby. Sean's perspective may have been draconian, but, "What the hell" he would say, "if you wouldn't be willing to die for a friend, he can't be a close one."

Ed and Sean could have brought dates, but Ed covered for Sean since he knew Sean had an affair going with Susan since early May, and Susan didn't want to share him with others. She was engaged to Stan but sleeping with Sean. It wasn't the best of arrangements, but she wasn't certain where the affair with Sean would lead and she was being practical. As she put it, Stan was reliable. A conservative tax lawyer, he would be a dependable even if not an exciting, husband. He was handsome and considerate, but a crushing bore. Sean felt it was just taking Susan time to understand that life on the edge is a whole lot more interesting than life with a fixture that was agonizingly predictable.

Ed asked what the attraction was between Susan and Stan besides his good looks. Sean suggested that she never answered that question in a fully definitive way. "It isn't the money," Sean proposed, "even though Stan does well in his practice. Susan has a ton of bucks more than Stan ever will. I think if they got married, Stan would work himself to death trying to prove something, but it would be a useless endeavor. Guess what she sees is dependability more than anything else. He's dependably boring."

"I can see that," Ed said, "but why does she see you on the side if she's thinking about something permanent with Stan?"

"Why? I'm amazed you have to ask. Ed I'm shocked. I may have to furnish a few references, old friend. Why, indeed?" Sean kidded, and then added, "besides great sex, I'll be honest and admit that I'm not sure, Ed. We have a terrific affair going, and other than you, no one knows about it because we are careful. I know she enjoys the time we spend on the side as you call it, but she has made it fairly clear that her intrigue doesn't extend to trust. She says I'm the kind of guy women have fun with but Stan's the steady type they marry. Whatever the hell that means.

"Which is all kind of nuts since she says she really cares about me, but feels that kind of caring could only lead to a broken heart sooner or later if we thought of any permanency to our affair. Maybe she's right, I don't know. To tell you the truth, it's been a long time since I gave any thought to a permanent commitment."

"I know what you mean," Ed mused. "She may well be right. Maybe you'll never get over the past. Have you ever talked to Susan about how you feel?"

"No, I haven't," Sean replied. "I don't talk about some things with anyone except you, because you shared them with me. So tell me why haven't you ever settled down or do you still subscribe to the old saying, if the Marine Corps wanted you to have a wife, they'd issue you one?"

"You may have something there, but I think it's more of a case where I haven't met anyone I can't live without who isn't already married. Besides you know when it comes to love, it is the forbidden kind that is most interesting. At least for a while. It's when all the obstacles are removed that it seems to lose its pizzazz and it's time to move on. Is that unrealistic? Maybe I'm just one of those people who finds monogamy unnatural, I don't know," Ed said, sounding a little wistful.

Ed's comments were directed towards the memory of one special woman who had been in his life. He knew from the beginning it was dangerous but the attraction led to an affair in spite of themselves. As so often happens, the relationship progressed to a point where judgment was lost in the blindness of forbidden love that negates reason. Eventually the ineluctable forces of passion and emotion led the lady to express the ultimate in desperation by professing a love so compelling she was willing to sacrifice everything necessary to marry him. Recognizing that he should not have allowed the situation to get that far out of hand, Ed understood how he had fallen victim to his own desires. But it took time, and then only through the greatest effort was he able to force himself to break off the relationship, accepting this as the only way to restore some semblance of personal worth to each of them. It took a long while but after much anguish the lady also understood why it was necessary and survived the death of spirit while Ed buried his anguish deep inside not even sharing it with Sean. It could never be the same for either Ed or his lost lady, but there would always be an enduring sense of love. The heart doesn't stop caring as long as the dream remains alive in memory.

Ed and Sean moved through the crowd and found Bobby Stein and Sam and Midge. Bobby's date was locked unto him like she had grown out of his side. "Lots of heavenly bodies out today I see, especially your date, Bobby. What's the lady's name, or is this private stock?" Sean challenged.

"The answer is, yes, and you lechers keep that in mind. Cindy meet Ed and Sean. Now say good-by to Ed and Sean. That's as close as you ever want to get to these Marines. A girl's not safe within hand to hand combat range of these two studs," Bobby said laughing.

"Hi Cindy. Been wonderful knowing you," Sean said smiling. "But don't believe a word of it. We're actually fairly harmless."

"You two will still be dangerous four days after you're dead," Bobby shot back. "So what have you been up to? I imagine Ed's been teaching our clean cut American youth to kill and destroy, but what's happening in the professional life of Sean, the wunderkind of criminal law?"

"Funny you should ask," Sean answered. "I got a call from an old buddy who went through much of the war with us in Korea. We kept in touch all these years and Friday he called needing help."

"Yeah," Bobby said. "What did he want? Did he kill somebody? That's what you guys are trained to do, isn't it?"

"Only bad asses like you," Sean chuckled. "Actually it involves his sister's son who's stationed at Camp Pendleton which is about forty miles north of San

Diego. He is being held in the brig on suspicion of rape and murder. That's all we know right now. Harry is willing to go to bat for his nephew. He says the kid has been a hard case for some time and he was hoping the Corps would turn him around. But right now he isn't sure. The family is close and Harry says he'll underwrite my fee. I'll scale it down considerably, or do it for nothing if I have to, but he doesn't have to know that now or else he'll worry that I might not work as hard."

"Doesn't the Marine Corps give the accused a lawyer?" Sam asked.

"Yes it does," Sean answered. "I told Harry the Corps would give his nephew a fine lawyer at no cost, but Harry said he didn't trust just anyone who might be assigned at random and he wanted me to take over. I'll make a few calls in the morning and see what else I can find out before I drive down there. Until then, that's as much as I know."

Sam noted, "I didn't see anything about this thing in the paper or hear about it from the other media." Sean said he hadn't heard anything on the news either, "But it happened only four days ago and in view of the Labor Day weekend, the Marines may have been able to keep it from the media so far. Camp Pendleton is for the most part exclusive federal jurisdiction so the Marines get the first bite on this thing. We love publicity as a rule, but not this kind. I can see how they might keep it quiet for a little while, but sooner or later the lid will blow off," Sean added. "See how much fun you rich cats are missing with your cushy practices and insurance scams."

He was making reference to Sam's opting for insurance underwriting and devising and marketing, new concepts. Sam did quite well devising or promoting esoteric insurance concepts such as key man life, deferred compensation and other exotic pension plans, and something, then new, called charitable remainder unitrusts. It reminded Sean of the nightmares they had studying estates in land and future interests in law school, along with the rule against perpetuities and the archaic Rule in Shelley's case, both of which sound like they predated the last supper. Bobby, on the other hand, had gone into securities law and was well on his way to becoming a multi-millionaire.

"You can give me the needle on insurance, Sean, but you can't jerk Bobby's chain," Sam fired back. "He's got the handle on this whole business. Securities law. Hell, he's already got his second boat. He's tapped a gold mine. His firm doesn't even talk to a potential client unless he's got big bucks. How many schmucks have you defended who didn't pay you a dime?" Sam asked. "No, don't tell me. I'll get sick."

"Thank you, Sam, and may your cock desert you at all the wrong times. When it does Midge, you can come to my place and I'll show you what an Irish midwife did with a circumcision that Sam's rabbi could only dream about. The Irish consider the male organ a sacred shillelagh and refuse to hack it up like some zealot did to Sam, also known as shorty."

Midge laughed, "I wouldn't know about that. Sam's my only experience and if he says it's six inches, who am I to quibble over a little difference in arithmetic."

Sam jumped in, "Midge, we'll talk later. The Irish are notorious kidders and I wouldn't want you to be misled by this miserable Mick."

Just then Susan walked up. "I've got to steal Sean away for a minute, gang. Got a friend with a criminal law question. Be right back," she promised. As they walked away and got out of earshot, Susan hissed, "I haven't gotten you alone all day. Closest I got was that perfunctory kiss you gave me when you arrived. I know what that tongue can do, you hypocrite. God do I want you. It's been five days and I am dying. Do you think I am oversexed?" she teased while looking around and smiling at nearby guests. "But all is not despair my blue eyed, Irish hunk. Stan is flying to Denver tomorrow for a few days on business. I'll drop him at L.A. International and see you at the Marina…about eightish."

"I don't know if you are oversexed, but I hope so," Sean answered devilishly. "I promise to be up and ready for you" he replied with a wicked grin.

"Just one warning, though, I am opening the door naked, so you'd better be alone. Which reminds me of the old joke about the Marine who was heading back to the states after being overseas for two years. He called his wife and said "I'll be home next week, honey, but make sure your mother doesn't answer the door or you'll be second.""

"Sean O'Ryan, you are incorrigible. Please don't ever change," Susan teased as she steered him into the house, into a walk-in closet, and kissed him with a passion and a promise of an interesting tomorrow. Then she left, making Sean count to fifty before breaking out and returning to Ed and company.

CHAPTER 5

Ed and Sean left Susan's mansion and returned to the Marina a little before nine. Sean gave John Crandall another call to set up a meeting with him and Jack Coleman and to pay a courtesy call on the Base Legal Officer before he went over to the brig to meet Lee Johnson.

"John, it's me again."

"Hey, Sean. Twice in one week, I must be blessed."

"You are you old reprobate, but not because of me. The reason I am calling is I thought I'd drive down in the morning and we'd get started on Lee Johnson. Can you set it up with Jack Coleman for about nine? We'll catch a cup of coffee and lay the groundwork. Also can you square it with the brig people so I can get in even though, technically, I am not Johnson's retained counsel until he approves me?"

"That's easy. What's your rank in the reserves these days? It'll be more impressive if I present you as a Marine officer," John responded.

"It's Major, I got promoted in July. We'll have a private wetting down tomorrow at happy hour, but just one thing, we are not, and I repeat, are not closing the bar. Okay? I really appreciate the help, old friend. See you in the morning at nine."

"You got it. Anything else you need in the meantime?"

"No, that's it, John. See you then. Semper fi."

"Semper fi to you too," John said laughing as they disconnected. Sean had a sense of foreboding about this case. Harry had warned him Lee was a hard case. Not exactly what he needed, a tough black kid accused - along with three white Marines - of raping a white woman and killing her white date. Sean wondered for a moment if he should have listened to Bobby. Securities law seemed attractive right about then, and yet the challenge was overriding the foreboding and he felt an equal amount of excitement. The next morning Ed shoved off at 0400 and Sean left at six to give himself enough time to meet John Crandall at nine. As he drove up to the Base Legal Office he felt at home having spent substantial time there on the supply officer matter.

Base Legal was located in the Twenty-Four Area of Camp Pendleton. As Sean pulled into a visitor's parking slot, John Crandall was standing on the porch that runs along the front of the "H" shaped structure that consists of two large World War II barracks on either side of - and connected to - a jury rigged center building turned sideways. It was an ugly monstrosity. Nothing like the lovely old courthouses one sees in the eastern United States, but fancy or not, it served its purpose and, as they have been doing since 1775, Marines could be counted on to do an outstanding job in spite of less than glamorous facilities.

In that context, although it may have been ugly, Base Legal was a model of functional efficiency, with the legal assistance and defense shops on one end of the left wing and the prosecution team on the opposite end which was separated by the law library. The courtroom covered the entire length of the right wing, and the center structure housed the Base Legal Officer, Colonel Gene Hanley, USMC, and his assistant, along with the enlisted and civilian administrative personnel. An adjoining patio furnished an office for the court reporters and the court-martial review officers.

"Hi, Sean," John called out to Sean displaying his usual wide smile and warm charm. "Have a good cup of joe for a change and not that namby-pamby stuff your one nighters make for you in the morning after too much nooky and not enough sleep."

"Thanks, John, I needed that. How you doing, old buddy?"

"Right fine, Marine. Looking forward to seeing *the Rock* again, but sure will miss the family. Okinawa is a long way from here especially now that the girls are growing so quickly. I hate to be away as often as I am, but they are turning out terrific in spite of it and I am proud as hell of them."

"I can appreciate that even though I don't have any kids of my own. At least none that I know about. Someday, if I ever settle down, maybe I'll have a couple just like yours," Sean answered.

"What the hell. Give Katie Dolan a call. You would have a marvelous wife if you landed her."

"I'll give that some thought. But back to business first. Where's Jack Coleman? And now that I think about it, I'd better pay a courtesy call on Colonel Hanley as a matter of protocol."

"Jack's in his office. We'll catch him in a minute. He's all primed and looking forward to teaming up with you. It's a good thing this Johnson kid is getting both of you. This one's a bear. I think the Marine may be hanging by his balls before this is over."

Sean looked at John evenly and thought he could have gone all day without that bit of pessimism, particularly because John had remarkable instincts when it came to evaluating the down side of a criminal case. "What the hell," he said with an air of false bravado, "wouldn't be any fun without a challenge. Isn't that what you always say?"

"Good thing you feel that way," John observed, "cause this one's gonna give you all the challenge you can handle."

They tapped at Colonel Hanley's door and he greeted them in his customary manner which was with a look that asked what the hell did they want and what were they doing invading his domain? That look would give second thoughts to Attila the Hun, but it was all a facade. Deep down Gene Hanley was one of the kindest men Sean had ever known. A graduate of the United States Naval Academy, he was selected by the Marine Corps for law school after several tours as an infantry officer, including Korea. It was his chiseled features and high and tight Marine haircut that gave him the look of a lean and mean, grunt Marine. He credited the image to a claimed heritage of part American Indian, but no one knew if it was true.

John spoke up. "Colonel, you remember Sean O'Ryan, who spent some time with us last fall. Sean's recently pinned on his oak leaves in the reserves and wants to host a little wetting down at happy hour at 1630 at the Seventeen Area O'Club if you care to stop over."

"Sounds like a good idea. Congratulations Major," Gene Hanley said, smiling at last. "What brings you down to the hallowed halls of justice this time?"

"I've been asked to represent one of the Marines accused in the rape and murder matter. His mother's a widow and hasn't the wherewithal to cover this, but his Uncle Harry Dixon is an old friend from the Corps and wants to retain me on the kid's behalf. I'll have to square it with the accused, of course, but I hope he'll agree since it will give me a chance to work with Jack Coleman again."

"Well, very good. Glad to have you aboard. I assigned Jack to the case because I share your opinion of him. I would have tapped John for this one as a defense counsel for a change if he was going to be available, but he's on his way to the 3d Division to try a different murder case. I think you and Jack Coleman will work well together."

"Thank you, Colonel. We won't take up any more of your time right now, but I look forward to swapping some stories with you at happy hour," Sean said while easing out of the office with John in tow.

"Salt of the earth. Don't let that look he gives at first fool you," John remarked as they set out for Jack Coleman's office.

"I know John. I've got nothing but the greatest respect for the Colonel. I've no doubt he'll give us a fair shake."

They found Jack in his office, feet up on his desk. He was reading the latest advance sheets from the United States Court of Military Appeals. "When all else fails, look up the law, hey Jack?" John kidded.

"Somebody around here has to. Not all of us can win on our good looks and charm like you do. Hi, Sean, good to see you again," Jack responded with a Harvard accent and a wide smile.

"Nice to see you too. Hope the client agrees to my assisting in this case. I prefer to be working with you instead of against you. Got tired of you giving John and me a bad time last time we worked a case," Sean replied, extending a warm handshake.

"The privilege is mine," Jack said in return. "You've built quite a reputation. I look forward to assisting you."

"I prefer to call us co-counsel, Jack. That way we assist each other. I never put stock in the title of lead counsel. Sounds too pretentious."

"Thanks, I appreciate that. Especially because we are going to have to go to the wall for this kid. From what I can see this one is going to be a bastard to try. I know we are technically starting with a presumption of innocence, but we both know there are two kinds of cases where that presumption is given nothing more than lip service. The first is child molestation, and the second is forcible rape.

"Seems like the accused has to get on the roof tops and immediately shout his innocence or everyone automatically concludes he's guilty. Glad to be working with you," Jack added with genuine feeling.

"I appreciate that," Sean said, "let's go get 'em. Only way to find out what happened last Thursday is to ask the person who should know more about it than anyone else. The key is to get him to be honest with us. So let's pay a visit to Corporal Johnson who is currently enjoying the hospitality of the barbed wire hotel."

As they exited Jack's office, Sean called, "Catch you later, John. See you at the O'Club at 1630."

"You're on. Good luck to both of you," John grinned, reinforcing Sean's serious concern about Johnson's chances.

"Have you had any contact with Johnson as yet?" Sean asked.

"Only to pass the word by telephone to the duty warden that I had been appointed to represent Johnson and would be over to see him this morning," Jack answered. "I've not talked to him directly, and I've never seen him, so I'm not sure what to expect. I'm told he's a tough kid, so I can only hope that, in spite of his reputation, he'll be cooperative."

They passed through the gate at the Camp Pendleton Brig after clearing with the duty warden and were ushered into a private interview room to await their client.

CHAPTER 6

September 8, 1964

Sean and Jack had been in the interview room for three minutes when they heard an unidentified voice sing out, "Sir, request permission to cross the line, Sir."

"Permission granted, shit bird," a second voice responded. Sean chuckled and commented, "The screws in this hotel give quaint nicknames to the prisoners."

At that moment Lee Johnson entered the interview room. Six feet two, give or take a half inch, and one hundred ninety pounds. All muscle weight. Good-looking face. His shaved head, mandated for all brig prisoners, took nothing away from his fine features. *Nice looking kid*, Sean thought. *Could be on recruiting posters.* Although fairly big, Johnson seemed pleasant enough. Then he spoke.

"Sir, Corporal Johnson reporting as ordered, Sir." Sean suspected the formality was for the guard's edification, so he closed the door to the interview room. "Enough spit and polish Corporal Johnson, we're here to help you, not stand on ceremony or lord over you. How about we do away with all suggestion of rank. Can we call you Lee?"

"You're not jivin' about that rank jazz?" Johnson asked.

"No, I'm not jiving."

"In that case, you call me Lee and I'll call you motherfucker," Johnson sneered.

Sean was surprised, but he wasn't going to let Johnson know it or get the better of him so he resisted the temptation to resort to boot camp discipline.

"I've been called worse, Lee, and God knows I've gotten it on with a number of women who were also mothers, so the label can't be all bad," Sean said calmly, but with a clear indication that he was not going to be intimidated.

"I bet you have, chuck dude. Can't tell the players without a scorecard. Know who the captain is by his uniform, but who's the dude in the civvies?" Johnson asked sarcastically.

"Since I'm the only one in civvies, I presume you mean me," Sean replied flashing irresistible Irish charm. Johnson was able to resist.

"Ain't no other chuck dude in civvies except you motherfucker. What's going down? Ain't expectin' nobody 'cept some captain named Coleman," Johnson barked.

Sean looked squarely at Johnson and was reminded how first impressions can be wrong. Although, initially, Johnson appeared pleasant, the Marine was clearly an angry young man. It was also apparent Sean had a long way to go to establish any trust. Right now the brig seemed like the best place for Johnson to keep him from being a danger to himself as well as others.

"This dude's name is O'Ryan. Sean O'Ryan. And you can stick the macho bullshit in your ear. If you've forgotten your military courtesy, at least have the decency to treat Captain Coleman and me with a modicum of civility. I was in the Corps before you got out of short pants, so knock off the John Wayne crap. I started as a buck-ass private at Parris Island and worked my way up to field grade. And I've got a hell of lot more ribbons on my chest than you'll ever dream about," Sean fired back. "But I'm not here to tell war stories or pull rank. I'm here because your Uncle Harry asked me to be. I don't know you but I know Harry Dixon, and I'd crawl eight miles over broken glass to help him. You read me, Marine?"

"I read you, Major field grade. Where's the plexi-glass insert for your naval? I hear all field grades need one to see where they're going, 'cause to make field grade you got to have your head up your ass," Johnson said with malicious delight.

"Now that's more like it, Corporal. Glad to see you have a sense of humor, and not just rhythm."

"Fuck you, man."

"Fuck you right back, man."

Johnson started to grin. "Maybe you're all right for a field grade chuck dude. How'd you know my uncle?"

"I'll tell you that if you'll tell me what a chuck dude is," Sean said smiling.

"Chuck dude? Fuck man, you don't know what a chuck dude is? This is 1964, man. You is a chuck dude. The captain's a chuck. You're white dudes, which means white motherfuckers, which means chuck dudes. It comes from the plantation days. The main white boss was called Uncle Charley. Fuck man, where you been?"

"Thanks for the explanation. And I'll stipulate to the fucking part, but I can't do anything about the white part. In any event, that's not why I'm here. You need to get a handle on the fact that it's to help you, not to dump on you. The way we are going at each other makes me wonder which one of us is the most fucked up. So what do you say we drop the color barriers and all move to the front of the bus. Your ass is in a sling, Marine, and right now, other than your mother and uncle, we are the only friends you've got in the world. "What do you say?" Sean asked without relaxing the bore them right in the eyes technique his mentor Jake Rogers had taught him.

"Okay, man. I'll go along with the program until I find out you're jerkin' me around," Johnson replied.

"All right, Lee. As we say in the grunts, let's get down and dirty. First of all, I know your uncle from Korea. We went through hell together and he saved

33

my ass more than once. That should give you some idea why I care for him."
Sean gave Johnson a challenging look and added, "Now let's talk about you. I
understand you will be charged with rape and felony murder, and they may throw
in aggravated assault as well. The First Sergeant of Headquarters and Service
Company will serve the formal charges on you today. The most serious
problems are the rape and murder charges, and they raise some important
questions."

Sean paused and then softly asked in a tone that was unmistakably serious,
"Did you rape a young woman last Thursday?"

"No fuckin' way, man."

"Were you involved in the beating of a Naval R.O.T.C. midshipman on that
same day, who was with the young woman?"

"No fuckin' way, man."

"All right, so far, so good. So where are we?" Sean asked, making a
deliberate effort to keep a sense of apprehension out of his voice. "For openers,
Captain Coleman and I will give you the full benefit of the doubt and stipulate
that we believe in your innocence. But that's not all there is. You have to be
brutally honest with us at all times. No holding back. No games, no lies, no
waffling, no crap. We can only help you if we know more than anyone else.
However, if we are the most surprised people in the courtroom because
something comes out you should have told us, you will be hanging yourself."

I ain't shuckin' you, man. And I'm not afraid to tell the truth. I got nothin'
to hide. Everything I tell you is gospel."

"Fair enough, Lee. Now for the next big question. If you didn't criminally
assault either the young woman or the midshipman, why were you found
unconscious in the area close to the dead midshipman and within a few feet of
the brutally battered and raped young woman?"

"I don't know, Major," Johnson replied in a much-subdued tone.

"What do you mean you don't know?" Sean pressed.

"What does it sound like? I don't know."

"O.K., what *do you know*?" Sean pressed harder, his purpose being to
accustom Johnson to cross-examination which quite likely would be even
tougher when some prosecutor was doing it at trial.

"I think I know how I got to where the M.P.s found me. I don't know how
the others got there. I was alone the last I can remember, and I fell asleep next to
Lake O'Neill."

"You were discovered at 2317 hours. Where had you been before that?"

"How much before?"

"Start with you going to work in the morning."

"O.K., I got to Base Recreation at 0730. The Lieutenant gave me the
morning shift at the Fifteen Area gym which opens at 0800. I went there and
stayed until 1200 when I was relieved by Lance Corporal Dorwinski to catch

chow. I got back at 1300 and handed out basketballs and other gear until 1630 when the night shift took over. I couldn't workout because I busted my hand last week. I'm supposed to be getting in shape for the basketball season. I was transferred from Division to Base to travel with the team."

"How did you break your hand?"

"On some chuck dude's head, 'cause he was talkin' instead of listenin' and no chuck calls me a nigger. Not twice anyway."

"Did you get in trouble?"

"Fuck, no. The dude ain't got balls enough to tell the man. Big mouth, no balls. Seen him yesterday in the next cell block, but don't know what he's in for."

"Getting back to last Thursday. You left off at 1630. Then what happened?"

"I went to the barracks and changed into civvies and went to the Enlisted Club. I started drinkin' around 1730 and kept drinkin' till I left several hours later."

"Sounds like you wanted to get drunk. Why?"

"Just wanted to that's all. Nothing' else to do. I was feeling down. My ex-pussy sent me a Dear John. Fuckin' bitch."

"How long were you at the club?"

"Don't know. Maybe four hours. Didn't check no clock. I was pretty drunk and started to get sick. Must have been after 2100 anyway. Went outside and started walkin' down towards Vandergrift and then headed for Lake O'Neill 'cause it was downhill. Tried to puke, but couldn't. I must a made it to Lake O'Neill, 'cause that's where they found me."

"What do you remember between the time you left the Club and the M.P.s rousting you at 2317 hours?"

"Nothin'. Just started walkin'. The rest is blank."

"Do you remember the M.P.s?"

"Yeah."

"How, if you were drunk?"

"I just do that's all."

"Can you remember everything that happened?"

"No, but I remember what happened after they beat and kicked the shit out of me."

"What happened before then?"

"I don't know. Must a slept a couple of hours. I passed out. But I remember coming to when they were beating on me with their nightsticks. And I remember one of them kicking me in my side and in my face. You can't tell by the ribs, but you can see my split lip and black eye. The last part ain't meant to be funny."

Jack and Sean got close to Johnson's face. There was clearly evidence of a black and bruised eye and a substantially split lip. "Why did they do that?" Jack asked.

"Fuck, they probably thought I had done the broad and the middie. I don't know. One of those motherfucker M.P.'s was one of my people. Goddamn Uncle Tom. Must get his rocks off bustin' drunk niggers heads," Johnson said more disappointed than angry.

"Lee, we won't use the "N" word if you don't. Is that a deal? Bad habit to get into, and we don't want you making any slips in court," Sean admonished.

"Okay. But you are still motherfuckin'-field-grade-chuck dudes," Johnson fired back and then started to laugh. Sean and Jack had finally reached their client.

Johnson went on to explain how the military police had handcuffed him and kept him lying face down in the dirt until the duty Provost Marshal arrived. That officer took one look and immediately ordered the area sealed off. He then called the resident F.B.I. agent at his home in Oceanside, as well as the duty officer at the local Office of Naval Intelligence (O.N.I.) - later known as the Naval Investigative Service (N.I.S.) - to report the crimes to the federal criminal agencies that would have an interest. He then ordered Johnson to be taken to the Naval Hospital for a pre-confinement physical examination and then locked up in the base brig. By 0200 the next morning Johnson had been visited by the F.B.I. resident agent, agents from the Office of Naval Intelligence, and agents from the Criminal Investigation Division of the Provost Marshal's Office.

Life of a military criminal suspect gets reduced to acronyms, F.B.I., O.N.I., N.I.S., C.I.D., P.M.O., M.P., and host of others depending on the crimes involved. It also gets the suspect a number of warnings under Article 31, Uniform Code of Military Justice, the military equivalent of the Fifth Amendment, later enhanced by the *Miranda* rulings. Johnson was no exception. The visits by the parade of investigators, tripping all over themselves, resulted in a minimum of ten separate warnings of his rights as a suspect. Each time Johnson said the same thing. A total denial of any complicity in the rape and killing and an adamant assertion that he could not remember anything between the time he had left the enlisted club and his being rousted by the military police as much as two hours later. His inability to remember posed a greater problem for Sean than a help.

Over the weekend Johnson was revisited by a myriad of federal agents several more times. They took hair samples, head and pubic; blood samples; finger, palm and hand prints; several dozen photos, front, side, back, face and full body, along with voice samples preserved on tape. All of this was allegedly done with Johnson's purported consent, but without providing him counsel before or during the seizure of these evidentiary items.

Sean asked him why he consented. Johnson replied, "Because I ain't got nothin' to hide. I didn't do these people. Plain and fuckin' simple. I didn't do these people."

"How do you know you didn't?" Jack challenged, deliberately accusatory. "You can't remember anything."

"Shit, Captain, maybe you should borrow the Major's plexiglass insert. You got your head up your ass too. Fuck, man! I would know if I got some pussy, willin' or otherwise, and I sure as shit would know if I was in a fight with some dude and killed him. What kind of a dumb, fuckin' question is that?" Johnson raged.

Sean and Jack both smiled. "Nice touch counselor," Sean said approvingly. "I'm convinced. How about you?"

Jack concurred and Sean appreciated Jack's effort to convince them that Johnson was telling the truth. He had touched the right nerve and Johnson's reaction was consistent with a truth-teller. A pathological liar would have finessed the question with a calm reclamor to the same effect but with a substantially different demeanor. Sean and Jack believed their client, and although things did look bad for Johnson, they were certain he was not playing games with them. Now all they had to do was prove they were right.

"What happens now?" Johnson asked.

Sean explained that a formal investigation under Article 32, Uniform Code of Military Justice would be conducted. The Article 32 Investigation is the equivalent of a federal grand jury in some respects in that it is designed to support the charging process, but that's where the similarity ends. Where non-classified material is involved, the Article 32 is an open proceeding. Defense counsel are present and the hearing is available to public viewing. This is contrary to grand juries which are conducted in secret and the target of the grand jury is not allowed to have counsel in the hearing room. Sean went on to explain that because there are four accused in this case there would be a minimum of four lawyers, and in Johnson's case, he had two attorneys since he had both appointed and retained counsel. The investigating officer is assisted by lawyer counsel as well, so there would be lawyers all over the place. "But most importantly," Sean advised, "the proceedings are eminently more fair than the grand jury."

Sean then added, "The investigating officer is sworn to be unbiased. His job is to collect facts relevant to the question of whether or not a crime has been committed and if there is sufficient evidence to indicate some involvement by the accused. He receives a broad range of information from both sides of the controversy, but the defense counsel don't have to offer anything if they choose not to do so. The investigation is an excellent discovery tool because it lets us know what evidence the government has, which a grand jury proceeding doesn't because it is conducted in secret."

To close the loop Sean also noted, "At the close of the proceedings, the investigating officer makes a recommendation to the convening authority as to what, if any, disciplinary action should be taken, or if the charges should be dismissed or expanded. The convening authority turns the whole package over to his staff legal officer (known as the Staff Judge Advocate in current parlance) for a brand new review and further recommendations. The entire matter gets thoroughly massaged before an accused ever ends up in a court-martial. In this way the Article 32 investigation is a far cry from most rubber stamp grand jury proceedings, and stands as a linchpin in the military system of criminal justice that is by far the fairest in the world."

Sean told Johnson that the investigation would probably not begin for a couple of weeks, and definitely not until the other government agencies completed their preliminary investigations. He further noted that there was no system of bail in the military at that time, and even if there were, it was unlikely Johnson could get out on bail because of the gravity of the charges.

"Will I be facing the death penalty?" Johnson asked, demonstrating serious concern.

"I don't think so," Sean answered, "but we can't guarantee it. There hasn't been an execution in the Naval Service for over a hundred years, although the Army had some as recent as the late fifties for a rape and murder that occurred during the Korean War."

Johnson sighed audibly, and with that, Sean and Jack left promising to be back in a couple of days after they did some digging. Johnson actually managed a smile and Sean concluded they had come a long way when Lee didn't bifurcate his farewell gesture by saying "Good-fucking-by."

When they got back to Jack's office, Sean called the local F.B.I. agent and was advised that the Bureau had deferred to the C.I.D. and the O.N.I. upon the advice of the United States Attorney for the Southern District of California. J. Edgar Hoover didn't feel the case was important enough for his agents to be duplicating the efforts of the other agencies. The crime happened on a military installation and all the participants, except the woman victim, were military so the F.B.I. concluded it might as well let the military handle it.

The F.B.I. agent confided to Sean a few days later that he was glad to get rid of the case since the other agencies were overlapping the Bureau's efforts. His observation was, "At the rate they are going, these clowns won't be able to find their ass with both hands in their back pockets." Funny thing, that's what the other government agents said about the F. B. I.

CHAPTER 7

Jack and Sean met Colonel Hanley and John Crandall at the Seventeen Area O'Club at 1645. "Talk about anything but the case. I've got to remain neutral and I don't want either side pinging on me before, during, or after I make my recommendations to the General," Gene Hanley admonished.

"Aye, aye, Sir," they each responded and then talked about the L.A. Dodgers and L.A. Rams. Someone suggested how lucky Sean was to live in Los Angeles where women grow on trees and are just waiting to get plucked. "Did you say plucked, or something that sounds like that?" Sean asked with a straight face. "Either way, it's a gross exaggeration, but one can only hope."

Among other topics Sean commented about the perception the general public has about the so-called hardheartedness criminal defense counsel exhibit towards the victims of crimes. "That's bullshit, of course, and the very people who complain the loudest are the first in line seeking defense counsel's services if they are personally accused. It's pure crap that defense counsel have no empathy for the victims of crimes."

Sean emphasized that the feelings of defenders have to be divided between the revulsion they feel about the crime, which feeling should be coupled with genuine compassion for the victims, balanced against counsel's sworn duty to protect the rights of the accused. "It sometimes is a losing battle, and unless and until someone is personally accused, he often overloads his identification with the victim," he added.

With these serious considerations out of the way, they turned to the more important questions, such as, who would win the National League? Would Maury Wills set another base stealing record? Would Goldwater beat Johnson for President or would all the things old Barry had been warning about come true in a full term with Lyndon B., the great manipulator and election stealer.

Sean demurred on a third beer because of the long drive back to L.A., and managed to break away by 1730 hours, promising to give Jack a call in the morning and wishing John Crandall a speedy return from Okinawa. Traffic wasn't bad until he got well into Orange County. Then it turned into the usual bumper to bumper for that time of day.

As Sean crawled along, he thought about Susan and how their affair had begun back in May 1964. He had known Susan's fiancé, Stan Lerner, for several years before Stan met Susan. She and Stan dated casually at first and then more steadily, until, in Sean's opinion, Susan's relationship with Stan took a turn for the worse and they talked of marriage. At that point Susan viewed Sean with caution. Admittedly, she liked him from the first day they met, but she equally distrusted him, viewing him as an incorrigible womanizer who would try to charm the pants off a female snake if someone held its head. The reputation was somewhat embellished, but Sean did have a hard time resisting attractive women and Susan had reason not to trust him.

He was particularly attracted to Susan, as might be expected, and he constantly had to resist the impulse to tell her just how interested he was. As time went on, however, he stopped resisting. In May, when Stan was out of town on business, Sean called Susan to convince her that a week alone in her big estate was cruel and unusual punishment. He suggested she ought to have dinner with him. She accepted, more curious than cautious. Halfway through dinner, and partly into a second bottle of St. Emilion, Sean used all of his savoir-faire in an effort to explain his long subdued feelings and how, quite frankly, he wanted to seduce Susan if he could. Eloquence may have been lacking, but he was sincere and figured that should count for something. His seduction technique missed its mark, however, when Sean looked at Susan and professed a long-standing interest in knowing her in a biblical sense, which he now would dearly love to address more fully in her bedchamber or his. The exact, but rather indelicate, words were, "Susan, I have been attracted to you for a long, long time, and, frankly, I want to fuck your brains out."

Susan feigned shock and surprise, but then laughed, "I'm sure you do, Mr. O'Ryan, but you're not going to. By the way, has anyone ever mentioned anything about your style? I'll give you high marks for effort, but your approach is anything but subtle."

"Damn, Susan, don't you know trial lawyers are masters of the persuasion game. You're doing serious injury to my ego. Hell, why else do you think I chose the litigator's life over the deadly work of a tax law like Stan? I was priming myself to become a quintessential seducer."

"You already have you Irish rogue, but you lost your case, counselor, quintessential or not. I don't need lip service persuasion, I need a good reason." Susan gave Sean a look that suggested she wasn't insulted, but, on the contrary, might be a bit flattered. Nonetheless, the proposal was not acceptable at the moment. He refused to be dissuaded, however.

"I'll give you the best reason of all," Sean pressed. "I don't believe Stan is all that interesting in bed. He's very good-looking, and definitely intelligent, but he doesn't impress me as a dynamo in the sex department. Maybe I'm wrong, but I'm willing to bet on it. As a result I think your responses in the sack are often more an accommodation than enthusiastic participation."

"I don't know whether that is a statement or a question, Sean, but either way, does it matter? I'm engaged to Stan. Nobody held a gun to my head and made me accept his proposal. I was convinced I was ready for that kind of decision, and there's a lot of reasons why I made it. Part of the deal, I presume, is that nobody else is supposed to be - quote, fucking my brains out, end quote - while I am engaged, or what you might call, promised to Stan," Susan said softly and with what Sean wanted to believe was a touch of doubt. He could see the opening but realized he had to use finesse because she wasn't buying his horny bull approach.

"Susan, what better reason could you have than the need to express yourself fully as a woman? This is a substantial need at any phase of a woman's life, and in your case you are still very young. Why should you be giving up something as wonderful as loving sex, or even unbridled sex for that matter. What's the old cliché, the worst piece I ever had was terrific." Sean then added before Susan could reply, "I'm not talking about your breaking up with Stan. I'm only talking about adding a dimension that is missing. There are all kinds of reasons why you might find marriage to Stan tolerable even without great sex. He's steady, and he's nuts about you. Maybe you just don't want to get back in the rat race and have to deal with the assholes who act out the find 'em, fuck 'em, and forget 'em routine. But that doesn't mean you have to live quasi-celibate if you can enjoy a little extracurricular fun that doesn't interfere with your so-called engagement. Don't you owe it to yourself to find out if life with Stan is what you really want?"

"I don't think you can have it both ways," Susan countered.

"Yes you can, provided you know the rules going in and live with them. Sort of keeping the airplane inside the envelope as my pilot friends say. You can have a lover on the side to give yourself to with complete abandon during your stolen moments, just so long as you understand that that's the alpha and omega of the arrangement. The only time lovers screw up is when one or both of the participants forget the rules mandating the limitations."

"Listen, Sean. I'm engaged to Stan. I'm supposed to be thinking about a commitment for better or worse."

"Bullshit. You're engaged, not dead, and if you are frustrated physically, you may be marrying for all the wrong reasons. And let me add, I'm not talking about some indefinable relationship that makes you suddenly less yourself simply because you made some promises to Stan. You are still free to do as you please. You don't owe Stan a damn thing, but you do owe it to yourself to find out if this is what you really want before you make the mistake of marriage."

Susan looked at Sean but didn't say anything, so he went on. "You are still young, engaged or not, and your needs might be dangerously sublimated but that doesn't change your person. There is nothing in human nature that makes the act of loving someone mutually exclusive. Don't let anyone tell you that you are somehow abnormal because you love two people at the same time. In this context I am talking about a unique kind of love, like man for woman, in a deep, emotional and sexual way. I am not talking about loving parents, siblings, or children at the same time. Obviously that's different."

Susan still didn't say anything but Sean could see that she was thinking about what he was saying, so he added, "In the sense of woman and man type of loving, that is husbands, wives, and lovers, I assume, maybe rightfully, maybe wrongly, that you love Stan, but it doesn't make you any less the sensuous woman I am convinced you are, and it certainly doesn't change your need to express that sensuality."

When Sean stopped, Susan gave him a strange look as she wondered silently, *What the hell is he saying?* Sean saw that he had to press on, but cautiously or Susan might rebel because he was touching an area she hadn't wanted to explore. "Look, Susan, I'm not trying to con you into bed. I'll admit I had hoped I could move you in that direction when I called, but now the conversation has taken an intellectual turn and the blood is back in my brain instead of my penis. So please hear me out and maybe you'll get a handle on something you have been avoiding. I truly believe you can love Stan and have a separate lover at the same time. Now you may not be in love with your lover, but you can have him. There is no need to limit your growth. The one man, one-woman theory is all right but it can be suffocating at times. Plato said, 'There's no greater or keener pleasure than that of bodily love, and none which is more irrational.' I agree with the first part but not the second. I think it is rational to keep the body, which is the soul's vehicle, functioning smoothly and in the manner in which it was designed throughout our long evolution. Sex is not a bi-product of evolution; it is a primary function, and by far the most pleasurable. So why commit to an exclusive relationship if it is incomplete? How do you grow from that?"

Susan interrupted, "Let me ask you a question, and don't take this as acquiescence in anything you are proposing. Particularly the seduction of Susan. How long have we known each other? Several years at least. I have been dating Stan for most of those years and now we are engaged. During that time you and I and Stan have done a lot of things together, parties and other socializing. I remember the wonderful ski trips to Lake Tahoe and the other fun trips to Vegas. But as far as you are concerned, I never trusted you because you clearly are a blatant womanizer. I admit I enjoy a lot of things about you and I admire your ability as a lawyer, but there are two Sean O'Ryans."

"Two?" Sean asked. "Some people find just one intolerable."

"You may be right," Susan replied, "but there are two sides to you."

"Is that right?" Sean mused.

"Yes, that's right," Susan went on. "Not in the sense of separate personalities, but separate perspectives. One is the consummate professional who wouldn't compromise his ethics for all the money in the world. The other, unfortunately, is the reckless bachelor who doesn't mind a trail of broken hearts. You are a paradox. At least I think you are, but maybe you're not. Maybe you are simply honest enough to do the things most men would if they could but don't have the nerve. I don't know. I just know I can't see you being serious about a monogamous relationship."

Sean started to speak but Susan waived him off, and he sat back and let her continue. "Now, having said that, let me ask you, what is your interest in me?

Surely you aren't pretending to be in love with me. I think you say things quite glibly when you want to get a girl's pants off, but what do you really feel for me? Don't answer. That's not the real question. Somehow I believe you may think you care for me as something more than a friend and God knows we've known each other long enough to have a pretty fair idea of who we are. But my question is, so what? So you care about me. What am I supposed to do about it other than let you fuck my brains out? What the hell is it supposed to mean after that?"

Sean felt as if he were seeing Susan for the first time. Although this beautiful woman had been in his life for several years, he realized he hadn't appreciated this side of her. He sensed that she was disappointed in Stan's lack of awareness of her total needs, but she was communicating something more significant than minor frustration. Rather, she seemed to be reaching out, but he didn't know what to do about it. He was bent on making love to her, but she was on a different track, and Sean hadn't planned on this kind of emotional response. The need for caution was clear because Susan was close to genuine anger over whatever it was that was bothering her.

"Susan, I don't know what to say. Hell I never had the nerve to confront these feelings in the light. I knew I cared, and I was fairly certain that marrying Stan wasn't in your best interest, but I didn't think it was my place to say anything unless you asked me. But I will now. Plain and simple, unless you are damn sure it's the thing to do, you should reconsider Stan's proposal. I say this not for my sake, or anyone else's, except your own."

Susan looked at Sean and softened perceptibly. "Sean, I'll take a chance on your sincerity, and I'll stipulate - as you lawyers say - that you are being honest and you mean only the best for me. I know you started out to seduce me and that you aren't making any promises. That's good, because I don't want any promises or complications. If I have any doubts about whether or not I should be marrying Stan, then I should find out in my own way and it shouldn't have anything to do with our wanting each other at least sexually."

"Our wanting? Each other?" Sean quickly picked up.

"Yes, Sean, I won't deny I am more than a little interested in finding out what it would be like to be in bed with you. I have wondered about that for a long time, reputation or not. And frankly I have thought that maybe I feel more than just friendship and I would like to know more."

"Susan, don't say these things unless you mean them and intend to do something about them. I'm not jerking you around about this. The blood is leaving my brain again and I am not going to be able to see that fine line between friendship and lust in a minute."

"Then I guess we should do something about it, Mr. O'Ryan. I have wanted to know more of you and now I have the courage, or foolishness, to find out. Maybe a little of each. I don't know where it will take us, but as the flyboys say, no guts, no air medals, and talking isn't going to resolve it. Just one thing, you

43

have not seduced me. This is my idea. I'm not just another filly in your stable. I persuaded myself. You - master trial lawyer - did not persuade me. You got that?"

"Yes, Ma'am," Sean replied. "Your place or mine?"

"Neither. Let's go some place neutral," Susan suggested. "Then if either of us has any regrets, we won't have a constant reminder around us."

"There will be no regrets," Sean confidently promised. And with that he paid the check and headed for the *Hilton* with Susan glowingly beautiful at his side.

CHAPTER 8

The Hilton, May 1964

Sean and Susan didn't talk on the drive to the *Hilton* but simply enjoyed romantic radio music that lent charm to the beautiful spring evening. In spite of past experience they were both feeling a little shy, but neither chose to say so. When they got into the room, Susan seemed uneasy and Sean sensed a personal reticence as well. He wondered why, since he had been in a first time situation many times before. But with Susan it seemed different. He genuinely liked her and he wanted to think that this encounter had more substance than just another opportunity to enjoy a lovely woman in the flesh. He smiled and took Susan in his arms, acknowledging that the man of reputation was a little nervous.

"I can't believe I am feeling like a kid. I've wanted to be with you like this from the day we met, but that was pure lust. Now that we are here, I'll be damned if I can get started. I hope you aren't having any second thoughts. It would shatter my ego."

"It's all right, Sean. I'm not having any second thoughts. It's just that I feel the same. We've been friends for a long time, and to be honest I have lusted after you too, so maybe we can finally explore our desires. Feeling a bit restrained is a natural reaction. Let's face it, I'm not surrendering my virginity. It's been a while since I did that. Besides, that status was terribly overrated. The alternative is much better, although the first time clearly was nothing to write home about. Thank God that's in the past. So I can stop acting coy or whatever, and you can start feeling studly again. I'm here, because you are, and we both want to do this, so let's relax and take it from there."

Sean smiled and took Susan in his arms without any further conversation. He kissed her tenderly at first and then with greater ardor as he started to fumble with her blouse and undress her. There is no more asinine endeavor than trying to disrobe a woman while at the same time attempting to take off one's trousers. There is no way to do it gracefully. Best to forget the dual effort and take off her clothes and then let her help you with yours, letting them lay where they fall, while enjoying the kissing, touching, and embracing, with maybe some teasing loving in the shower along the way. Nothing like a warm woman under running water to heighten the anticipation of delights to come.

They did it all. The undressing, the kissing, the touching, and then the shower, after which Sean dried Susan with a large towel and her beautiful skin glowed from the combination of warm water and pulsing blood flowing through her lush body in response to his passionate caresses. Then he led her to the bed and lowered her gently. Unless approached with consideration for one's partner, the ultimate sex act can be fairly selfish, and in Sean's life at times it was. But it was different with Susan. As he touched and tasted her, and then filled her with himself, he realized that their lovemaking had taken on something akin to a totally giving experience that he had known before in the sense of offering and not just taking. Unless you have been there, it is difficult to define. But it clearly is more than a physical thrill. It is an emotional high that takes you well beyond the confines of the environment of two bodies engaged in touch and taste and nerve sensations. It is akin to ethereal.

Sean had known the phenomenon he referred to as an *out of body experience* only once before. That was another time with a love of infinite dimension. Now he sensed it again with Susan and he was amazed. It was - as he held Susan, still tightly fully consumed by her - that he felt he was out of his body and he seemed to be watching from a place above them as if he had been mystically transported to the top of the room as a supernatural hologram. He could see himself and Susan enclosed in each other. And on her face he saw the sweet look of caring and pleasure mixed in the way that only humans, who are joined in body and soul, can achieve.

Susan's long, dark hair formed an adornment on the pillow and Sean's face was buried in it as he surrendered all effort to take up his weight. He collapsed against her beauty and he looked at her with a feeling he could not explain. He concluded that this had to be the meaning of born again. To go out of yourself and renew the spirit that is the soul striving for evolvement. He had made love to Susan with a passion that was not only on a different plane, but also of a different universe. It was then that Sean understood what had happened to him once before in another time when he was deeply in love and he knew he loved without reservation. He didn't believe he was in love with Susan in the same way as yet, but he did care with a greater depth than he had expected.

Susan opened her eyes and looked at Sean with an expression that needed no words. Only when she finally spoke did he return to his body and joyfully accept her straightforward statement that this adventure would be revisited soon. "All I can say, Mr. O'Ryan, is that you certainly know how to spoil a lady. I don't know if I will ever be the same, but it is too sweet to let such concerns intrude. If I start to worry about what might be rather than what is, it will diminish the moment, and this moment was meant to last no matter what might happen from here on."

"I'll take that as the ultimate in compliments," Sean said smiling, "and I'm not going to worry about tomorrow either. What we are about right now is the only reality. Making love to you is all I am concerned about." He kissed her tenderly and held her gently while bringing her down from the plateau of her passion until she fell asleep in his arms, lost in this special experience.

As Susan slept, Sean glanced around the room and noticed for the first time that there was a radio on the nightstand next to their bed where fantasy had become loving reality. He reached quietly to turn it on so as not to disturb Susan, and was grateful to discover that the previous tenants were persons of taste as classical music drifted softly through its electromagnetic magic. The adagio from the ballet *Spartacus* was being played by a symphony orchestra and the poignant melody seemed appropriate for the combination of euphoria and melancholy Sean was feeling at that moment. The splendor of a loving experience was coupled with a concomitant sadness that this relationship, like so many others, might be fashioned out of gossamer too fragile to survive the reality of life beyond their safe harbor in the *Hilton*.

He didn't want to think about that reality, but the long and often painful progression of Sean's life, filled with all of the vicissitudes of which the poets are fond of reminding, gave him pause. He was acutely aware of the many circumstances where dreams can come true and then die in almost the same space of time. Although he had no illusions about the depth of his love for Susan, he felt something more than just the strong friendship he enjoyed with her to up this time and more than the euphoria and joy of wonderful sex with a lovely and special partner. For the first time in a long time he felt vulnerable, and this was disturbing because he wanted no more loss and pain.

Often his relationships as a lover were entered into with either blind passion, or by a "what the hell" attitude, let's give it a go, and if it worked, then fine, and if it didn't, then at least it was worth the effort. In this way some lovely women came into his life, and some left. And some, he discovered, would remain forever in secret places in his soul even though no longer physically present. He suspected that the matter of Susan would take on that proportion. But he promised himself to be on guard. Maybe she would decide not to marry Stan, but Sean convinced himself it shouldn't be because he was taking Stan's place. He cautiously assured himself that this affair would be kept in bounds. And he was confident that Susan shared his views on this.

****

September 1964

That was four months ago. Susan was still engaged to Stan but no wedding date has been set. Sean was confident the continuation of the affair that started at the Hilton was influencing the delay. But he was equally certain that he and Susan had come to terms with the limitations they agreed were necessary so they could enjoy the ecstasy of stolen moments without falling victim to the complications that affairs produce. This wasn't always easy and Sean's desire to make love with Susan had a way of manifesting itself at inappropriate times. He realized this sort of thing is what causes relationships to get out of hand and leads to notions that maybe one is not fully alive unless the other person is with him.

47

Such notions are a precursor of thoughts of marriage, which sometimes works, but too often doesn't. As he pleasantly recalled that special night in May, Sean noticed he was approaching the Marina and still had a little time left to shower before Susan would be arriving after she dropped Stan off at the airport.

Susan rang the bell at eight fifteen with a small suitcase in hand which she had sequestered in the trunk of her Mercedes convertible so her husband would not see it as she dropped him off. As planned, she had placed his luggage in the back seat, which was easy to do with the top down. Sean, who was naked as he opened the door, embraced her playfully as she walked in. Susan laughed and suggested that undressing should be easy since it was going to be all one sided.

They didn't make it to the bedroom. The oriental rug in the living room was revisited and their lovemaking continued its golden climb. Later they would move to the bedroom, but at the moment they were lost in loving; immersed in each other with no reservation or shame, enjoying the wondrous gift that God has given to men and women which allows them to express completely the feelings generated from being unreservedly merged physically, spiritually, and emotionally.

Sean awakened several hours later with Susan wrapped in his arms. He looked at the time displayed on the alarm radio that had just come on. The love theme from Tchaikovsky's *Romeo and Juliet* had awakened them and its sensuous sounds blended with their romantic embrace. He kissed her and felt a passionate response. She felt the same and they loved again, and then lay quietly for a few minutes. Then Susan spoke softly, "One for the road, Mr. O'Ryan? I presume you are off somewhere. Why else would you be waking us in the middle of the night?"

"Gee, Suz. Had I known you were going to seduce me so early in the a.m., I would have set the alarm a whole lot earlier. What a nice way to start the day," Sean responded with a warm smile.

"My pleasure sir. Anytime, just anytime at all."

"How about tonight? I should be back fairly early."

"How about we just stay here all day," Susan countered.

"Wish we could, Suz, but I've got to drive down south. I'll be back by eight at the latest, and a whole lot earlier if traffic permits. I'm headed for Camp Pendleton again, which is why we are up so early, but I'll be on the road back to you by four-thirty, I promise."

"What is this case about?" Susan asked, but then added quickly, "no, don't tell me. Save it 'till later. I don't want to hear about some bad ass while I am enraptured by you. You have landed, Marine, and the situation is well in hand. And in me too," Susan chuckled in a sassy way.

"You got it, dear lady. Besides I don't talk about my cases until they are over, so no point in changing now."

They showered and then Susan made coffee while Sean shaved. He left at six thirty sharp with a promise of another night of pleasure in a little over twelve hours. Susan lingered a while to enjoy the magnificent sunrise in Sean's apartment. He had to hustle to get to Pendleton by nine, but it was worth it.

CHAPTER 9

September 9, 1964

Driving down to Camp Pendleton Sean's thoughts of Susan were warm as he considered the good rapport they enjoyed, but he had no idea where they were heading. They had talked briefly about their relationship but he couldn't get past the feeling that they should view their affair as just one of those great sex things with no discernible future. Susan admitted she had been giving serious thought about whether or not she should marry Stan, but she emphasized it wasn't because her attention had been diverted by Sean. And he had no qualms about the limitations they had imposed particularly since a great physical relationship is much more enjoyable without responsibility attaching. Sean wondered how people could claim to be enjoying the moment while they constantly worried about whether or not it was going to be this way tomorrow or ten years later. It was supposed to be only fun and games with Susan. And Sean was not thinking of marriage even though he had grown increasingly in love with of her. He assumed that when Susan was ready, she would marry Stan, who was steady, and the fun and games would peter out over a course. When they did, he and Susan would remain friends even though no longer lovers. Until then he found it exciting making love to a beautiful woman, particularly when he wasn't supposed to be. There's something to be said for the fruits of original sin.

As Sean continued south-bound the ugly aspects of Interstate 5 on the southern fringes of the Los Angeles metro area gave way to rolling hills around El Toro. With traffic lighter he was soon enjoying the beauty of the ocean as he rolled past San Clemente and reached the outer boundaries of Camp Pendleton. Thirty minutes later he arrived at Base Legal and found Jack in his office going over the investigative reports furnished by the O.N.I. and the C.I.D. Jack greeted him with the news that word of the crimes had hit the wire services. As a result the Commanding General called a press conference and asked Colonel Hanley to preside in order to avoid suggestions of any predetermination of guilt and to guard against comments that might come back to haunt the general later.

"Ah well, this was bound to happen sooner or later. I'm surprised it was low keyed as long as it was. The Labor Day weekend no doubt helped. I imagine the *L.A. Times* will pick it up. Maybe it will be buried in the back. It's a sad commentary that rape and murder are no longer news in a metropolitan area of several million people," Sean noted, and then added, "by the way Jack, have you had a chance to check with counsel for the other accused to see if they will let us talk to their clients?"

"I have, but right now everyone is under wraps, although I do have the names of the other players. They are, Lance Corporal Thomas Panos, Lance Corporal Anthony Fennelli, and Private First Class Rick Cox. Panos is represented by Captain Frank Chase; Fennelli by Lieutenant Dan Richardson, and Cox by Captain Dusty Burns. They are not inclined to jerk us around, but right now they are sure to play everything close to the vest. You are the only civilian counsel involved so far."

"What are the victims' names?"

"The young woman is Chrissy Long, age nineteen. The deceased midshipman was David Hall, age twenty-one."

"Something is nagging at me, Jack, but I can't isolate it. Maybe after I read the reports, it will get clearer. In any event at this point I believe Lee Johnson has been honest with us so somehow this has to make sense. I don't think he is trying to deliberately mislead us. And in the meanwhile Sergeant Major Ed Tabor is checking with his contact in the Provost Marshal's Office to see what he can find out unofficially. The cops don't put half the stuff they know in the reports."

Jack had a copy of the AP wire that had gone out from San Diego which basically said no more than a rape (victim's name withheld) and a homicide (victim named) had occurred on Marine Corps Base Camp Pendleton, Thursday last, and four Marines had been implicated and charged. One Marine, a Negro, was apprehended at the scene of the offense, Lake O'Neill, which is near the Naval Hospital on the base. The other three Marines, all Caucasians, were traced through a uniform cap found at the scene, which bore a name and serial number stenciled in the headband. It was not revealed how this discovery led to the apprehension of the remaining two Marines. An investigation was continuing. It was obvious to Sean that the Marine, whose cap had been found, blew the whistle on the other two. He wondered what kind of deal was made with the snitching Marine and what he may have had to say about Johnson.

One of the O.N.I. reports had a statement by one of the accused, Thomas Panos, in which he implicated the other two white Marines, Fennelli and Cox, but completely denied that he personally took part in any of the conduct that resulted in the rape of Miss Long and the death of Midshipman Hall. He claimed he had only been with the other two when they ran across Hall and Long, but he didn't get into the fight with the midshipman and he swore he never touched the woman victim. Surprisingly, while Panos also implicated Johnson, who he said was at the scene but had not been in the company of the three other Marines prior to their encountering Hall and Miss Long, he waffled on the details of Johnson's participation. The most he would say was that he remembered a Negro Marine being at the scene and participating with Fennelli and Cox, but he hadn't been with them earlier in the evening. Panos did not elaborate on what he meant by participating other than to say that Johnson had got it on with the other two

Marines. When pressed to answer if he meant Johnson was involved in the fight and rape, Panos only answered, "Yes."

Panos's counsel still would not let him talk to Jack and Sean, so they went over to see Johnson at the brig to discuss the reports and Panos's so-called admission. "Did you know Panos, Fennelli or Cox before that night?" Sean asked as Johnson settled into the chair across from him in the interview room.

"I knew Fennelli from the Division. We were in Delta-One-Five."

"Were you friends?"

"Hell, no. He's an asshole. Always mouthin' off. Got an attitude about coloreds. We didn't like each other, but that's because he don't like 'spades' he says. Claims he's from the South, but it's South Philly. He's an asshole."

"You ever get in a fight with him?"

"Nah, he's too chicken. Mouths off a lot but only gets it on with people smaller than him. I did knock his buddy on his ass last week outside the 'E' Club, but Fennelli backed off. That's when I busted my hand."

"What's his buddy's name?"

"I don't know. Might know him if I see him."

"Could be one of the other two," Sean commented to Jack. "We'll check it out later."

Sean went over the reports with Johnson, but Johnson couldn't add anything to his earlier observations. They prodded him to keep working on his recall the best he could. As Sean and Jack were about to leave, Johnson spoke up. "I don't think there was anything else, but something strange keeps slippin' in and out of my head. It's kind of mixed up."

"What's that? Don't sweat how it sounds. We'll figure it out," Jack interjected.

"It has to do with a girl. I don't remember but I think I remember her screaming. Maybe I was dreamin'. I was pretty drunk, but I remember something that sounded like screaming and then - strange fuckin' thing - I remember smelling perfume, like a woman was close to me. What the fuck, I must a been dreamin'."

"Could mean a number of things," Sean said. "But it's interesting. Let's see what we can do with it, and in the meanwhile keep trying to remember anything else you can."

Jack and Sean left the brig and went back to Jack's office. "I don't like the smell of perfume part, Jack. Sounds like he got real close to the girl unless he really was dreaming. If he did get close, why? He says he didn't do anything to her." Once again, they went over the reports that had been furnished by the O.N.I. and C.I.D. Each contained the usual warnings. Property of the United States Government. Official Business. Not to be copied or disseminated, which meant God help the person who lets the press and other undesirables see one word of this. The only admonishment that was missing was burn before reading.

After carefully reviewing each report a couple more times, they both came to the same conclusion. What was missing was more important than what was there. Panos exonerates himself, but implicates the other two white Marines; then waffles on Johnson. Something was wrong. He doesn't clear Johnson, but what he doesn't say loomed large. Panos responded to questions that seemingly harmed Johnson, but not with the precision they would have expected, and he didn't elaborate on details when questioned.

Q. Did the Negro Marine take part in beating of the midshipman?
A. Yes.
Q. Did the colored Marine participate in the assault on the young woman?
A. Yes.
Q. In what way?
A. I don't know. He was just fighting with the Navy guy and I saw him make it with the broad.
Q. How did he make it with the woman?
A. I saw him on top of her or her on top of him, same as the other guys were doing.

***

In reading the reports, it was obvious the agent had employed the often used tactic of asking the suspect questions and then typing the questions and answers in the agent's own words, paraphrasing the actual language used. At the same time the agent makes deliberate mistakes in spelling and other typographical errors so that it is necessary to have the suspect initial corrections of the typos, purposely made by the agent, to give the appearance that the language employed throughout the statement was, in fact, that of the witness. This manipulation is done to meet the interrogator's design and often traps the unwary.

"I sure would like to talk to Panos right now," Jack said, "but it looks like we are going to have to wait until the Article 32 Investigation and then we can only hope his counsel puts him on the stand. If he gets cute, I promise he'll leave the courtroom with a new ass," Jack said making no attempt to conceal his anger at Panos's murky implication of Johnson.

"I'll second that. Something is really fucked up here. Either Johnson is lying his head off, or Panos is. I wonder what Panos's motives would be," Sean responded. He then gave Ed a call to see if he had heard anything from his contact at the Provost Marshal's Office.

"Just one thing," Ed advised, "but I don't have the full scoop so it is still fairly raw data. My inside man is checking it out for more details. He heard through the grapevine that the Negro M.P. who rousted Johnson, probably the one who kicked his brains out, had the hots for a girl Johnson was dating. He doesn't know anymore than that, but he thinks the girl dropped Johnson and has been doing her thing with the M.P. This might explain why he gave Johnson a little extra attention when they rousted him at Lake O'Neill. He's going to follow this up and keep me posted. Don't know if it will have any bearing on the case, but any lead is better than nothing."

"That's right Ed. Thanks for the help. I'll be in touch."

"How 'bout that, Jack? The jealousy monster rears it's ugly head and Johnson gets his ass kicked. Be nice to tie it in somehow," Sean mused. "When's the Article 32 set to start? I have cleared my calendar as best I could for next week, so I'll be available whenever you give me the word."

"Last word I got, it will go off Monday at 0900," Jack advised. "The investigating officer will be Major Pat Carothers. Hell of a fine guy, and you can bet the farm he will play it by the book. Pat used to be a fleet boxing champion and has a chest full of medals from World War II and Korea. I have no question he'll be fair, so even if we can't get the charges against Johnson kicked out at the pre-trial, at least we'll know where we are if the case gets referred to a general court-martial."

"Sounds good," Sean nodded. "Guess I'll head back to L.A. now and see you bright and early Monday morning. I'll try to get here about 0800 in case there is anything we need to talk about before the formal proceedings start. In the meanwhile if you hear anything, give me a growl. We've got a few days to nose around. I'll get back to Johnson's uncle and see if there is something in Johnson's past that will help us. You dig around Division and Base and see what you can come up with. If not before, I'll see you on Monday."

******

On the drive back Sean's thoughts shifted from Johnson to Susan and he started to feel subtle messages of desire flowing through his chest and down into his loins. The sexual relationship was so strong that even if he did think about her in other terms, such considerations were overwhelmed with overinding lustful urges. He understood how it is harder to break off a relationship based on sex than one based on fragile emotions mistakenly thought to be love. Great sex can really screw up one's thinking and Sean tried to figure which of Susan's attributes he appreciated as much as her physical beauty. *She clearly is a strong, independent woman gifted with an exceptionally bright mind that is a match for her beauty*, he admitted as he reflected on these qualities. He also admitted how much he appreciated being with her for reasons unrelated to physical attraction, particularly after making love when they would engage in long talks. But he hadn't allowed himself to approach the relationship with any serious considerations beyond an ever growing affection which he was confident was love enhanced by their wonderful sexual rapport.

While he had willingly accepted the idea of marriage to someone else a few years ago, those plans hadn't worked out. Now he was dedicated to the freedom he enjoyed as a single man which gave him unlimited time to devote to his profession, as well as to date a number of different women. Having no present desire to give up that freedom, he accepts their friendship and sex as the controlling aspects. Because the physical responses in and of themselves are great between them, he rationalizes that this is reason enough in and of itself.

The traffic was better than the day before, but it still took three hours to make the trip. As he pulled into his garage at the Marina, he saw that Susan's car was there which meant she was up in the apartment. He had given her a key a few weeks ago with an open invitation to use it anytime. This was not intended to be a symbol of surrender, but a gesture of affection and appreciation of their relationship.

As Sean entered, Susan was standing on the balcony watching the magical display that evening produces. Sunsets and sunrises are special gifts as a result of the positioning of the apartment with a wide array of windows on either side which provides a double exposure, east and west. When the morning light streams through the windows welcoming the sun from the east, it unites in a spectrum of colors with the westward vista of sea and ships. As twilight approaches and the sun dips into the Pacific, it sprays red fire across the gray water and sends tongues of gold leaping upward to caress the masts of pleasure boats snuggled in their slips, and then reaches for Sean's apartment in a shower of sensual delight. He shared the sunset with Susan for several minutes, holding her from behind in a warm embrace as they faced the sea. Then she turned and they ascended in a sudden rush of passion revisiting the oriental rug in the living room which manifested greater beauty than the weavers ever dreamed of. Afterward, they lay quietly still joined in loving repose as the retreating light clothed their nakedness in darkness.

CHAPTER 10

September 12, 1964

Ed Tabor drove up to spend a couple of days with Sean the weekend prior to the start of the Article 32 Investigation. Susan was tied up with Stan, so Sean called Joy, the lush redhead he had met at the *Ambassador*, and set things up for Joy and Gerry to take in a Dodger game on Saturday night. It was designed to be a casual date with hot dogs and beer, and the four of them had fun just being themselves without any fancy airs. Joy was an avid baseball fan and knew more about the Dodgers than Sean did. Gerry was less of a fan but found Ed fascinating and didn't worry about whether Sandy Koufax had a no hitter going into the seventh inning.

After the game they had a drink in a little bar in Santa Monica and then moved on to the apartment Joy and Gerry shared. When they arrived, Joy and Sean sat in the living room and talked for an hour or so while Ed and Gerry disappeared somewhere in the back. Joy was mildly surprised that Sean hadn't tried to hustle her, but he assured her it had nothing to do with her desirability. "If desire were the only consideration, I would have been all over you," Sean said smiling. "I just thought you might like a date for a change where the guy wasn't all hands and hot breath. I'd like to see you again, and I want you to know that you can be appreciated for yourself and not just your terrific body."

"You have no idea how nice it is to hear that. What a treat not having to fight off some turkey who thinks he is owed something just because he spent a few bucks on wine and dinner. I'm not sure how much of a fight I'd want to put up with you, however, but it is nice not to have to."

"Thanks for the compliment," Sean answered wondering if he was being genuinely decent or if he was enjoying so much sex with Susan that his natural inclination to hustle other women was slowing down. But then he studied Joy's lovely face and figure and decided he really hadn't lost any of his normal appreciation of beautiful women. "I had a lot of fun tonight, Joy, and I'd like to see you again. I know it's an old line, but when I say I'll call, *I will*."

"I believe you, Sean Fitzpatrick O'Ryan," Joy said smiling. It was an invitation Sean couldn't resist and he took her in his arms and kissed her softly at first and then with greater emphasis. Joy responded in a most promising way and Sean felt confident the next time would be sooner than he had anticipated. Ed and Gerry finally reappeared. Ed was smiling as he and Sean left about one in the morning.

They slept until nine, and then after breakfast they met Bobby Stein at his slip in the Marina and spent the rest of Sunday with him and Cindy, still the woman of the moment, cruising down to Laguna Beach and Newport, stopping for a late lunch and a couple of beers along the way. They returned to the slip about seven and headed directly to the Marina. Ed shoved off for Oceanside, and Sean went to bed early knowing he had to get up at 0500 and on the road for Camp Pendleton.

The Article 32 hearing was called to order by Major Pat Carothers. He had been introduced to Sean earlier in Colonel Hanley's office, and Sean noted that Jack had not exaggerated when he said Pat had a chest full of medals, which included five purple hearts. Seems like Pat was consistently in the right place at the wrong time, and he literally came out a bloody hero on many occasions. Sean liked him immediately; tall, good looking, strong build, he resembled the *after* Charles Atlas ads one used to see in pulp magazines, only with a close cropped head of brown hair worn *high and tight* Marine Corps style.

They then moved into the hearing room. Lee Johnson and the other three accused were there under guard, a precaution the brig was carrying to the extreme. All four detainees had been brought in with their hands cuffed behind their backs and led jointly on a long lead chain that gave them the appearance of a Georgia chain gang. Incredibly, one of the guards assigned to Johnson was not certain if he could remove the handcuffs even when Sean asked him if he thought it might not be a good idea if Johnson was able to sit at counsel table and participate in his own hearing. The guard said he would have to call the warden. Sean advised him that the warden and the guard would be standing tall before the General in five minutes flat if he didn't unshackle Johnson. Pat Carothers overheard this exchange and barked, "Get your head out of your ass, Marine, and do what counsel asks." The guard sensed Pat's short fuse and jumped to the task.

The opening salvo began after the preliminary jurisdictional observations were read into the record. The court reporter was using the stenomask system wherein she repeated every word into a hand held mask that fitted over most of her face so her voice was muffled and didn't disrupt the proceedings. Her words were then tape recorded. The Marine Corps hadn't gone to the more sophisticated systems as yet and Sean found it interesting to watch this very pretty woman perform a strange oral ritual that looked like she was trying to eat out the insides of a large cylindrical piece of fruit. "Life imitates sexual art," Sean whispered to Jack with a smile.

Counsel for the investigating officer was Major Brendon Bryant, a wild and woolly Irishman who could have led a Saint Patty's day parade in Dublin. Sean immediately felt a kindred spirit and thought, "If this guy turns out to be an asshole, I'll get him excommunicated." His fears were unnecessary. Major Bryant proved to be a highly capable but genuinely decent and likable lawyer. Which may be an oxymoron in some circles. But the description fit.

The first witness was an agent from the Office of Naval Intelligence, the O.N.I., who introduced the reports of that agency and the statement of Panos.

Sean decided not to attack Panos's statement as yet. He couldn't get any mileage out of that procedure at this point, and he decided to save his shots for cross-examination if Panos took the stand. Panos's counsel was still playing things close, so Sean and Jack had to wing it.

The next witness was an agent from the Criminal Investigation Division of the Provost Marshal's Office. He set the scene of the crime for the record and provided pertinent physical details about the geography and the victims. Nothing earth shaking except Sean had to pin him down as to whether the agent had any indication as to when any and all of the participants may have arrived at the scene. The witness stated he knew nothing about this and couldn't tell from the investigation who was first to arrive, the victims or the accused, nor whether the accused were all together, or if one had been there before anyone else. Sean knew he wouldn't know, but it set the stage for later inquiry into that important element.

Forensic and lab personnel who performed various technical experiments were then called to testify. The autopsy report of Midshipman David Hall was introduced but the pathologist was not present, so Jack and Sean saved for trial any attack they might have on the post-mortem. The autopsy revealed that David Hall had died from a laryngeal hemorrhage caused by severe blows to the larynx either by instrument or shoe clad feet. He would have died even without the laryngeal hemorrhage if he had been left unattended because of a subarachnoid hemorrhage at the base of his skull, which caused massive internal bleeding.

Additional forensic reports summarized physical findings as to the young woman victim. Miss Chrissy Long suffered severe trauma to her face, throat, and skull, including a fracture of the skull, a knife wound to her throat, deep bruises on her arms and legs from repeated blows, and a clear violation of her genitalia, which reflected manual abuse of her vulva and vagina as well as unquestionable acts of intercourse. At least three separate strains of human male semen were found deposited in her vaginal canal indicating that a minimum of three persons had sexually imposed themselves on the victim and had experienced orgasms.

The reports were devastating causing Sean to feel repugnance towards the other three accused. He had to be careful or he would lose objectivity about Johnson as well. Sean and Jack had to believe their client was innocent and whoever was responsible for killing David Hall and brutalizing Chrissy Long, Johnson was not. To this point the case against Johnson was still questionable even though he was found at the scene and Panos had suggested in his written statement that Johnson was supposed to have participated in the crimes. Panos had not yet testified but Sean felt confident Panos would say no more than he did in his statement to the investigators. Thus Sean was carefully considering if they wanted to attack him at this stage. It looked like they had best wait for trial where the impact would be greater and Panos wouldn't have time to manufacture reasons to bolster his earlier account of the events.

A blow to any complacency they might have felt came when Major Bryant introduced a sworn statement from Chrissy Long. Sean and Jack had not seen the statement, which the government counsel only obtained the day before. Because she was still hospitalized and not available for in person testimony, the victim's sworn statement could be substituted even though not subject to cross-examination. Sean didn't like the rule, but it served a practical function. Chrissy Long's sworn statement read:

AFFIDAVIT

My name is Chrissy Long. I reside in Los Angeles, California, and I make this statement under oath from my hospital bed in UCLA Medical Center where I am a patient.

Present are Major Brendon Bryant, U.S. Marine Corps, a government attorney, and Agent Stanley Reeves, Office of Naval Intelligence. I make this statement of my own free will. I understand it will be used in an investigation being conducted into the death of my fiance, David Hall, and into acts of violence and other crimes committed against me on Thursday, September 3, 1964 at Marine Corps Base, Camp Pendleton.

On that night I was in the company of David Hall to whom I was engaged to be married. David was a Naval R.O.T.C. Midshipman, who had elected the Marine Corps option. He was performing his summer cruise by participating in Marine training at Camp Pendleton for six weeks. He was due to finish training on Friday, September 4, 1964, the day after he was killed.

I was visiting David and staying at the Guest House on the base. We were going to return to Los Angeles on Saturday morning. On Thursday, we had been to the Officer's Club in the Del Mar area. David had officer club privileges as a midshipman. We had dinner and then David drove me around the base to show me some of the areas where he trained. We ended up in the area of the Naval Hospital, which is near Lake O'Neill. We parked the car and went for a walk along the lake. It was a beautiful evening with bright moonlight. We were in love and the setting was very romantic.

We saw no one during our walk until about a half hour after we had started. We were headed back to the car when we came across three Marines, all of whom were in uniform. We didn't say anything, but one of the Marines made a rude remark to me. David, who was in uniform, admonished the Marine. There was no question that David's status as a midshipman was recognizable, but the Marines all laughed and called him a sea scout and a swabbie and told him to "fuck off."

59

David reprimanded the Marines for their conduct, and I urged him to let it go and just get us out of there. I think David would have done so, but one of the Marines approached and tried to grab me. David yelled at him and then the Marine hit David without warning. David defended himself and the Marine and David got into a fistfight.

Within seconds thereafter one of the other Marines jumped in and started to hit David, who fell to the ground. Then both Marines started kicking him in the face and head. I do not remember what the third Marine was doing, but I believe he also came over and either punched or kicked David.

I was screaming and, without thinking, I ran over and starting hitting them, but it was to no avail. I was punched in the face by one of the Marines, and fell to the ground. He then picked me up by the hair and punched me in the stomach and as I fell, he pounded my arm. As I lay on the ground, he kicked me in the head at least once and maybe twice.

I don't remember what happened to David after that, but I think he also was kicked by one or more of the three Marines as he lay on the ground. It was a nightmare, but I thought they would leave us alone after that I lost consciousness for a while. I cannot say how long, but when I was once again aware of what was happening, I realized I was bleeding from my nose and mouth. I prayed they would go away, but one of them said he was going to finish what he had started and was going to show me what a real man was like and why I shouldn't hang around sailors. He then stood over me and opened his trousers to reveal his sex organ.

He then threw himself on me and tore away my panties. I was wearing a blouse and skirt and sandals but no stockings. He tore my blouse and bra, and he roughly handled my breasts and then reached down and grabbed my crotch with his hand and forced his fingers into my vagina. I screamed and he hit me with his fist in the face and then produced a knife whose blade sprung open and he pressed it against my throat warning me not to scream again. He cut my neck with the knife and I could feel my tears and blood running down my shoulder. Then he forced his organ into my vagina and after a few seconds, he grunted, and I sensed he had reached a climax. He lay on top of me for a minute or two and then got off and said I was ready for the next taker.

I was filled with shock and I cried, "Please leave me alone." But it didn't do any good. Another man then got on top of me and placed his organ inside of me and repeated what the other one had done. After a brief time he too was finished and a third man got on top of me and had intercourse with me. I believe he reached a climax as well.

The first man who violated me then dragged me over to a little hill and then took me behind it where another man was lying. This man was not one of the three who had first violated me. This man was dressed in civilian clothes. He was brown colored. The first man threw me on the colored man and said he could have me. He said something like, "Niggers deserve a fucked up woman, and this bitch is about as fucked up as you can get." Then he laughed and I fainted. I woke up sometime later. I don't know how long it was. The colored man was on top of me but he wasn't saying anything. I was able to push him off and I rolled a few feet away and fainted again. That's the last I remember until I was being placed in an ambulance by some Navy personnel dressed in white uniforms. I was then taken to the Naval Hospital where I had surgery and I remained hospitalized at Camp Pendleton about six days until I was transferred to the UCLA Medical Center at my parents' request.

I do not know the names of any of the men who were involved in killing David or attacking me. I know that three white males were present along with a Negro male. I believe I could remember them if I saw them again.

Since I was unconscious part of the time, I do not know if the Negro had anything to do with David, but I do know that I was thrown on top of him and then fainted. When I came to, he was on top of me. I could see that the fly to his trousers was opened and his penis was exposed. This is all I can remember at this time.

/s/ Chrissy Long

Subscribed and sworn to before me an officer authorized under Title 10, United States Code, to administer oaths, this 13th day of September, 1964, at Los Angeles, California.

/s/ Brandon Bryant
Major, United States Marine Corps

****

Panos's counsel did not put him on the witness stand, which was a smart move. The other two counsel followed his lead and kept their clients off as well. Sean also decided against putting Johnson on. There was too much they had to find out before he could successfully present a defense of innocence in this matter, starting with some items his client seemed to have left out. He concluded that the investigation could only serve as a discovery device, and there was no way he was going to get a dismissal of the charges against Lee Johnson at this stage.

The defense having no evidence to offer, the investigation was adjourned. As expected, Pat Carothers recommended a general court-martial for all four accused. Colonel Gene Hanley gave the investigation a thorough review and concurred in that recommendation to the Commanding General.

The General agreed, and Johnson and the other three accused were referred to a joint trial by General Court-Martial as a non-capital case. Commencement of the trial, of necessity, would be delayed until Chrissy Long was well enough to testify. This meant that Johnson would have to stay in the brig awaiting trial, but it gave Sean and Jack extra time to dig further into the charges and come up with a game plan. Ninety percent of the actual trial of any case is preparation. And it makes all the difference. Sean often remarked that a lawyer who doesn't thoroughly prepare can damn well plan on losing. He had learned that from a master trial lawyer eight years earlier. "If we are going to get Johnson acquitted we have to start with an acceptance of the hard fact that in this case we have to prove his innocence," Sean said darkly to Jack. "This shouldn't be the case but in this instance it is what we are faced with and we've got a hell of lot of work cut out for us. We can pray for success because we believe in our client's cause, but God isn't likely to do the work. That's our job. It reminds me of the words of wisdom from the great poet and playwright, Will Shakespeare, which he set forth in *All's Well That End's Well,* where the actor notes, *'Our Remedies oft in ourselves do lie, Which we ascribe to heaven.'*

CHAPTER 11

August 1956

Jake Rogers, L.A.'s premier criminal defense attorney, taught Sean the importance of in-depth preparation some eight years earlier in 1956 when Sean clerked in Jake's office following his first year of law school.

Upon meeting Jake for the first time, Sean was surprised that Jake wasn't as tall as he had expected. Other lawyers talked about Jake as if he were a giant. Actually he was only five foot seven, but when he fixed his steel gray eyes on you in his patented cold, uncompromising stare, he got a lot taller. Witnesses responded to that look with body language not likely to be missed by the judge and jury. Sean believed only a pathological liar could meet Jake's eye's and not reveal uneasiness. This technique was only one of many employed by this legendary defender of persons accused - sometimes rightfully, sometimes wrongfully - of criminal conduct.

Jake had the dashing good looks of the old matinee idols before movie stars decided to adopt the shaggy dog look of the sixties. His coal black hair was sprinkled with gray and lent an air of credibility to a highly competent attorney who had been tested and challenged in the toughest of all arenas, the criminal courts. He maintained his stamina for such battles with daily runs and weight training. His reputation was larger than life and Sean felt honored when Jake first turned that look on him. He was expecting a somewhat softer opening, but it was his turn to be tested by the master. The first of many challenges Jake handed him.

"I am impressed by your resume, Mr. O'Ryan. Good grades, member of the law review, a Marine Corps Officer, and a Bachelor of Arts, with honors, from UCLA. Are you as good as you resume suggests?"

"That sounds like one of those, when are you going to stop beating your wife, questions," Sean replied. "Is it intended to be rhetorical, or are you setting me up? I've heard you are the world's greatest cross-examiner and I think I should be careful. By the way, please feel free to call me Sean." All of this came out sounding more cocky than Sean had wanted even though he tried to remain low key. However, knowing what he had in mind for his life, Sean wasn't disposed to kowtow to Jake Rogers or anyone else just to get a law clerk job. Or so he thought. With his usual stubbornness he pretended he didn't give a damn what Jake Rogers thought, but he knew it wasn't true. He did want to work with this lawyer of legendary fame, and learn from him. The opportunity was golden but at that moment he was doing his best to screw it up.

"Well, thank you, Mr. O'Ryan, but there's no need to get testy. You are among friends. I appreciate your willingness to stand tall when challenged," Jake replied. "But a word of caution, don't let anger cloud your judgment."

Jake didn't seem to be lecturing so much as guiding, and Sean listened. "All that does is give your opponent an edge. It's all right to feign anger for show. Juries like to see some fire in counsel. They watch T.V. and movies and think all trials are that way. It's crap, of course, since many trials are fairly boring and the leeway counsel enjoys in staged productions is seldom tolerated in a real courtroom. So keep your head and don't let your emotions rule."

Jake then smiled disarmingly and said, "No offense, but I don't think I have the right to call you Sean until I earn it, and that won't be until you have earned the right to call me Jake. I'll let you know when that is."

"Yes, Sir," Sean said softly, accepting the well-deserved rebuke.

"All right, let's get back to fundamentals," Jake went on. "First of all, being on the law review is an honor, but it doesn't mean you can make it in the trial arena. You want to be a researcher, wave your law review credentials around and go work for a law-publishing house. You want to be a trial lawyer, show me what you have done in moot court and trial practice, especially in your senior year. My firm doesn't need people who come alive only in a library. I want people who love to fight for causes and won't roll over just because everything is crashing down on them. People who are willing to say *stick it in your ear* when challenged."

Rogers paused and fixed the look on Sean. "Trial work is rough and tumble. This doesn't mean you can't be a gentleman, because you should always be that even when there are humongous assholes on the other side, and believe me, there are far too many of them in the law today. Just don't sink to their level. But you don't have to back off when it comes time to stand up and be counted. I believe at least half the lawyers who try cases have no business in the courtroom. Not only are they inept, but they don't know the rules of evidence, and they don't have the heart for intellectual battle, so they try to make up for their incompetence by running roughshod over witnesses and other counsel. They are a disgrace to the profession."

Jake was well into the lesson and Sean was in awe. He got the feeling that Jake could convince anyone of anything, and for a brief moment Sean began to doubt his personal qualification to be taken on by the Rogers firm as Jake commented while looking at the transcript attached to Sean's resume.

"I'm impressed by your grades, which indicates you are bright, but the question is, how are your guts? How willing are you to go to the wall for something you believe in, especially when everyone wants to lynch you along with your client who they believe is guilty?"

"That's why I'm here, Mr. Rogers. I remember a little guy named Willie Earle, a victim of vigilante injustice down in South Carolina back in 1947. My guts are firmly in place having been fine tuned by the Marine Corps," Sean responded politely but firmly.

"Okay. Tell me about the Corps," Jake said pleasantly, but to Sean it sounded like an order.

"I joined in 1949. Got commissioned; served on active duty, and now I'm a member of the organized reserve. I drill one weekend a month and spend fifteen days active duty each summer wherever my unit is training. I'm a rifle company commander; my present rank is Captain."

"Did you serve in Korea?"

"Yes, Sir."

"Did you see combat?"

"Yes, Sir."

"A lot."

"Yes, Sir."

"Ever kill anybody?"

"Yes, Sir."

"How long were you in Korea?"

"August 1950 to November 1951."

"Have nightmares about it?"

"Yes, Sir."

"Want to talk about it?"

"No, Sir."

"Get wounded?"

"Yes, Sir. Twice."

"Why did you stay in the Marine Corps Reserve?"

"I like the Corps. I think I'm needed."

"Want to work for me?

"Yes, Sir."

"Why?"

"You're the best and I want to learn. I'm not trying to suck up to you when I say this. I hope to get good enough to be taken on as an associate in your firm when I pass the bar in a couple of years. I think I have a lot to offer to you as well as to take from you. It's a two way street."

"What do you have to offer now?" Jake asked pleasantly.

"What do I have to offer? For openers, I'm bright, a hard worker, stubborn, a lousy loser, and I intend to be a hard assed gladiator, while remaining a gentleman, of course. I know this lacks humility, but as we say in the Corps, it's hard to be humble when you're the finest. Naturally I'm not in your league, but I want to be, and I intend to be. That's why I want to work for you."

The cold went out of Jake's eyes and he smiled engagingly. Sean wondered if this was another of Jake's techniques designed to turn a tough witness into a mere mortal, but he had Sean hooked. "All right, Mr. O'Ryan, you sound convincing, but I have one more question. What is the most important virtue for any working relationship to succeed?"

"That's easy, Mr. Rogers. First and foremost, it's loyalty. I work for you, I'm one hundred percent loyal to you, otherwise I shouldn't be here."

"Welcome aboard, Sean," Rogers said with genuine kindness. "By the way, call me Jake. We haven't talked about money, so let me tell you it isn't much as a clerk. It gets better as an associate if I keep you on after the bar, but there are no promises about that at this stage. We'll see how you develop. In the meanwhile, you'll be getting something money can't buy clerking for me," Jake promised. He kept that promise.

Over the years Sean became Jake's disciple and he taught Sean more than he ever learned in his formal courses. He made mistakes, of course, but Jake never got on his case. All criticism was constructive and Jake fashioned him into the lawyer he always believed he could be, patiently insisting that Sean never give up the dream and encouraging him to pursue his potential as a man dedicated to the law. As a consequence of this unselfish devotion, Sean was immersed in the process of becoming a highly accomplished criminal defense counsel.

He never regretted exploring an interest in criminal law, but that interest wasn't spontaneous. He had checked out several areas of practice before he sought a position with Jake Rogers' firm, and, in time, he came to believe that justice could only be served by protecting the constitutional mandates of due process and fair play, and particularly, by safeguarding the right to competent counsel. He discovered that it is the essential participation of counsel which ensures that prosecutors will make an effort to be honest and not subvert the burden of proof, which the law wisely imposes on the accuser rather than the accused.

Sean's experience also convinced him that the highest calling in the law is to try cases in which counsel protects his or her client from oppression and deprivation of life and liberty. He realized that criminal defense was the only format that consistently met this challenge. Personal injury work for the plaintiff is important, of course, but full of potential for fraud on both sides. Besides, Sean was an admirer of the great Edward Bennett Williams, and he appreciated Williams' observation about why he gave up personal injury work saying something to the effect that there are just so many ways you can get hit in the ass by a streetcar.

In his search Sean also found insurance defense work truly distasteful, especially since it appeared that many practitioners of that art sell out to the insurance industry because the work, however unfair the defense, is steady. Not all, of course, but many lawyers who engage in that practice become devoid of any expression of human compassion. It doesn't matter how badly the victim was racked up or how outrageously someone was raped physically or economically by malpractice artists. All that matters is how cheaply the case can be settled or how the lawyers can two block recovery by whatever means, thereby allowing the tortfeasor and his insurance carrier to skate.

Finally, considerations of corporate work, tax counseling, securities law, and agency work evoked all the excitement of a frozen enema and were easily dispelled. Then Sean lucked out; Jake Rogers took him on as a law clerk. Then later as an associate. And ultimately as a partner during Sean's sixth year of criminal law practice. From the day he was employed by Jake he never thought of his role as work and he shared the observation of super lawyer, Louis Nizer, that whatever you are doing, "It's only work if you'd rather be doing something else."

From the beginning Jake impressed on Sean that the right to counsel means competent counsel, and not shysters who fatten their files with active cases but only average a few hours with a client before throwing him to the prosecution. His disgust with such counsel is the reason Jake insisted that continuances may never be sought by his firm unless absolutely necessary to complete an investigation and gather evidence. Jake viewed continuances for any lesser reason as nothing more than devices for greedy attorneys to build up a caseload at the expense of the client. As Judge Learned Hand said, "Justice delayed is justice denied," and Jake made it plain that unnecessary delays, especially when the client can't make bail, deny the right to speedy trial.

With these principles and ground rules firmly in place, Sean viewed himself as a latter day Don Quixote, willing to tilt at the windmills of injustice with the same starry-eyed idealism, but he hoped, with a whole lot more success.

****

Autumn 1958

Three weeks after he was admitted to practice law in 1958, Sean got his first personal taste of what seeking justice was about. He was standing in one of the Departments of the Los Angeles Municipal Court answering, "Ready for the defendant, your Honor," in a preliminary hearing on a charge of first-degree murder lodged against a street beggar named Arthur Curtis. He called himself, Art, and he claimed he was descended from George Washington. The origin of that claim was doubtful, but of no consequence other than to reflect on his credibility.

Art, whatever his ancestry, was discovered in Griffith Park going through the clothing of another transient who was still wearing that clothing but who earlier had given up any objection to an invasion of his privacy as a consequence of an eight inch butcher knife ventilating his heart. Art should have noticed this intrusion into the victim's breathing habits, even if he hadn't authored it, but he was either oblivious to the violence or simply chose to disregard it in his search for a few token valuables that might be on the deceased's still warm body.

Art's timing was rotten, unfortunately, and he was caught in the act by a brace of Los Angeles policemen. Promptly arrested he was booked into the County Jail. He denied any complicity in the killing and was assigned a public defender three days later at his first appearance before a judicial officer. At that time Art reaffirmed his innocence with such vehemence that the Chief Public Defender, a friend of Jake, called him and pleaded with him to talk to Art, and, if he was convinced that Art had any kind of chance at trial, to take on his case pro bono because the Public Defender's office was already up to its ass in alligators. The P.D. lamented that this one was going to be a tough nut to try and would be another difficult drain on the P.D.'s resources.

Jake felt it was time to add another pro bono case to his office docket, so he and Sean went over to visit Art at the County Jail. Jake thought this would be just the case for Sean to lose his virginity as a trial attorney. They took Art over the coals for two hours delving into his background and attacking his story from every possible angle. Surprisingly, he stood up well and in the end it was unanimous. All three of them, Jake, Sean and Art, believed in Art's innocence and Jake accepted the case. This is how Sean came to be making the opening gambit at the preliminary hearing in the defense of Arthur Curtis on behalf of Jake Rogers and Associates, counsel of record.

Jake wasn't present at the prelim in this one because he knew as a matter of course that Art would be bound over for trial in the Superior Court and he wasn't going to make any tactical moves at the prelim. So he let Sean wing it, believing you learned more by doing than watching. Sean didn't care that the chance of avoiding a bind over was slim to none. He was ready and eager to launch on his first solo flight. The Deputy District Attorney who presented the case for the People under a charge of first-degree murder in violation of Section 187, California Penal Code, was thorough and brief. She introduced evidence of the violent death of the victim, known only as John Doe, by stabbing in the heart. The post mortem report, which eliminated any other cause of death other than a stab wound, also indicated advanced cirrhosis of the liver. The victim would have died within the year if he had not been prematurely dispatched violently in the park. As a result of some excellent forensics by the Medical Examiner, undertaken within minutes of the discovery of Art and his silent companion, the time of death was placed within fifteen minutes of Art being caught in the act of heisting the corpse. The two L.A. cops were precise in their testimony recalling what they had observed. All Sean's hoped for clever attempts at cross-examination were useless.

"No, sir. We did not see the defendant stab the victim, but we saw the knife and fresh blood on both the victim's and the defendant's clothing. The defendant was kneeling over the victim, and also had blood on his right hand. My partner and I saw no one else and observed no tracks leading away from the body to indicate that anyone else had been in the area. The grass was wet and a fine cover of dew was undisturbed except for the footprints of what appeared to be the victim and the defendant."

Both officers testified in a straightforward, convincing manner. Things did not look good for Art. One of the officers continued, "My partner and I made a special effort to locate anyone else who might have been in the area, particularly because the defendant denied he had stabbed the victim. He claimed he found the victim that way just before we arrived and that the blood on his hand and clothing was from going through the deceased's pockets."

"Were any identifiable fingerprints found on the knife?" Sean asked.

"No, Sir. I was advised by the police lab that there were some smudged prints but nothing they could lift."

Sean didn't put Art on the witness stand since it would have been a futile gesture at this point. The preliminary hearing could only serve as a discovery tool in this instance as it does in many cases. This was particularly true since the prelim judge was old *Numb Nuts*, otherwise known as the Honorable Lincoln Dominick Smitts. The "Honorable" part was an oxymoron. Only that portion of the legal community who never had the misfortune to have to deal with him ever referred to him as anything but *Numb Nuts*. Short, pear shaped, arrogant, incompetent and generally biased in favor of the prosecution, it was rumored that no preliminary conducted by *Numb Nuts* ever settled in favor of the defendant. His bind over rate was about ninety-eight percent, so there wasn't any point in trying to resolve the charges at preliminary hearings with *Numb Nuts*.

Some people are born to be judges and early on demonstrate a natural ability to be fair and reasonable. As they progress on the bench, it is apparent they work seriously to improve on their natural abilities. Others, however, have absolutely no business as judges, and it is amazing how lawyers in particular and the public in general tolerate the abuse these wretched creatures inflict. If *Numb Nuts* were a truck driver, the kindest thing one could say about him was that he was double parked all his life. He was just another political flake who wouldn't know Blackstone from Clarence Darrow, but somehow managed, while damn near starving to death in private practice, to suck up to the right politicians and get a political appointment to the bench and then continue to succeed himself over the years in unopposed judicial elections. Through it all he managed to rise to the level of his own incompetence until he believed he was truly worthy of being a judge and that he had evolved into a legal oracle whose pronouncements bore the imprimatur of infallibility. Thus it was that old *Numb Nuts*, the would be pope of the Municipal Court, bound over Sean's client on murder one. Sean turned to Art and genuinely expressed, "I'm sorry, but at least now you'll get a real bite at the apple."

Later Sean drove back to the office on Wilshire to report to Jake. He knew what Jake was going to say. "This was expected, so now get busy on saving Art's ass since we are convinced he is innocent." To which admonishment Sean would immediately guarantee an acquittal without the slightest idea how this could be done. Young lawyers are notoriously naive in their belief that innocent defendants have nothing to fear from the criminal justice system. But naive or not, to their credit they learn to reject out of hand the fiction perpetrated by prosecutors that ninety-seven percent of all defendants are guilty as charged even though many are acquitted. There is no way this mythical statistic has validity, but it serves as a sop to the erosion of sensitivity that results from prolonged exposure to the prosecution side.

Sean told Jake that Art had said something a bit strange after he was bound over for trial to the effect, "It ain't worth it, Mr. O'Ryan. I didn't kill nobody. You did your best, but it ain't worth it." Art shook his head after he said this, as if some thought had gotten stuck between his brain and his voice box.

"What isn't worth it, Art?" Sean had asked, not understanding what was behind Art's lament.

"Nothin', just nothin'. Fuck it. Ain't worth it." Art continued to ramble as a Deputy Sheriff cuffed him and led him back to the holding tank. Sean didn't know what Art was thinking, but he was determined he was going to show Art that he was worth it. Sean was going to the wall for his first real client in need of help.

Art was not convicted. Sean would have liked to report that it was because of his hard work and dedication to his client's cause. But it wasn't. Art hanged himself in his cell that night. No one on either side of the bars tried to stop him. Largesse is low on the priority of the hosts and guests at the County Jail. Sean believed Art was innocent. That was six years ago in 1958, the fateful year in which Sean learned other painful lessons about life and the tenuous hold we have on it.

CHAPTER 12

September 17, 1964

Sean called Lee Johnson's uncle the morning after the Article 32 investigation was completed. Harry was at work so Sean didn't detain him, but he did make it clear they had to talk about Lee as soon as possible and it would be a good idea if Lee's mother was also available. Sean suggested she probably would be more comfortable if they met in her home. Harry called back and confirmed and they agreed to meet at seven that night.

Sean couldn't do much on the Johnson case for the rest of the day, so he turned to a couple of other files. One involved a poor Mexican who was several degrees below poverty level. He had walked into a Bank of America branch with a toy gun stuck in his belt, which was hidden by a shirt worn outside of his trousers. He handed a note to the teller that said he had a gun and she was supposed to give him a thousand dollars. He then lifted his shirt enough so the teller could see the butt of the phony gun. She gave him some money, maybe a couple hundred in tens and twenties and he ran - not walked - to the door. This was the third mistake he made that day. The first was trying to rob a federally insured bank. The second was using a toy gun and then only asking for a thousand dollars. This guy had no imagination; he risks a dozen years in prison by holding up a federally insured bank for a miserable thousand dollars. The third mistake was running to the door. A security guard intercepted the robber's one hundred and twenty-five pounds and decked him with one punch.

The rest was history, and now Sean's client had less to feed his wife and six hungry kids who live in Mexico. It seems that the client had availed himself of the hospitality of the United States without telling the U.S. Government about it. Sean, who was handling the case pro bono, had real problems with this client. Pro bono cases often are the hardest since they leave the attorney with limited resources with which to work. The best Sean could hope for in this case was a reduced charge of unarmed robbery because of the unreal gun. He wondered why these amateur robbers bother with a weapon, for show or otherwise. Most of them wouldn't use it even if they had a real one, so why do they risk enhancing the sentence with a bogus claim of being armed?

Sean called the Assistant U.S. Attorney handling the case to see what he could negotiate. He offered a guilty plea with imposition of sentence suspended for a full five years, with one hundred eighty days to be served in the local slammer for inducement, along with voluntary deportation. This way his client would have the five years hanging over his head in case he got stupid enough to cross the border uninvited ever again. Mere illegal entry would trigger the five years federal prison time, so it offered something to both sides. Besides the poor jerk didn't even get out the door, and no one was in any danger. Hunger robs people of their common sense. The tragedy is that there were seven innocent victims of his stupidity. His wife and six kids. *Probably is a Catholic, which accounts for all the kids. Maybe the Pope will feed them while my client is away*, Sean mused.

******

Sean arrived promptly at seven at Lee Johnson's home. Lee's mother was a handsome woman and Sean could see a lot of her in Lee. Harry greeted Sean warmly, and once again they felt the glow that old warriors sense even though war is a distant memory. He and Harry had faced great risks together. Harry almost called Sean lieutenant, but caught himself. "Old habit. I know you're a major now, but you'll always be that shave tail I went through hell with. The image of you trying to make the man come out and push the kid aside will always be there."

"No sweat, Marine. If it hadn't been for you that kid wouldn't have lived to become a man. You call me anything you want," Sean responded, and then turning to Lee's mother, extended his hand and said, "Mrs. Johnson, it is a genuine privilege to meet you. I'm only sorry it has to be under these circumstances."

"I'm sorry it has to be this way too, Mr. O'Ryan, but Harry told me so much about you and I feel good having you on Lee's side. He's had some problems, but I know he wouldn't do anything as evil as they say. He wasn't always the best kid, but that's not the same as being a bad one." Mrs. Johnson said this somewhat sadly, but not apologetically. It was obvious she felt great concern for her son and was willing to tell Sean whatever he needed to know to help him. But she also felt confident that Lee Johnson was falsely accused and she didn't have to apologize to anyone about her efforts to raise her son without a husband's assistance. Lee was only eight when his father died. "Where would you like to sit and talk, Mr. O'Ryan?"

"Tell you the truth, Mrs. Johnson, I've always been partial to kitchens. If you don't mind, the kitchen will be fine. By the way, please call me Sean. If we keep things so formal, Harry will be saying 'sir' again just to give me a bad time."

"Why, thank you, Sean, and please won't you call me Esther?"

"I'll be happy to Esther. And if you've got any extra of that good coffee I smell, I'll take a cup."

They sat at the kitchen table and began with a desultory conversation about Lee Johnson, his boyhood and general background. Eventually Sean moved into an area that he realized might be painful but it was necessary. "Has Lee ever been arrested by civilian authorities?" Sean asked this because he sensed Johnson had been in some trouble along the way, but no one had volunteered any information to this point; not his client, nor Harry. All Johnson had told Jack and Sean was that he had no prior record.

"I was afraid you might ask that, and at first I was tempted not to say anything, but I believe you when you say we have to be honest and open about all of this, as hard as it may be to talk about," Harry said with obvious reluctance.

"What was Lee arrested for and when was it?" Sean asked.

Harry decided he should get the story going and suggested that Esther fill in the blanks. "It was a juvenile matter. There was this young girl who the guys on the team referred to as the village pump. She was alleged to have screwed the entire football team, but I doubt it. Not because she might not have been willing to, but some of the players wouldn't have her even if she were willing. Also I always suspected she was prejudiced against nonwhite players. I don't know how willing she would be to make it with them," Harry said uneasily.

"One night one of the guys made a date with her. He said it was with the understanding that they would be going to his house because his parents were away for the weekend, and a few other guys would be there. She agreed to let them have intercourse with her - what we used to call a gang bang in the old days - not that I have any first hand knowledge of such things mind you." Harry added this last part because Esther gave him a blistering look of surprise.

He then continued. "Everything was going according to plan until Lee arrived about fifteen minutes after the others, who were all white kids. When everyone had gone around except Lee, he thought it was going to be his turn, but the girl objected and it was fairly obvious her objection was based on Lee's color. The guys started razzing her and said she ought to find out if what they say about black cock is true. After a while - they said - they got her curiosity up and she consented to let Lee have her. He did. Unfortunately his timing was bad because as he was doing it, the girl's mother and father returned from their weekend trip earlier than expected."

"Then what happened?" Sean pressed.

"And then all hell broke loose, of course, and the worst part is that the little tramp accused Lee of taking her against her will even though it was obvious she had consented to the others. In short, Lee was the only one charged with anything. At first, he was charged with rape, but it was reduced to sexual assault and the case was kept in the juvenile system because he was only sixteen. A hearing was held and not one of those other four white kids would testify for him. The girl stuck to her story and Lee was declared a delinquent. But I understand that doesn't amount to a criminal conviction under California law, and the Marine Corps didn't find out about it. When he enlisted, he said he had never been convicted of a crime."

"Technically, that was true, Harry. The juvenile proceedings are not criminal in the ordinary sense of the California Penal Code and criminal convictions arising under it. But a declaration by the juvenile court becomes a matter of record, even though sealed. So there is a record somewhere. The bad part is that Lee's conduct is the kind that can come back to haunt him if we try to put his character in issue. He can be asked - not on the basis of a prior conviction - but on the basis of prior acts of misconduct, if he has ever been charged with any sexual assault. It makes the jury think that if there's smoke, there's more smoke, and sooner or later there's fire. They think that if he engaged in sex without permission once, he's a good candidate for doing it again," Sean explained.

"Holy, shit," Harry said. "It's a good thing we told you. Do you think you can do something about it so it won't come out?"

"I'll sure as hell try, Harry. Regrettably it changes some of the tactics I had considered, but we can work around it. So don't worry about it." Is there anything else that Lee was ever arrested for, juvenile or otherwise, that either of you know about?"

Esther spoke up. "A couple of times he was brought home by the police for curfew violations or for fighting, but I don't know of anything he was ever arrested for other than that lying tramp who said he had forced himself on her. No good whore."

"I understand how you feel, Esther. But I need to know how this affected Lee? Did he change? What was his reaction?"

Harry jumped in. "I'll tell you what his reaction was. It was to develop or maybe confirm a simmering distrust of white people. He felt he got shit on, and he was right. A couple of the kids told him later they were sorry they hadn't spoken up for him, but they blamed their parents who told them not to get involved or the girl might claim they all raped her. They said they were scared, and the girl wasn't exactly playing with a full deck, so they couldn't take any chances."

"I can see where this would be of little consolation to Lee," Sean said. "I assume this simmering distrust erupted into a full blown fixation ultimately, and from the go rounds I have had with him, I can only conclude he would have trouble accepting any white man on faith, including Jesus himself if he came back."

"You got that right Sean," Harry chimed in. "I told him his attitude was going to get him more trouble than it would ever resolve, but he just continued in his mad as hell, distrustful way. I'm surprised he made it through boot camp, but he wanted to get away and because of me he thought the Marines were the only outfit where a tough kid would be appreciated. One of his drill instructors at San Diego was a Negro. I think that helped him over the rough spots. But here he is again, facing the white man's justice. I'm really worried."

"It's not white man's justice, Harry. It's the Corps'. I admit we don't have a lot of Negroes in the Corps, but we're getting more everyday. And for the most part they are damn good men and women. Times will get better. Hell, we didn't get our first Negro Marine until 1942, and that says something about the Corps which was founded in 1775. We were slow learners, but we finally got around to it. Now we pride ourselves on the point that all Marines are green and no other color distinctions are acceptable. I admit there are some old timers who think there are light green Marines and dark green Marines, but that's bullshit. We aren't going to cure prejudice overnight, but we're getting there."

Harry and Esther chuckled at the play on words. Sean hoped he had persuaded them that Lee Johnson would get a fair shake in his court-martial every bit as much as the three Caucasian Marines would. And he was determined to make sure of it. Esther asked about the victims, and Sean admitted that they were seemingly fine people and had been brutalized in the worst fashion imaginable. He emphasized that there was no defense to such outrage other than innocence, which is what Sean and Jack have been asserting and would continue to strive to establish even though technically the burden of proof was on the other side.

They visited a while longer and then Sean left with the promise that Jack and he would do everything they could to acquit Lee of the charges. He assured Harry and Esther of his firm belief in Lee's innocence and how this belief bolstered his normal resolve not only to protect the system, but also to fully protect his client against false or misleading accusations. Sean couldn't completely relieve their anxiety, but at least they could be assured that neither they nor Lee Johnson were alone in this.

******

Sean called Jack Coleman as soon as he reached his office the next morning.

"Jack did you find out anything new over the weekend?"

"Wish I had more to report, Sean. Only one thing. It's a little peculiar. Not that there is anything wrong with the situation, but its still peculiar when you consider Johnson's understandable distrust of white people.

"What's that, Jack? You going to tell me or just leave me on the edge of my chair?"

"Sorry, just sort of thinking out loud. What I am talking about is the girl that Johnson used to date, for want of a better word. Her name is Jill Thompson. Blond, blue eyed, and very white," Jack replied.

"You gotta be shitting me. Johnson was dating a white girl?"

"That's affirmative. Miss Thompson is a white woman, actually a young, white woman. Age about seventeen or eighteen. I hope its eighteen, we don't need any statutory rape charges added to anything else. In any event she now dates, and I use the word advisedly, Sergeant Stanley Williams, the big, Negro, military policeman who rousted Johnson at Lake O'Neill with his feet and nightstick."

It was normal to hear Jack make reference to someone as a Negro even though it contrasted with developing attitudes and changing times in 1964. The black power movement was taking hold and slogans were appearing extolling *black as beautiful*, and black pride. But before this time, the country had grown up with the words *Negro and colored*, and it was hard to adjust to the emerging terminology. Prior to this, at least in civilized company, one always referred to blacks as Negroes. Some people would hand you your head if you called them black when Sean was a kid. It was considered a word of derision, but in 1964 the expression had crept into the vocabulary and the term *colored* was becoming archaic, although the NAACP still employed the locution *colored* in its title. Thus, like Jack did, Sean still used the word, Negro, simply as a matter of habit. Although the crossover was becoming more common, Sean felt it sounded strange to say black when talking to people who were as light as any white person he knew. Social mores take interesting turns. In years to come, the term black would be replaced with other preferences of refined designation such as, African-American.

Jack interrupted Sean's thought processes, and advised, "I didn't intend to make a social commentary about Lee Johnson and Jan Thompson in any of this."

"I understand that, Jack. I know you have no problem anymore than I do with a white girl and a black man, or vice versa, dating or getting married for that matter, if that's what they want to do. The only inconsistency I see in Lee Johnson's case is what you referenced. It is strange to visualize Johnson involved with a white girl considering what I found out a few days ago."

Sean went on to explain what he had learned from Harry and Esther. Jack expressed surprise and not a little dismay at this latest development. "Glad this is a secure phone, Sean. I wouldn't want the prosecution to know about this. I presume we will be doing everything we can to keep it a well guarded secret."

"We sure will, Jack, but it does give us a problem with the introduction of character evidence. While the prosecution can't open the door with it, they could use it if we do. We'll have to think about our tactics on this one."

He then aadded, "Got anything else right now?"

"No, that's it for now," Jack replied. "When are you coming down?"

"Towards the end of the week, either Thursday or Friday. That gives us a couple more days to dig around. Let me know if you latch on to anything. We will have to go over and talk to Johnson and see if there is more to this than I got from his family. I'll keep you posted. Semper fi, and all that good stuff."

Sean hung up the phone and swung his chair around to stare out his window overlooking Wilshire Boulevard. The window covered most of the outer wall and provided his office with host of light emphasizing the rich, dark brown paneling covering the other three walls. A built in bookcase filled most of the wall to his left as he faced inboard. Jake generously had given him a magnificent mahogany desk and two beautiful leather client chairs that sat directly in front of the desk. A large leather couch ran along the wall to the right, above which his degrees and bar admissions were neatly hung to impress himself, if no one else. The couch occasionally came in handy when Sean worked late - or to entertain a lady in a pinch - after everyone had left the office. As he took in the dynamic panorama of movement created by the busy people on Wilshire, he reflected that Californians never seem to light for long. They just keep coming and going. He wondered where they all came from? And where the hell are they always were going? A world of constant motion. *Must be the great weather,* he concluded. *No one wants to stay indoors in a climate like this. Got to be on the go, even with no place to go.*

Sean realized that this daydreaming wasn't solving the new wrinkle of Johnson, the black man, dating Jill Thompson, the white woman. Which made Johnson more of an enigma considering his distrust of white people generally and his resentment of how he was treated by another white girl and her four candy assed white friends when he was charged with sexual assault as a juvenile. He concluded that only Johnson could give him the kind of insight they needed into this development, assuming that he knew himself. "We'll just ask and see; what else can we do?" Sean said, thinking out loud.

The rest of his day was filled with wheeling and dealing on a couple of other cases, including the would be bank robber. Sean struck gold on that one. The Assistant U.S. Attorney agreed that the poor guy deserved a break, speculating that this probably was the only one he was ever going to get in life. So he went with the five-year suspension of imposition of sentence, coupled with one hundred seventy-nine days local jail time as a condition for probation. This way the client couldn't get any good time, which is usually five days a month on any sentence of one hundred eighty days or more. In addition, the client had to agree to voluntary deportation back to Mexico. Thus, if he ever made even a simple illegal border crossing, he had a minimum of five years prison time hanging over his head.

Sean then turned to the next case and worked late finishing his final preparation for the bench trial coming up in the morning in the United States District Court in which he was defending a young Mexican-American charged with assault and resisting arrest of a Border Patrol Officer. The trial wouldn't last more than a day and then he could concentrate on Lee Johnson exclusively.

He hadn't heard from Susan for a few days, but that was normal in this type of affair. They had grown closer. But they had no sense of any new considerations, like falling in love. They continued to enjoy a great sexual rapport, but neither wanted any complications at this point. Susan was still engaged to Stan and would probably stay that way. In addition, she was busy at

Sullivan industries as the Vice President in charge of Marketing and Development.

Susan also was teaching as an adjunct professor at one of the local state colleges. She did this not for the money, which she had no need for, but strictly for the sheer love of teaching. At the same time, Sean was more involved in his profession than he was willing to admit. Thus, his personal relationships were subordinated by design. He knew that Susan wouldn't be disposed to being second or third in any one's life if they ever thought of marriage to each other. As a consequence, they were able to appreciate such limitations as were necessary to keep the affair free of interferences or distractions.

This was better for Sean because he hadn't forgotten a special woman named Jean, and the special love they had shared even though substantial time had passed since they first found that love back in 1955.

CHAPTER 13

September 1955

Sean met Jean on their first day of law school at UCLA, the same day he met Sam Mann and Bobby Stein. Sam is Jewish, brilliant and deceptively low-keyed. Behind the relaxed facade a passion burns in a tightly controlled way. Bobby Stein, another gifted Jewish gentleman, is filled with boundless energy. Best described as bright, quick witted, outgoing and charismatic, he could serve as the prototype for God's chosen people. Dynamic and blessed with an inexhaustible enthusiasm for life, it has been suggested that Bobby sleeps in overdrive. The contrast between Bobby and Sam is simply a matter of approach. Equally gifted, they share a common bond formed out of insatiable interests in everything.

Sam had discovered a fiery Jewish lady named Midge, who is anything but the stereotypical Jewish American princess. Midge got Sam's attention immediately as she got his interest and his schwanz to stand up at the same time. By the end of their first year of law school Sam and Midge were married. Good thinking on Sam's part. Smart for Midge too, but then Midge was always as bright as Sam but shrewd enough not to let him know it. He probably did anyway.

The greatest treasure that first day was Jean. Sean learned unconditional love from her. As Dante wrote in *The Divine Comedy*, it was a love that *moves the sun and other stars.* It was through Jean that Sean was born again spiritually. He had drifted away from much of the dogma that shaped his early spiritual perspectives, especially after the emotional experiences of the Korean War. But he still harbored religious myths such as those that mandated that romantic relationships were supposed to be exclusively loving responses rather than merely sexual ones. Indoctrination by the Catholic Church delivered, ad nauseam, about the immorality of sex outside of marriage would haunt him from time to time even though generally he had given up feeling guilty about sex. Fundamental purists would probably attribute this to a hardening of the conscience, but Sean thought this was a smoke and mirrors attempt to keep people on the straight and narrow to preserve the control of the clergy. Sean felt that if conscience is shaped by suggestion, such as *The Ten Suggestions* Moses carried down from Mount Sinai, then conscience could be refined, rather than hardened, by enlightenment.

When he met Jean, he fell deeply in love and rose out of the ashes of his moral conflicts. His evolution into what he refers to as a recovering blind faith Roman Catholic found full development in her. As a result, loving did not cause him to lose his true faith in God but rather enhanced it so that he understood what

Catholic, in the sense of universal, rather than parochial, fully meant. To Sean, this was sharing an abiding faith in the only thing central to his salvation, which salvation was complete through the incarnation of God by the assumption of a separate human nature supplemental to, and subordinate to, His divine nature, and sacrificing the human side on the cross. He understood that salvation was not his for the earning, but rather an unconditional gift.

Thus he remained a Catholic only because he believed in the *miracle of transubstantiation* which resulted in a real - not merely symbolic - presence of the God/Man manifested under the specie of bread and wine. All the rest of Catholic doctrine became unimportant. It mattered not what anyone else wished to believe. They could convinced themselves that the Pope is infallible, and Cardinals and Bishops too, if that is what they want. He didn't. They could think birth control is immoral. He didn't. They could advocate that women should be denied the unfettered choice of what they alone, as a matter of exclusive right, will do with unwanted pregnancies. But Sean believed in informed choices and free will, while at the same time recognizing that accountability went along with freedom of choice. Thus if one chooses wrongly for the wrong reasons and truly contrary to his or her conscience, then he or she will have to answer for such irresponsible choices in an afterlife. In this way none of the illogical and intellectually limiting concepts proffered by the Church was of personal relevance to him any longer, including such questions as to whether or not Mary was conceived without original sin or remained a virgin all her life *after the birth of Jesus*, or if Jesus had blood brothers and sisters. In essence Sean had recovered from all of the non-essentials in his relationship with God, and that recovery started with loving Jean.

The name Jean derives from the Hebrew word for *gift of God*, and, if ever there were an instrument of God's love at work in Sean's life, it was she. Five feet four inches tall, with wide brown eyes and lush dark brown hair that complimented her lovely face. It was her eyes most of all, however, that said so much about Jean and captured Sean the moment they met. There were a couple or so seats left in the center of the auditorium as first year students filed in for freshman orientation that first day of law school at UCLA. Sean deliberately pushed in ahead of Sam and Bobby so he would be next to the lady with the mesmerizing look.

"Is this seat taken?" he asked.

"No, help yourself."

"Hi, I'm Sean O'Ryan, and these two bums you don't want to know because they will distract us from more important things like, are you in love, engaged, or married, and if not, what time can I meet you tonight for a beer and some interesting conversation?"

Jean gave him a long stare and then smiled. "Have you always been this shy, Sean? I wonder if we can converse at all if you don't come out your shell."

"I'll try, honest. What do I call you besides the lady with incredible eyes? I mean, we surely will be in some of the same classes and, of course, we will be sitting next to each other for three years, so we ought to be on a first name basis. Don't you agree?"

"Let me guess, Sean, your favorite radio show as a kid was gang busters. Right? My name is Jean. And that's the only part of the scenario that you've gotten right. First of all, I don't know if you are in any of my sections, and secondly, what makes you think I would want you to sit next to me for even a semester, much less three years?"

"Well, Jean, I'm very pleased to meet you, and I submit most humbly that when two people are immediately attracted to each other, they ought to follow up on that attraction. Now certainly I am attracted to you, and since I am single, tall, not bad looking, and won the last war for you as a Marine, it stands to reason that the attraction has to be mutual," Sean countered with a smile.

"I'll say this, Sean O'Ryan, you couldn't have been anything but a Marine with that line of conceit. I've known a few other Marines and one thing is consistent, you all are insufferable about your Corps. What do they do, open the top of your head when you first join and fill it with guts and glory?"

"No, ma'am, just with an awareness of who's the finest and if you make the team, you get bragging rights for the rest of your life."

"I was right, you are insufferable, but I suspect I won't be able to do anything about it except ignore you. But that would probably be harder to do than just saying, yes, I'll have a beer and some conversation with you. But please, no talk about the Corps. Is that a deal?" Jean replied with a chuckle. "Oh, yes, one more thing. You can't marry me. This is only for a beer. I've met your kind before, and heard all the promises," Jean added with good humor.

"You got it. Only a beer. I know just the place. The *Vin and Grog* over on Wilshire. By the way, as reluctant as I am to introduce you to other guys, let me point out that the handsome guy on my left is Sam. He works there. Bobby is the other good-looking stud on his left. He drinks there. If we treat Sam right, he'll give us one on the house every now and then."

"Sam and Bobby, say hello to Jean."

*****

Sean met Jean at the *Vin and Grog* at seven that night. She lived out on Beverly Drive and thought it would be better to bring her own car on their first date. Sam and Bobby were already there; Sam behind the bar, and Bobby working on a couple of co-eds on the other side. One was Midge, who none of them knew at the time but it turned out be Sam's lucky day. Her friend was Tracy, who immediately fell for Bobby. It wouldn't do her any good over the long haul, but she'd have fun until he wandered off to new interests.

81

A lot of friendly banter went back and forth for a couple of hours while they all got better acquainted. The process was guarded at first, but the formation of solid friendships was present from the start. Midge was enamored with Sam, and he couldn't see past his penis after a while. Good thing he was on the other side of the bar. Bobby and Tracy hit if off well, but then Bobby would hit it off with anyone. He oozed energy and charm and didn't have to work at it. He reminded Sean of Ed Tabor in that sense. Two guys who gave the impression that they never made an enemy in their lives. Sean couldn't say that for himself, but then he took refuge in the old saying that you can measure success by the number of and kinds of enemies you've made. It's probably bull. But if there's anything to it, Sean could be called a smashing success.

Sean learned a lot about Jean's background. She was open and candid about her life. Twenty-four years old. A graduate of the University of San Francisco, majoring in psychology, earning a Bachelor of Science with distinction.

She married a college sweetheart in the Catholic Church, although she wasn't a Catholic, after the usual red tape for dispensations and all that nonsense. The marriage didn't work out. Not that they didn't like each other, but love was a one-way affair. Good for him, lacking for her. After two years, Jean felt like she was in a perpetual straight jacket and had to leave. It was difficult because her husband adored her, but it was better done sooner than later, and they were still young. Jean decided to go to law school after three years of working with psychologists. She felt she could help people better as an attorney than if she went back to get a doctorate in psychology. A most fortunate decision for Sean. He told her a little about himself, but with only a small portion of the candor she was willing to share. The essentials were there, however, and Sean noted that Jean was pleased that he was single and the complication of marriage wasn't lurking in his background.

They stayed until ten and then agreed they ought to get some sleep since they had an early class in the morning. Midge and Tracy, who were in the undergraduate program at UCLA, accused Sean and Jean of being party poopers. So Sean reminded them that staying until the last dog was hung was all right in the easy phase of education like undergrad, but professional school students had to get their butts home for some beauty rest. Torts class at eight a.m. was going to be tough enough and they ought to be bright eyed and bushy tailed. But even at that Sean hated to say good night to Jean especially because he wasn't going to be driving her home and he figured he wouldn't be able to give her a proper first date kiss. As he walked to her car and then fumbled around like a virgin in a whorehouse, Jean resolved the problem by saying, "Sean, you want to kiss me, and I want you to, so stop acting like it's your first time and take me in your arms."

He kissed her. Then holding her tightly, added several more. It was a joyful beginning, and he wasn't sure how he managed to let her get into her car and finally leave. Jean wasn't certain either. He walked back to the *Vin and Grog* and had another beer. Sam, Midge, Tracy and Bobby were still there. Sam took one look and said, "So much for going to bed early. I wonder why? Oh, Christ. The man's in love, or in heat. Can't tell which in this light." Sam was very perceptive.

The next morning Sean arrived at the law school fifteen minutes before the start of torts class so he could have time to talk with Jean. As he entered the lecture hall, he was pleased to see she was already there and had saved a seat for him. "Hi," Sean said feeling strangely awkward. "We went home early to get some sleep, right? So why couldn't I sleep? I think I'm in love, but I must caution you I am an incurable romantic."

"Gosh, let a handsome stranger buy a girl a beer and the next thing you know he is throwing himself at her feet." Jean smiled, and then added, "Ah, the story of my life. Kings and Princes, showering me with gifts and promises of undying affection. It has been a terrible burden. I wonder how I survive."

"All right, smart ass. You'll be sorry you made fun of my advances. But seriously, knowing what a romantic fool I am, what would you do if I did fall in love with you?" Sean teased half seriously.

"I don't know, Sean, maybe fall in love back, but it's too early to tell. I mean twenty-four hours and nothing but fun. There's more to love than that. But I will say it was a good start. And whether it's infatuation or whatever, I'm pleased you are sitting next to me and I suspect I will want you to be for the next three years."

"Me too, Jean, and I mean that. You're right. It is a good start and I know one thing for sure, we are going to be friends. Who knows, maybe we'll find friendship progressing to something more. So here we go. I was reading the catalog and we are going to be subjected to three years of all kinds of interesting things like torts, estates in land, past and future interests, real and personal property, fiduciary administration, trusts and other estates, code pleading, civil and criminal procedure, tax, evidence, constitutional law, corporations, agency, and what seems like a couple of bakers' dozen of esoteric law courses on our way to becoming hotshot lawyers."

"I'll settle for just becoming a plain lawyer right now," Jean replied. "You know how tough the bar examination is in California. But I'm determined to survive law school and make it through the bar exam my first time out."

"No point in dreaming small," Sean said softly. "I respect your determination, and I'm glad to see you have a handle on your professional goals as well as your personal life." Sean said this while thinking how hard he was going to work at being a large part of both.

"Welcome to my world, Mr. O'Ryan. I must confess I really am taken with you. Only one thing worries me. Will our attraction be a distraction? We've got to bust our balls, me figuratively, and you literally, to make it through law school. We can't let that focus shift."

"Ah, what the hell, we won't. We'll let the relationship take its course, but our goals will be professional life first, I promise," Sean assured.

"Thank you, Sean. I think this is the beginning of a beautiful friendship, and if we get along in the hugging and kissing department as well as we did last night, we are going to have quite a friendship," Jean responded with a warm and promising smile. At that point the torts professor approached the podium and said, "Good morning ladies and gentleman. Welcome to the law and the discovery that most of the things you thought were legal probably aren't, including many of the things you love to do most." The class laughed with genuine amusement, although somewhat nervously, as well, over what this introduction might portend.

Thus it began. The first of dozens of required and elective courses on various aspects of the law over the next three years designed to divine the mysteries of the law, which the professor defined as an attempted solution to the recurrent problems of human behavior administered through a system of justice. He stressed the importance of this methodology so that *civilized* people could turn to the justice system in order to right wrongs rather than resort to the six-gun.

Sean was excited and he glanced at Jean who was clearly sharing his enthusiasm. He could see the sunlight streaming from the skylight and refracting off the lecture chair in front of her as it swept up the tawny colored grain and planted a deep hue of brown and gold in Jean's eyes. For a moment he marveled at those eyes - those incredible eyes - which he was convinced had to be a true reflection of an exceptionally evolved soul. The warmth Sean was feeling as he looked at her added to the delight he experienced from their blossoming relationship, all of which made concentrating on mundane matters such as civil wrongs arising out of negligent conduct seem relatively unimportant. He should have been assimilating the introductory and definitional comments of the professor, but Sean was more concerned with the wonder of what Jean looked like naked. The lady wasn't just eyes, and he longed to savor her mouth again and find out what she tasted like everywhere. Her breasts were full and formed a desirable balance with her lovely, womanly hips, tush and legs. His desire to know her fully was reaching urgent proportion, which made him wonder how he was going to keep his promise to focus primarily on professional pursuits.

The lecture continued for fifty minutes. Sean forced himself to concentrate at last and managed to get a few notes. In the other two classes they shared, contracts and personal property, he did a little better, but only if he didn't sneak too many peeks at Jean's inviting chest. Sean often joked that he was weaned too early and, as long as he could remember, he had this insatiable desire to return to the breast. There are worse afflictions, of course, and he was certain this sure beat the hell out of a foot fetish.

The weeks went by in this fashion. Classes together; study time in the library, and then a couple of beers at the *Vin and Grog* with Bobby and Sam, and then later, some fairly serious necking and petting. After three weeks of *drive me up the wall* restraint, Sean point blank asked Jean if he could make love to her all the way with no holds barred. They were sitting in a coffee shop and he was pressed tightly against her thigh even though there was enough room in the booth to park a small truck.

"I thought you'd never ask. I have wanted you since day one, and you wouldn't think I had been married the way I was being coy about the idea of having sex with you. We came pretty close the other night when you took me home. Unfortunately my roommates were there, but I was ready to find out a whole lot more about you. I think we can get on with our discovery anytime you want just so it's within the next ten minutes, 'cause I don't think I can wait any longer. I want your *bod* Marine, and I've got just the place to get it. My friend Karen is back East and I've been watering her plants. I have the key to her house, which is full of many pieces of furniture, especially a great big bed, and there's no one to intrude. Let's do it," Jean coaxed.

Sean didn't need an order. They were out of there. It was difficult to drive with Jean's hand on his inner thigh, but somehow they survived the trip to Karen's house and left a trail of clothing from the front door to the bedroom. His desire to know what Jean tasted like was fulfilled and he became fully one with her on the first of many magnificent, loving liaisons. From that memorable beginning the next two years passed in a succession of hard work and close friendship and - best of all - loving to a depth he hadn't thought possible as they grew as close as two people can without his intruding on that part of her that would always be a little mysterious.

As he discovered more and more of Jean, the more he loved. They shared proximity of thought, effort and love that sustained them through the miserable grind of law school. That combination of love and discipline took them to their senior year and they each had a fair idea of what they wanted upon graduation. It was at that time that Sean proposed marriage and Jean accepted without hesitation, suggesting only that they wait until after they graduated and took the bar examination so they wouldn't have the distractions normal to being newly married.

Sean agreed, and he bought Jean a diamond he couldn't afford and she had trouble seeing. Okay, so it wasn't the *Hope diamond*. It was the thought that counted, along with the promise of forever, to which he happily surrendered. It wasn't quite as simple as loving and asking, however, because Sean was still mired in the terribly erroneous belief that, because he was a Catholic, he was supposed to marry in the Catholic Church otherwise he wouldn't be truly married. The problem with that idea of marriage in the Catholic Church was that the Church hierarchy contended that Jean's marriage to her first husband in a Catholic ceremony was presumptively binding as a sacrament even though Jean was not a Catholic. A real theological Catch-22, which no doubt, was designed to maintain the tight canonical controls that have been deeply entrenched over the centuries. Thus according to the archaic rules of the church, Jean presumptively was not free to marry again in the Roman Catholic Church unless a declaration of nullity of her first marriage was obtained through an annulment process. That was 1957, and the church was not giving away annulments. And it wasn't selling them either.

Sean had a plan, however, and it didn't call for summary execution of Jean's ex-husband even though the thought had a certain practical appeal. He assured Jean that there had to be a way around this, other than marrying outside of the Church. That latter obvious solution had been ruled out by his irrational goblins of fear and hell fire. Sean had yet to discover that marriage is only a sacrament when it results in an external, *unconditional manifestation of a subjective intention to be married*. This manifestation is the essential sacramental sign that flows from an expression - through one's conduct - of a willingness to embrace the sacrament in the full context of two people indelibly becoming one by fully consenting, only after lengthy deliberation, to be fully united in the eyes of God until death do they part.

In that context it is unlikely that marriage becomes sacramental at the time of the ceremony for most people. Often it takes years to turn into a sacrament, and then only when the participants are unreservedly willing that it should.

As a consequence the phrase *until death do us part* cannot be accepted without question. It is mysterious at best, in much the same way that many things allegedly attributed to Jesus are. To literally take the expression *until death* to mean bodily death, denies any other possible and more realistic meaning, such as *death of the spirit* rather than the body, particularly when one considers the limitations of human judgment at the time of entering into a so-called contract of marriage and a lifetime commitment. It is not idle comment to say that one seldom, if ever, fully knows another until he or she lives with him or her.

Being uniformed as to this fine distinction at that time and being blindly naive, as well as without understanding any logical basis as to why it was so, Sean accepted the assertion that he couldn't morally marry Jean until they had straightened out her status. He should have just disregarded it all, of course, but after his then twenty-seven years of hell fire and damnation indoctrination, he wasn't disposed to blithely ignore the threat of excommunication.

"Jean, I think the best thing is to fly to Chicago and talk to Dan O'Flarety. He is the Jesuit priest who has been my spiritual advisor since I was fourteen. He knows everything about this bullshit and I am confident he'll have a solution. You want to come along and see my mom again and meet Father Dan?"

"I would, darling, but the firm is in the middle of the Hughes' appeal and the deadline is fast approaching. With twenty-five million at stake I don't think they would let me go right now. You know how stressed lawyers get when their slave law clerks aren't burning the midnight oil to make them look brilliant. Tell your Mom hello and that I look forward to seeing her soon, especially now that her son has finally asked me to marry him. Honestly Sean, sometimes you take the longest time to do things," Jean teased with a devilish grin.

"Hey, babe, a gentleman's supposed to take a long time. Haven't you heard the expression that nice guys finish last? Leo Durocher meant in baseball, but I always thought it meant in bed. Never heard any complaints out of you so far."

Before Jean could slip in a rebuttal to his sassy remark, Sean added, "But seriously, honey, I think I should go and see what can be done. I'll fly out tomorrow. I called Dan and he said to come on down. He's the greatest."

"I love you, Sean, and I'm not worried about this. We'll make it work. Two people don't love like we do and let it get away."

"I love you too, dear lady," Sean whispered as he embraced her with more desperation than he had ever felt. "More than I could tell you in a thousand lifetimes."

CHAPTER 14

August 1957

Sean flew to Chicago and went directly over to Jesuit High to meet Dan O'Flarety. "Ah, Sean, my favorite hopeless case. How you doing, son?" Father Dan held out his arms and greeted Sean with affection and warmth. "Are the ladies still leading you around by your cock? Wouldn't surprise me a bit. I hear you made a name for yourself in Korea. That doesn't surprise me either. As long as I can remember, if you weren't screwing, you were fighting."

"God, it's good to see you, Father." Sean said hugging his old friend.

"Sit down, Sean. Try the spiritual chair, it's still in service."

The spiritual chair was the most comfortable place to go to confession. You had a problem, you took it to Dan. You needed to go to confession, you came to his place and sat in the spiritual chair. Anything less than bank robbery got you three hail Marys for penance. Sean recalled a time back in high school when he had gone to confession one Saturday afternoon in the spiritual chair, and within an hour had to go again. It seems he met this girl in the parking lot after leaving Dan's room, and...and...well...that's another story. Sean was reluctant to go back to see Father Dan, but he was supposed to go to the Holy Name Society Mass and Communion the next morning, so he waited until evening and then went to the local church to go to confession in a regular confessional. Just his luck, however, Dan was the only priest hearing confessions, so Sean disguised his voice and went through the drill. When he got through, Dan asked, "Is there anything else, Sean?"

"I often wondered how you knew it was me, Dan? I thought I had that fake voice down pretty good."

"It wasn't the voice I recognized, Sean, it was the sins. I'd heard them all from you many times before. I knew it had to be you," Dan said with a wide grin. "I suspect the outcome would be the same today. You need to go to confession?"

"Thanks anyway, Dan. I'm not here for confession, and I don't think you have that much time anyway. What I'm really here for is your help and advice. I can't think of anyone who can provide them better."

"Well, thank you," Dan replied, "nice of you to say so, even if you seldom took my advice. Praise Jesus, you were a stubborn one." As he spoke, Dan looked at Sean in the same way he had over the years, with humor and patience, and a touch of what Sean always suspected was too much understanding, as if to say, "You dumb Mick, will I ever get through you." Sean didn't resent the look. He would have wondered what was wrong if it weren't there. But it made him feel like he was fourteen again as he took in the familiar scene. The same comfortable, book cluttered room Dan lived in at Jesuit High hadn't changed since this extraordinary priest first arrived many years ago and started to teach young men how to survive in tough, immoral world. Their friendship was instant and lasting. Dan was one of a special kind. There are a lot of good priests, and regrettably there are some bad ones, but Dan was one of the great ones. A brilliant, but totally self-effacing, gentle, man. Generous with himself, his time, and his forbearance, he was one of those rare individuals who lived for others without a thought of what might be in it for him. Priests like Dan never make Pope.

"So, who is the lady, Sean? I know there has to be a woman involved as sure as I know the English stole Ireland."

"The lady is Jean, and I am madly in love with her. We plan to marry next summer, but there's a slight hitch. She was married to a Catholic in the church, but she wasn't a Catholic. They got some kind of dispensation. I checked with the Chancery Office in Los Angeles about her status and was told she would have to get a declaration of invalidity of her former marriage before we could marry in the Catholic Church. I understand that means going through an annulment process. I think it's ridiculous and I'm willing to fight city hall, so what do I do?"

"Well, it's nice to hear you are finally thinking about going through a ceremony and not just the consummation. God only knows how many sweet young things thought you'd get around to the ceremony after you deflowered them, but that's something else. As for Jean, first it has be determined if she has any grounds for an annulment. Even though she isn't Catholic, it is the validity of her first marriage that is in issue not her religion. Then she has to petition Rome. It's a long, involved procedure with no guarantees. I can tell you it won't be easy and there is no way you can work this out by next summer. It often takes years."

"Oh, fuck, Dan. That's the last thing I needed to hear."

"I know, Sean, but you have to face even unwelcome facts. So let's see if Jean has any basis for annulment," Dan replied. Sean responded by going over as much of Jean's background and her marriage as he knew. At the end, Dan wasn't optimistic. "I don't see much here for a formal annulment, Sean. The Church is pretty stingy when it comes to pronouncing the invalidity of marriages. Actually that's a bit misleading since it is the - in fact - invalidity of marriage that is the key. And that already exists with or without the Church's say so. If people aren't sacramentally married, they aren't. Nobody can make it any less or more so.

"Thus the Church's pronouncements granting annulment are merely the official recognition of that existing invalidity. But neither God nor man gave the Church the ability to declare what is or isn't a marriage in fact. If it is, it is, and if it isn't, it isn't. However the Church can assist people is discovering if they are truly, sacramentally married, and if not, assist them in straightening out the defects, or recognizing that the so-called union cannot be fixed. In this way the parties are permitted to dissolve their invalid relationship civilly as well as through the annulment process, and they may marry again in the Catholic Church hoping they get it right this time around.

"I'm sorry to note, however, that the Church is slow to grant such recognition, and truly, only grudgingly awards annulments. In time we may get enlightened, but amazingly, this far into the twentieth century, we still proceed as if we were in the dark ages when it comes to recognizing the need to nullify seriously questionable marriages."

At this point Sean wanted to denounce the arrogance of the hierarchy who set themselves up as the self-anointed, infallible guardians of God's will, like they would know what that is, but he resisted. Dan didn't deserve that sort of diatribe, although he would have listened patiently. He always did. Then without waiting, Dan advanced to a workable solution even before Sean could ask if there was an alternative to annulment.

"Now don't give up hope," he said. "There is a possible solution. This involves a doctrine called the *Internal Forum Solution*, which is little known outside of Canon Law, but every bit as valid as an official proclamation of annulment if done in good conscience. This is how it works. The technique is used when a couple is genuinely convinced in conscience that their marriage is not what a marriage is supposed to be to make it a sacrament, but they don't have enough evidence to prove it in a formal tribunal. The parties discuss their situation with a qualified priest, and if they are able to come to the honest conclusion in their collective conscience before God that there is justification for ending their marriage, they may return to the sacraments with the priest adviser's blessing and they are free to remarry.

"I should note," Dan continued, "that it's a very informal procedure. There are no records kept. A sort of do it yourself thing. So in the event the parties change parishes, the new parish priest might not recognize the act as having been sincere, and you could not force him to allow you to remarry. So the best bet is to remarry in the parish in which the priest assisted you with the *Internal Forum Solution*, or, if necessary, don't tell the new priest about the old marriage. It would not be a lie of omission if you look at it logically. For example, if Jean were asked if she had been previously married, she truthfully could say no, meaning not sacramentally. I am not suggesting this, of course, but it could be a last resort."

"Dan, you old son-of-gun, this is great," Sean shouted.

"Let me add," Dan said, "the only person who knows what she can say in good conscience is Jean. No one else can speak for her, but this is a way around the long annulment process. And I should emphasize that when the Church grants an annulment, it never, and I repeat, never says there wasn't a marriage recognizable at law. The annulment process and the *Internal Forum Solution* merely declare the nonexistence of a *sacramental* marriage. No more, no less. A lot of people mistakenly think that somehow an annulment bastardizes children and negates pre-existing property rights. It does neither. All it does is free the parties to remarry in the Catholic church and return to the sacraments if they have been away."

"You are the greatest, Dan. How come people aren't told about this?"

"I don't know, Sean, maybe because the top brass hates to let go of the controls, but we lowly ones keep hacking away at it, so there may be hope yet."

With the formal business concluded, Dan and Sean visited for another hour. Dan broke out some beers from his private stash and Sean felt better than he had in a long time. The black cloud that seemed to be following him around had disappeared. He called Jean as soon as he left Dan's place, but she wasn't home, so he left a message with one of her roommates to tell her he had found the answer and that he loved her madly and would be home tomorrow and everything was just fine. In the morning he went through another of those emotional goodbyes with his wonderful Irish Mom, and then headed back to Los Angeles and the dawn of a new era. On the plane he opened a letter Jean had given him before he left. She had asked him not to read it until after he had finished talking to Father Dan and he was on his way home to her. He was happily ready for her thoughts and more impatient than ever to marry this magnificient woman. The wait seemed terribly long now that the impediments were about to be resolved. Jean's letter read:

Sean dearest,

As I write this letter, I do not know if you will have had any success with Father Dan. I hope so for your sake, because I want you to be comfortable with your decision to marry me. I don't want theological ghosts haunting your determinations.

On a few occasions we have discussed your feelings about the Catholic Church. In spite of your protests, I know you are steeped in the traditions that underscore your faith, and you would be troubled marrying outside of that faith.

If it will help, I offer you some insight into my feelings. To begin, I admit I only gave lip service to the Catholic aspects of my former marriage.

Most troubling was the mandate that I had to accept that union as a lifetime commitment. I wondered how I could possibly know how to do that at age nineteen. I was too young and too inexperienced. As a result, there was no hope for that marriage after a while.

But now, with maturity and growth stemming from that failure, I am able to commit to you in a way I never understood before. In that sense, now wiser and older, I freely give myself to you. This is substantially different from the mental reservations and conditional qualification of my former attempt at marriage, and when the *raison d'etre* vanished, that marriage passed into history, never to be reprised.

I come to you better informed about the essence of marriage and I choose to give myself to you without reservation. I love you body and soul. Every fiber of my womanhood, my heart, my body, and my mind are ineluctably caught up in the being who is Sean. I have become one with you with such totality that, in many ways, I have become you. So you see my darling Irishman, even if we never go through a ceremony, I will forever be a part of you, and - in that mysterious way of love - all of you. We need no ritual to affirm this. We are already one.

I appreciate that convention dictates some formality, however, and thus there will be a ceremony of your choosing. I hope it will be Roman Catholic so you can close the loop on your religious odyssey that started long ago with the Baltimore Catechism. I want this for you.

For me, I want only you and I thank God every day that you came into my life. I pray that this is His will, although mostly I find an understanding of His will to be difficult at best. But even when I cannot divine it, I submit to God's love and feel confident that He will guide me through.

You once mentioned that you accepted the concept of God as all-powerful, just, and merciful, but you hesitated on "loving." Not that God didn't love us, you opined, but that His disregard of the suffering and the incredible evil that plague the world seemed markedly inconsistent with the concept of perfect love. You expressed it in terms of an indifferent God. I think these feelings started in Korea, but you never talk about the war.

I too have thought about God over the years, even substituting some of my own terms for the more common ones. But terms are irrelevant whenever one addresses a concept as awesome as "The God" or "The One and Only God." Particularly when I think that we have created that awesome, Supreme being in our own image and likeness rather than truly and fully accepting that we were created in His.

In any event, I strongly believe in God, and while I don't always know what His will is for me, I try. I do know I could not become a Catholic because I do not accept certain doctrines. It doesn't matter, however, because they are not important in my personal and unique relationship with God anyway.

But I know that the Church is important to you, and I respect your feelings. I make no demands of you. We each find God in our own way, and while He sees things as they are, we often see them only as we are conditioned to do. If we are diligent, however, we will continue to grow and we certainly will learn from each other.

Someone once said, "Time is just nature's way of keeping everything from happening at once." That bit of wisdom is worth savoring. Time is on our side, my dearest, so we can make things happen in good order and not haphazardly. Maybe we will even uncover some of the mystery of our God.

Right now I don't have any answers, but of one thing I am supremely confident, and that is my love for you. Whatever you find out from Father Dan won't make a difference in that context. I will love you with or without a religious imprimatur on our love. I feel married to you right now. And as a matter of unequivocal choice, I want to be with you forever and ever.

Sean Fitzpatrick O'Ryan, I love, cherish, adore, and idolize you, and having given a lot of thought to the matter, I like you too. Come home to me, my darling.

Jean

******

Sean called Jean as soon as he landed. She happily advised that everyone was gone for the weekend so please come straight over and ravish her. The invitation was irresistible. He was still holding his suitcase when she answered the door and Sean asked if he should put it down before or after the ravishing. Jean thought it might be a good idea to free up both of his hands so he could concentrate on pleasure as she pulled him through the doorway. She then led him to her bedroom and they loved completely. After they finished, Jean lay softly against Sean and he held her for a long time with either speaking. The warm closeness was the only communication they needed.

Sean had come to Jean and he loved her with an intensity he hadn't thought possible. His odyssey was complete. The long search for love came to rest in her and he wondered why he had been singled out to be blessed with this exceptional human being. But he accepted her as a gift from God, who he had to admit could not have been indifferent. At least not this time.

******

93

Their senior year of law school was filled with the many demands imposed on third year law students and it passed quickly. Busy was a common condition, but they were never too busy to delight in stolen moments in which they would hide and lose themselves in each other. Lying together after their lovemaking was an emotional refuge that took them far from an intrusive world.

Graduation finally arrived in June 1958, but the final test was yet to come. Immediately after graduation they embarked on a bar review course and at the end of July they wrote the California bar exam feeling confident they would be among the thirty-five to forty percent projected to pass, although they wouldn't know for several months. On the third and final day of the exam, with their hands seemingly ready to fall from their wrists after writing an infinity of words on the law, it was over and they emerged from the sterile examination hall ready for some well-earned relaxation.

Sean suggested the recently opened *New Coventry Hotel*, which had tea dancing on Wednesday afternoons until eight. He figured they could lower the stress factor with some drinks and dancing and then catch dinner later.

"Sounds good. I'd love to go dancing, my gallant knight," Jean responded happily. "We can finally talk about our wedding without having law on our minds."

The hotel was popular but they were able to find a cozy spot under a fancy skywalk suspended over the rectangular inner courtyard. Their table had easy access to the bar and dance floor, so they gladly exercised both options. The music was the kind you rubbed bellies to while slow dancing. That kind of dancing meant you held the lady close and you didn't boogie around the floor doing your own thing as though you had misplaced your date but never noticed.

"I'm glad the band plays a lot of ballads, Jeanie, because tonight I just want to hold you close and feel your body tightly pressed against mine. I love the part where we dip and I climb on your thigh. Got to be careful though, or it'll show."

"Sean O'Ryan, you rascal. All this time I thought it was *my mind* you craved. I had no idea there was something else on *your mind.*"

The lovely strains of *Moonlight Serenade* that followed a medley of *As Time Goes By* and *Stardust* trailed off and the orchestra leader suggested it was time to swing as he signaled the downbeat for Duke Ellington's *Satin Doll*. This was Sean's cue to take a break and make a head call. Several golden beers had made a journey through his kidneys without a pause for color-coding and he was overdue. He took Jean back to their little nook and excused himself with something eloquent like, "I'll be right back, darling, I have to whiz."

Jean was kind enough to smile lovingly at the madman taking urgent leave, and said, "While you're gone, remember I love you."

The orchestra was in full swing as Sean worked his way through the crowd to the men's room. *Satin Doll* never sounded livelier and he noticed a fair gathering of people up on the skywalk keeping time to the rich beat. "If they get any more enthusiastic, they'll be registering on the seismograph at Cal Poly," he said to no one in particular.

He was just finishing in the rest room when the area shook violently as though an earthquake had struck. But he realized it wasn't the slow, rambling movement that quakes often start with. This was sudden; accompanied by a deafening roar. It felt like a freight train had crashed through the roof. Sean was alarmed and he rushed out of the men's room into a hell he hadn't seen since Korea. An obscenity he will never stop seeing the rest of his life. The skywalk had broken loose, and came crashing down, hurling dozens of people unto the inner court and on top of dozens of others.

The screams of agony *from the dying* and *for the dying* who were buried under a mountain of steel, concrete and glass, added to the indescribable terror generated by the sickening panorama of broken, bleeding bodies, some decapitated, some limbless, some simply crushed flat.

Sean looked for Jean, but everything was blood and bone and anguished cries. Orientation of what was the original geography of the inner court wasn't immediately possible. He climbed over the rubble of stone and steel cutting his hands and knees without awareness of pain, feeling only the terror that filled his soul with a frantic frenzy to find Jean and take her away from the madness. He found her at last, lying in peaceful repose amid the violent carnage near the cozy spot where he had left her. Her incredible eyes were open and she was looking at him as she had so many times, full of love and giving. But she didn't see. Even in death she would not deny Sean those eyes that drew him to her that first day.

He learned later that Jean had died instantly when a steel reinforcing rod had whipped free of it concrete tomb and sang a death's song as it swung in a deadly arc and sawed mercilessly across Jean's cervical spine severing all signals between the stem of her magnificent brain and her vital organs. Sean thanked God for sparing her pain, and then cursed Him in the same breath for His outrageous indifference. Part of Sean died that day with Jean.

With her invalid Mother's permission, and because she had no other family, he buried Jean in Forest Lawn, along with a part of him that will always be hers alone.

He visits her often. He knows she hears him as he tells her he will love her always.

Two months after that descent into hell the bar results came out. Jean and Sean had both passed. He took the announcement to her grave and told her. He was certain she was pleased. He buried it beneath the headstone in a metal cylinder along with a poem he had written to her and the memory of a love that would never die. It read:

Jean

Courtly lady of my delight,
      You came through an opening of my heart,

And never more a world of black and white,
      Only areas too gray to distinguish.

Right or wrong - lawful or illicit. What can it
      matter? I have judged. I was judged.

My case was pled in your eyes as I appealed to you
      With subtle motions even I did not understand,

And two lives merged into one.

Surely the tribunal on high can be moved
      To compassion for bodies and souls forever joined.

Courtly lady of my delight,
      To love you, is to know why there is a God.

To leave you is to descend to the depths of hell,
      The hell that results - not from loving -

But only from losing.

What greater hell than losing you?
      Is there no appeal from this cruel sentence?

God is love.
      Why would God destroy love?

Courtly lady of my delight,
      Be my advocate.

Plead for me before the bar of understanding,
      Seek to acquit me of my pain and torment.

Free me from the prison of my despair.
      Make me whole once again,

To touch, to taste, to love,
        To be one with you, forever.

Courtly lady of my delight,
        Plead our cause,

For it is right and just.
        Speak for us,

As I cry for you. Consume me
        With your very being.

I need you. I love you.
        I am you.

Precious lady of the law,
        Plead our love in a heavenly writ,

So that Heaven's Court will declare in judgment
        What we have always known in our hearts,

Love forever affirmed.

CHAPTER 15

September 1964

It has been six years since Jean died. Sean has avoided extended romantic involvements by deliberate choice. Even his relationship with Susan was being handled cautiously. The excitement was high, but the risk of over emotional response was being carefully guarded against.

Heading to Federal Court where he was to meet a client who had been charged with assaulting a Border Patrol Officer, Sean returned to cold reality and he pushed thoughts of Jean deep into his heart as he had done countless times. A bench trial was on the calendar for his young Mexican-American client, Ricardo Martinez, who had been born in El Centro, California. Martinez had been stopped by an INS officer in El Indio. The officer demanded proof of citizenship. The young man repeatedly told the officer he was a native born American, but he had no proof on his person since, like any other American, he was not required to carry a copy of his birth certificate. *The Man*, as the Border Patrol agents are referred to by street people, didn't believe him and attempted to put Martinez under arrest, allegedly because he fit the description of a *coyote*, a name given to people who run illegal aliens, called *pollos*, past the San Clemente check point fifty miles north of San Diego. Ricardo Martinez resisted the officer but lost the battle after being subdued by the officer's partner with a few well-placed persuasions on and about his head and shoulders with a six-cell flashlight.

He was booked into the Metropolitan Correctional Center. In time his U.S. citizen status was clarified, but he was charged, nonetheless, with assault on the officer. Sean called several other native born Americans as witnesses to show a pattern of abuse arising out of the so-called smuggler profile. Each of these witnesses similarly had been rousted at various times by *The Man* simply because they rode around in large, old, low slung cars, and they fitted the Border Patrol profile for smugglers. Their testimony was helpful in convincing the court that the officer had gone too far in his enthusiasm to apprehend an alien looking young man with a dark complexion, black hair and brown eyes, who looked just like millions of other Americans. Finding no probable cause for the stop of Martinez, coupled with the fact that he was legal in every sense, the Judge ruled that Sean's client had the right to resist an *unlawful arrest*. Sean thought the Assistant U.S. Attorney would have shared this insight as well, but he didn't.

Thus, Ricardo Martinez, natural born citizen of the United States of America where justice is supposed to be color blind, had to undergo the indignity of arrest and trial. Judgment of acquittal was entered and justice was served, but Martinez will always have an arrest record even though the arrest was illegal and the resisting charge resulted in acquittal. This is one of several areas where the justice system sadly fails to protect.

Sean received no fee for the case, which was referred pro bono by an attorney friend, Hank Ramirez, but the feeling that comes from seeing innocent persons vindicated is its own reward. He appreciated being involved in a manner more significant than acting as a hired gun on behalf of the highest bidder no matter how unworthy the cause.

Sean drove down to Camp Pendleton on Friday, and he and Jack immediately went over to the brig to see Lee Johnson. Sean asked Johnson why Chrissy Long said she could see his penis exposed when she regained consciousness at the scene of crime. He said he didn't know, suggesting maybe he had forgotten to zip his fly after taking a piss. Sean knew the jury wasn't going to like that answer, but Johnson couldn't provide anything better. Not disposed to give him room to make up less plausible explanations, they left.

"Something is really fucked up here, Jack. For the first time I feel Johnson is lying to us. Not about the rape, but about his attraction to Jill Thompson, a young white woman. Something doesn't sit right. Do you think he could have raped Chrissy as a vengeance thing?"

"I don't know," Jack replied slowly, "but I share your misgivings. If he is jerking us around, he's doing a damn good job. Until this visit, I would have bet my life on his telling us the truth. Even if he didn't take part in the fight and the initial attacks on Chrissy, he could very well have had intercourse with her after she was thrown on him. Maybe when she was unconscious."

"That's my concern too," Sean answered. "Even if Chrissy was unaware, it would be non-consensual rape. That old juvenile rape charge is disturbing."

"What ever happened to the other kids in that juvenile thing?" Jack asked. "How did the girl explain their presence?"

"That aspect wasn't pressed by Lee's counsel at the time," Sean explained. "The district attorney's position was that it didn't matter if she consensually fucked everyone of the L.A. Rams on that day, it was rape if, when it came Johnson's turn, she said no and he forced himself on her. None of the other kids would testify that she willingly consented to Johnson and his ass was grass. I can see where getting even might enter into his thinking when he was drunk and pissed off. Hell he had just gotten dumped by another young, white woman."

"We've got a problem. And Johnson's got a bigger one," Jack said shaking his head.

"You're right, Jack. Let's go see Major Bryant and find out if he wants to go with us when we interview Chrissy Long."

They went over to talk to Brendon Bryant who had been counsel for the investigation officer, Major Pat Carothers, at the Article 32. Bryant now would be the prosecuting attorney, technically known as the trial counsel, at the general court-martial of the four accused. The case was still referred as a joint trial and none of the counsel wanted to ask for enlisted members on the court as a means of getting a severance. Each attorney would have preferred a severance because there is the danger of guilt by association in a joint trial, but the risk of adding enlisted members is sometimes a greater. Usually some crusty old Sergeants Major or First Sergeants are added because one-third of the court has to be enlisted if the accused is enlisted and asks for them. More often than not these old timers are tougher than commissioned officers when they sit on a jury.

Major Bryant was most cordial. A good-natured Irishman, he brought his barroom charm and demeanor to the courtroom; always ready for a good fight, but friendly and likable. Sean found it refreshing to work with a considerate attorney on the prosecution side.

"Sean and Jack, good to see you again. I suspect you have come to pick my pocket so what is it you want to fleece me out of. Be glad to help, but no deals. You want to make an offer to plead guilty in exchange for a thousand years without parole, I'm your man. Otherwise, no deals. You've got the right to propose a pre-trial agreement, but I'll dig in my heels unless it hangs these guys by the balls. Now what can I do for you?" Brendon asked with good humor and a big Irish grin.

"How about you go fuck yourself, you Irish bastard," Sean replied with equal good humor.

"Ah, eloquence from defense counsel. I love working with poets," Brendon laughed.

"Seriously, Brendon, we're going up to talk to Chrissy Long tomorrow and want to know if you want to come along," Sean said.

"Well I would if she is willing to talk to you, but the last she told me is *mox nix*. No way she will talk to you. I told her she had a right to refuse to be interviewed by defense counsel but please do not say that I said she should refuse. She promised she wouldn't put me on the spot."

"Oh hell. Just what we needed. How about we give her a call, with you on an extension, and we ask her if she has changed her mind?" Sean suggested.

"Sounds reasonable," Brendon responded. "She's at home now. Left the hospital two days ago. You guys get on the phones on those other two desks and you can ask her, but I don't think she is psychologically ready to talk to you. The trauma is still pretty raw."

They called and pleaded with her, but Chrissy persisted in her refusal to be interviewed by the defense team. Sean wondered who had gotten to her. Chrissy had a right to refuse, which, unfortunately, is one of the shortcomings in the military criminal law system which doesn't unqualifiedly allow the defense to depose complaining witnesses or talk to them if they refuse to do so. This gives the prosecution an unreasonable edge because so much of what defense counsel learns from the witness must then be done in open court. That's the last place you want to go on a fishing expedition. The old rule of never ask a question on cross-examination that you *don't want to know the answer to* takes a beating when the witnesses have been uncooperative before trial.

"Well, thanks anyway, Brendon," Sean said after they had disconnected.

"Anytime fellas. What else can I do for you?"

"How about a trial date?" Sean responded. "Now that Chrissy is home and in spite of her physical and psychological trauma which is understandable, I presume she'll be able to travel and appear in court one of these days. What do you think Brendon? When will your key witness be ready?"

"Let's see when the judge will be available," Brendon replied. "Then we can coordinate with the other counsel."

"I suggest we shoot for the middle of October and keep our calendars open for that period," Sean proposed. "This provides flexibility to accommodate everyone's interests, and doesn't keep our client hanging around the brig any longer than necessary."

"What's the difference, he's going to be there for a lot longer when the trial is over," Brendon said needling Sean.

"Brendon, how about you dangle your nuts over an alligator pit. That's just about right for a Mick like you," Sean fired back with a big grin on his face as they shook hands and then left.

"We have a little more time now, Jack, but I don't know what the hell else we can do. The other counsel won't let us talk to their guys, and Chrissy Long won't talk to us. I don't think I've ever gone into trial with more shots in the dark than this one. We have our work cut out for us, and most of it will have to be done in the courtroom rather than before we get there."

"I know, Sean. This one has turned into a lion's den. Sorry we won't be tooling up to L.A. to talk to Chrissy Long, but I'll keep digging down here and keep in touch as I go," Jack said somewhat apprehensively. Sean understood. It was hard to be optimistic, but they did have the one thing going which helped keep the adrenalin flowing. In spite of some nagging feelings, they still thought Lee Johnson was innocent. It was just getting harder to prove, although technically they weren't required to do so. Unfortunately, reality overcomes technicalities in some situations. With that problem unanswered, they said goodbye.

Sean drove up to Los Angeles thinking about Susan because he was horny and it had been a while since they made love. As he pulled into his garage at the Marina, he saw Susan's Mercedes. She wasn't in it, which means she had gone up to the apartment. "What the hell, that's why she has a key," he said softly. "This is a nice surprise especially since I have been thinking of her in a sensuous way."

CHAPTER 16

He opened the apartment door and saw Susan standing on the balcony watching the ever-spectacular panorama of boats and sea. As he walked to the French doors leading to the balcony, it was Susan's first awareness that he had arrived. She turned and looked seriously depressed.

"Hi, Suz," Sean said as cheerfully as he could, and then moved to take her in his arms. She didn't resist but he could tell from the kiss that her concentration was decidedly elsewhere. He didn't press the point. Everyone experiences mood swings. Sean thought this was just one of those days. "It's good to see you, even if you are sort of down. What's happening?"

Susan looked at him with a pained expression. "Sean, tell me honestly, does the name Chrissy Long mean anything to you?"

He hesitated for a moment trying to understand how Susan had heard the name, and then answered truthfully, "Yes, Susan, I know the name."

"I was afraid of that," Susan said sadly. "I know Chrissy very well. She was a student of mine last semester. Unlike most other students, I got to be friends with her. She is a lovely person and we hit it off, not as a professor and student, but as genuine women friends."

"Well that's good, Susan, but unfortunately it means you know what happened to her," Sean answered.

"And to her dear, gentle, boyfriend," Susan added. "I presume you know his name too. It was David Hall."

"I know."

"Of course you do. That's why you have been going to Camp Pendleton isn't it? You must be involved in defending the scum who raped this beautiful girl and killed her friend."

"I won't deny I am representing one of the Marines accused in that case, but I've got to take issue with your characterization that he is scum," Sean replied a bit too sharply.

"I just found out about this today," Susan said, her voice rising. "And I went right over to see Chrissy. I don't know if you are aware how much seeing her has devastated me. After I talked with her, I started thinking about your trips to Camp Pendleton. Chrissy was raped at Camp Pendleton. Her boyfriend was killed there. All this happened around the time you suddenly got a new client who just happens to be a Marine, who just happens to be a black man, who just happens to be accused along with three other Marines of rape and murder." Susan was almost shouting now and her anger and frustration were undisguised.

"I'm not going to lie to you, Susan. I didn't even know you knew the victims. Hell, you know I don't talk about my cases, and this case was no exception. I wasn't aware of a connection between you and Chrissy Long."

"I'm glad you recognized her name, Sean. I was afraid you had lumped her into the category of just another victim who rates infinitely below the rights of your precious criminals."

"That's a low blow. You know better than that. I sincerely would have said something long before this if I had known my client was accused of committing acts of violence against someone you knew. I wasn't deliberately keeping this from you," Sean replied calmly, although he too was growing angry. He knew what Susan was feeling and it wouldn't do any good to jump all over her.

"Maybe you would have said something, but that doesn't change the most important consideration, does it?" Susan challenged.

"Like what?"

"Like the fact that you still would have represented one of the animals who did this to Chrissy whether or not you were aware I knew her and felt terrible about this," Susan shot back.

"First of all Miss Sullivan my client is not an animal, and secondly, of course I would represent him whether you knew the victim or not. It's my job."

"Job be damned, and I don't believe he isn't an animal. Chrissy told me what all four of those bastards did. They brutalized her and beat her boyfriend to death. Tell me, if they aren't animals then what the hell are they?" Susan was close to crying and Sean wanted to hold her and comfort her, but he didn't move. It would have made matters worse. "Which one of the bastards is your client, Sean?"

"My client is a Marine named Lee Johnson. He's black, and the other three accused are white. I don't know if the other three are innocent or not. But I am confident that Lee Johnson is, and I'll work my ass off to make sure he stays that way all through the trial. He has a right to this, and he has a right to have me protect him. Damn it, Susan, the Sixth Amendment hasn't gone out of style has it? Or maybe we should just suspend it for this case," he said not as calmly as he would have preferred.

"That's bullshit, Sean. You give me this innocent crap. But I know you, you'd do the same if this guy admitted every fucking detail. For all I know maybe he has. Either way you'd do it, because you have this fucking Irish crusade stuck in your craw and there's no hope for you."

"Please try to understand, Susan, this is what our system is all about. I learned that a long time ago when I was seventeen and I read about a little guy named Willie Earle down in Greenville, South Carolina. The name may not mean anything to you, but he was the victim of vigilante injustice, which sounds a lot like what you are proposing for my client. You think your friend Chrissy was treated badly, let me tell you about Willie Earle, a poor, drunken, epileptic Negro who was accused of killing a white taxi driver. A band of white men, other taxi people it was said, broke into a nearby local jail and beat him and stabbed him five times. Then they blew his head off with a shotgun. Why he was suspected is not clear, but the mob didn't wait for the niceties of due process. So what happened to them? In the long run, nothing," he answered with disgust. "Thirty-one white men were arrested and put on trial for lynch murder as either principals or accessories. Not one of them testified at trial, nor were any defense witnesses produced. The prosecution had twenty-six signed statements the defendants made to the police. These statements were read to the jury, and almost no argument was made by the defense counsel except some asinine pleas for white supremacy. After all this, the jury deliberated for only five hours and acquitted every one of the defendants. Hardly democracy in action, unless you believe that all men are created equal, but some are more equal."

Susan looked at Sean and seemed confused. Tears were forming in her eyes. "I have been trying to understand."

"And I'm trying to help you understand."

"But you're not helping me, Sean. All you are doing is giving me a bunch of pious platitudes about rights and duties, and some other person's injustice many years ago. I'm sorry about Willie Earle, but right now it's all unreal."

"No it isn't, Susan. It's very real. I'm talking about a young man's rights and my duty as an attorney to respect and serve those rights. I took an oath to do this." Sean tried to respond more calmly because Susan's anxiety level was reaching a danger point and she might walk out without letting him explain.

"How about Chrissy's rights? She was brutally raped by four animals. How about David's rights? He was killed trying to protect her. Nobody took care of their rights. Don't victims have rights?" Susan's voice cracked with anguish.

"Of course they do, Susan. Above all else they have a right to justice. A right to be vindicated. An absolute right to have the persons guilty of those terrible crimes punished to the full extent of the law. But note the key elements here, which are persons *guilty* of those crimes, not just accused of them. There's often light years between accusation and guilt in fact. You're angry because I'm protecting my client from a lynching based on accusation alone."

"Sean, you drive me crazy. You and your voice crying in the wilderness. You and your fucking crusades. Just once in you life can't you admit that some truths are self-evident. Your son of a bitch client was caught in the act. Chrissy told me he was there when the police found her. The other animals were caught later, but they all were caught. And they're all guilty. If you choose to ignore this hard fact because of your goddamned idealism, you are fooling no one but yourself." Susan was over the edge now, and Sean didn't know how to reach her short of acquiescing in everything she was saying.

"Susan, I know it looks bad right now, but there's a lot more to a case than presents itself at first. I believe in this young man. I believe he's innocent, as bad as it looks at the moment. So I've go to help him. It's my duty. It's his right to have me as counsel. I'm not turning my back on the victims. I'm only making sure the right persons are brought to justice, not the wrong ones."

"Sean, I knew you had some crazy ideals, but I didn't realize how much I don't know about you. Sometimes I think you are a lunatic idealist. How could anyone understand how you can willingly represent a murderer and rapist, who everyone knows is guilty?" Susan's voice, filled with desperation and despair, told Sean he could not win in this battle of emotions.

"Not everyone knows he is guilty, Susan. I don't know it, and neither does he. I can't think of two more important people in that equation. And let me point out something, if I don't protect the system as well as my client, then it's just one more incursion into all of our protections." Sean was speaking calmly now, having abandoned any hope of out shouting Susan on this. "If you fuck with the system when it's Lee Johnson's turn, where will you look for protection when it's your turn? It's easy to be accused, you know. But where does one turn for safety when she is innocent and we've allowed the system, which was designed to protect everyone's rights, to be destroyed by a passion for revenge?" He looked at Susan with sadness because he knew he was addressing principles she had no interest in at the moment.

"Sean, this is just more of your blind idealism. I'll tell you what I think of the system as you phrase it. I think it was a system originally designed to protect as you say, but it has gotten out of hand. All too often it overprotects so that justice can no longer be served. With all your forensic skills and the cockamamie rules of evidence you have spoken of many times, your bastard client could get off even though he is guilty as hell. I have something to say about your system, counselor. Fuck your system! It doesn't focus on truth, it focuses on rules and structured procedures by which guilty men go free and thumb their noses at justice. How many times have I heard you say jokingly that the last thing a guilty man wants is justice; he wants acquittal. Justice is way down on the list of wants at that moment. What kind of system is that?" Susan raged.

As calmly as he could and with an effort not to patronize, Sean replied, "Susan, there may be better ways to do this, I don't know. Maybe the French have a more realistic format where most of the case is persuasively worked up by a magistrate judge before the actual trial begins. But I doubt it, because this tends to shift the burden of proof by the time the main trial starts, and the accused, while technically still presumed innocent, in effect has to prove his innocence or he's had it. Maybe the American system isn't perfect, and I'll be the first to admit it needs work, but it does accomplish one major goal, it keeps the burden of proving guilt on the accuser." Sean wasn't discerning any change in Susan's demeanor and he could only hope he was getting through a little, so he continued. "Sometimes the burden falls short and the accused does walk away even though he is guilty in fact. But that doesn't make the system wrong. It actually strengthens it. Keep in mind that a system that only convicts and never acquits is not a system of justice, it is a system of tyranny and oppression. I'm sure you can see that."

Susan looked at Sean with her beautiful green eyes now saddened by the burden of these terrible crimes and his role in their resolution. She hesitated for a moment, fighting back tears and a choking sensation that made it hard to speak.

"Sean, this is hopeless. When you are like this - so gung ho for protecting a system so few people understand - I wonder if I ever knew you at all. How can anyone truly accept what you are doing?" Susan was crying softly now, and he didn't know how to help her.

"Some people can, Susan. Some would."

"I suppose that means, Jean," Susan snapped, catching Sean unaware. "She probably lapped up every fucking thing you said."

"Jean? What do you know about Jean? I never talked about her with you."

"You never talked about Korea either, or no name village, or the Chinese soldier you killed to save him from hopeless pain, or all the rest of your personal war. But I know about it all," Susan said sadly, accusing him with a look that rebuked his unwillingness to speak of these things.

"How do you know?"

"Ed told me."

"Why would he do that?"

"He felt he owed it to me and to you. He felt I should know you better if I was going to continue being involved the way we were. Ed's wiser than all of us. Don't be angry with him. He was right to tell me."

"I'm not mad at Ed. Hell, how could I be? I'm just not sure I wanted you to know," Sean said softly and with a feeling of great sadness.

"I think we need some time apart to sort things out, Sean. I don't know how long. At least until your current crusade is over. I don't think I can handle making love with you while you are involved in this filthy case. It's like the scum and dirt have rubbed off on you notwithstanding all of your noble bullshit."

"Susan, don't do this. I won't talk about the case. Hell, I don't anyway, you know that. I'll leave it at the door when you are with me. We have a good thing going, why let this case hurt our relationship?"

"I'm sorry, Sean, I can't. I don't know if it's the end of our affair or not, but I need some distance from this horrible spectacle you are engaged in. I need to think. Please don't try to contact me. I'll call you when I've sorted all this out. That's the best I can promise. I'm too sick at heart to even pretend I can understand right now. I apologize for mentioning Jean. That was cruel. I know how hurt you were."

Susan turned and didn't look back. She paused at the door and dropped the key to the apartment on the entry way table. The sound of metal striking wood was like the blade of a guillotine falling. He saw the door open and close behind her. After a long moment as he replayed the heartbreak of her leaving, he went out on the balcony and watched the setting sun extend a last golden embrace as it sank into the ocean leaving a long, lonely trail of dying light.

******

Sean fell asleep in his favorite chair by the unlighted fireplace. He didn't know how long he had been sitting there thinking about Susan and Lee Johnson and Chrissy Long and all the madness that intruded on the love affair he and Susan had shared. He awoke with a start a little after nine plagued with the nagging feeling he had harbored since he first met his client, and he decided to call Jack Coleman at his home in Carlsbad.

"Sorry to bother you so late, Jack, well actually it isn't all that late. But I need to know if you can recall something from the ONI report on Chrissy Long."

"No problem, Sean, what is it you need to know?"

"Do you remember if she was described physically in that report other than the effects of being battered and raped. Does the report suggest what she looks like normally?"

"Yeah, I remember generally. Female, age 19, long blond hair, blue eyes as well as the description of the results of the assault, like various bruises on her arms and legs, cut on her throat, skull fracture..."

"Whoa, stop right there. We haven't seen Chrissy Long in person, but you do remember her being described as having long blond hair and blue eyes?"

"I'm sure of that."

"O.K., Jack, that's what I need to know right now."

"This tie in somehow? I recall that Jill Thompson also has long blond hair and blue eyes," Jack commented.

"I don't know. Just a nagging feeling. I'll let you know what I come up with. Thanks, Marine."

Sean hung up and called Lee Johnson's mother. "Esther, Sean O'Ryan. Sorry to bother you so late but I have a short question and I'll let you get back to whatever you were doing."

"That's all right, Sean. Happy to do anything I can to help."

"I appreciate that. Tell me, what did the girl look like who accused Lee of rape when he was a juvenile?"

"Oh my...Let me see. I always thought she was kind of slutty looking but preppy at the same time. I suppose some of the boys would think she was cute. She had a well-developed figure and long blond hair and blue eyes. Does that help you at all, Sean?"

CHAPTER 17

Sean tried to put this latest development into perspective and balance it against the difficult scene that had been played out with Susan. He had to admit her reaction wasn't unusual. Most people who have been victims themselves, or close to victims of violent crimes, have a hard time appreciating the criminal justice system and its necessary safeguards. Sean had been there himself and had wrestled with some serious questions after Jean died. Jake Rogers recognized his concern during that terrible period, and guided Sean through valuable lessons about the law and the criminal justice system.

It was September 1958, and Jake had directed Sean to take a month off before coming back to work while he waited for the bar results. "It'll be several weeks before you find out about the bar. I'm confident you will pass, but right now I want you to take time away from the law and do some serious reflecting on your life. Nothing will bring Jean back, but she will always be a part of you. I think you need to sort some things out before you get back on the mission you started a long time ago."

Sean accepted Jake's generous offer and spent a month in the summer of 1958 with his father, Seamus O'Ryan, who lived in Santa Monica with his second wife and their only child, Sean's sister Catherine, then a lovely, young lady of eleven. Sean had a lot of love to give, and the sad loss of Jean had left him with a surfeit of loving feelings, which he showered on Catherine. This wonderful child had been the primary object of his love and affection before Jean. Catherine knew Sean was deeply hurt and she infused the healing process with an intuitive acceptance of the love she had willingly shared with Jean. It would take a long time to recover, but Catherine gave him direction.

Catherine's Mother, an innately kind lady, was exceptionally gracious during Sean's visit. Seamus O'Ryan had separated from Sean's mother when Sean was nine, and had been a stranger for many years, but he welcomed Sean into his home, not as a prodigal, but as the son he had somehow misplaced and only now was able to view with pride. In the process Sean's youthful impressions were confirmed. He wasn't certain of the source of those impressions, but it wasn't his mother. She never breathed an unkind word about the handsome, dashing, Irish rogue she had loved and married.

This stranger Sean finally came to know was undeniably a rogue and an incurable romantic, as well as a philandering womanizer. Like father, like son? Sean wasn't sure. He admitted that he had been before he loved Jean, and probably would be again as he labored over the discovery that *unconditional* love is filled with a great deal of risk and pain. But as he progressed in understanding, he came to terms with his father's strengths and weaknesses. The elder O'Ryan was a generous man, but with a serious fault. If you needed help, he was there to give you everything he had. But if you needed him for himself alone, and nothing else, he wasn't always there. A brilliant man who broke many hearts with a lot of promises, Seamus discovered early on that his charm and good looks often allowed him to get away with more than he should have. Sean couldn't change any of it, and didn't want to.

One evening, after a few beers and everyone else had gone to bed, Seamus asked Sean about Korea. Sean said he would share his experiences if his father would share his war with him. He did and Sean did, and for the first time Sean learned how heroic his father's wartime service had been. 1942 in New Guinea, Seamus was awarded the Army Distinguished Service Cross, the second highest medal the Army awards for valor demonstrating extraordinary bravery above and beyond the call of duty. The following year he saw more action in the South Pacific on another island, winning a Silver Star and his third purple heart.

At times parents take on heroic proportion through the sacrifices they make in giving to our needs. But Sean hadn't viewed his father in that context until they talked about their personal wars. Only then did he realize that, in spite of seeming neglect, his father in many respects had given of himself in a personal way. Not only to Sean, but to millions of other sons just like Sean, by presenting them with freedom and providing a model to demonstrate the worthiness of guarding that same freedom for their own sons, even at great personal risk. Like father, like son? Sean hoped so. This then was the common denominator of two blood line warriors sharing memories of their personal, bloody wars that furnished Sean with a deeper appreciation of the bigger than life legend he had only known in memory as Seamus O'Ryan. And he loved him.

At the end of that memorable month, Sean returned to Jake Roger's office. The bar results were imminent and he was gearing up to be a real lawyer at last. The emotional scars had slowly formed, and while he knew part of him would always be with Jean, he accepted the fact that he had to seek out new challenges. In the secret recesses of his heart where she will always reside, Jean told him he must. His plans at the moment, however, did not include risking love again. The venture seemed too great and the wounds still too raw.

Jake welcomed him back with effusive charm and graciousness. Sean should have been alert to the signals Jake was sending, but he was happy to be back and he missed them. "Good morning, Sean, it's good to have you back. I'm not going to ask you how things went. I'm sure you reached deep down on other occasions and did this time as well. All of us will cherish the memory of Jean, but if you live in the past, you die in the past, and right now there's work to do."

"Thank you, Jake," Sean said with genuine appreciation. "I'm ready to go, and I'm grateful for your generosity in keeping me on the payroll even though I haven't produced a thing for you the past month."

"No sweat, G.I., as the ladies of the night would say in Japan in the good old days. At least that's what I'm told. Naturally, I have no personal experience with such sportive ladies myself, you understand," Jake said with a mischievous grin.

Then he paused and stopped smiling. "I've got to break some news to you. News that won't sit well, but it involves something very important and is in keeping with what you and I are all about. I'm sorry to have to hit you with this as you walk in the door, but it's happening right now and there's no way to put off discussing it."

"Oh? What's happening that I'm not going to like?"

Jake fixed his eyes on Sean and said evenly, "I have taken on a new client. He has been indicted by the grand jury while you were away. There were several others indicted as well, but they posed a conflict of interest and I would only accept this one client." Jake continued looking steadily into Sean's eyes, and said softly, but not apologetically, "You will not be working with me on this case. Not now in your last few weeks as a law clerk, nor as an associate in a few weeks when you are sworn into the bar." It was the first time Jake had directly advised that Sean was staying with the firm, and while he felt a fleeting elation, Sean was filled with apprehension at what Jake was saying.

"As far as you are concerned this case has the plague and you will hear, see, and know nothing about it from anyone or anything in this office. I'm building a Chinese Wall around you so there will be no conflict of interest," Jake added.

"What is this all about, Jake"? You've got me hanging from a cliff."

"Frankly, Sean, it's a matter in which you have an emotional interest, but that's not the principal barrier. The main problem is that while you were not a witness to the origins of the incident, you were a percipient witness to the terrible and ultimate consequences. Thus, although it is a remote possibility, in the unlikely event you should be called as a witness by the District Attorney, we both will have been protected from any ethical conflict. I have cleared this with my client and he has given me the go ahead should this happen. In the meanwhile, I've got to keep you completely insulated from any involvement."

"I understand the ethical requirement, Jake, but you still haven't told me what the case is," Sean said trying to remain calm although he sensed what this case was, and then Jake confirmed Sean's fears.

"My new client - who is charged with manslaughter - is the design engineer involved in the skywalk that collapsed at the *New Coventry Hotel* where Jean died."

"What the fuck, Jake. Are you jerking my chain? You are going to represent the guy who may be responsible for Jean's death?" Sean shouted. His disbelief was bordering on anger and his question was deliberately accusatory.

"Yes, I am, Sean, and I'm glad you qualified your outrage with the phrase may be responsible. At least you haven't decided to summarily execute him," Jake fired back.

Sean started to speak, but Jake held up his hand and said, "Hear me out on this. "You know that an indictment presented by a grand jury doesn't mean a fucking thing other than the prosecution, with its stacked deck, convinced some good people who haven't a tenth of the facts that somebody has done something criminal and ought to answer for it. Secret proceedings are an abomination when they are used to indict. They might be all right to investigate community matters and keep things non-public so innocent people don't get hurt. But as a tool to indict, they serve as an archaic relic of Star Chambers and Inquisitions, and are equally outrageous."

Jake paused for a moment as if to clear the disgust from his voice and then continued, "Only one side of the story is presented to a grand jury and prosecutors aren't eager to submit exculpatory evidence to balance the plethora of damning evidence they selectively present. This is because all gray areas can disappear when one has been a prosecutor too long. If a prosecutor loses a balanced perspective, the world appears black and white, and justice becomes synonymous with conviction. Any suggestion that acquittals are indispensable to a fair system are dismissed as radical heresy. This mind set corrupts the criminal justice system, and winning at any cost becomes the goal. You know what happens to ethics at that point."

Once more Jake paused, clearly disturbed by the tactics of some prosecutors, and then added, "Most men and women who represent the federal government or the People of California are fairly honest in their dealings with defendants, but there are a number of truly bad prosecutors who are willing to hide, and sometimes even destroy evidence, or conspire with witnesses to get them to say what they want to hear. Obscene deals are cut with scum who are far worse than the individuals taken to trial, and canons of ethics that mandate that the prosecutor's role is to serve the proper ends of justice and not simply to convict are ignored as nonexistent." Jake's disgust was growing as he said this. He then went on, "Maybe if prosecutors had to switch roles and defend criminal cases every two years or so, they would appreciate that justice and acquittal are not mutually exclusive concepts."

"I understand this, Jake, but Christ, your client may have caused all of this horror with a fucked up design or engineering. How can you represent him?" Sean asked, still visibly upset.

"I can represent him because he is entitled to my services, and you know it. Note the emphasis here on my services. I am doing this, not you. You are totally out of this, so don't let your feelings get in the way." He then emphasized his next point just in case Sean wasn't getting the message. "I looked into this long and hard before I accepted the client. I even bounced the design plans off of my engineering experts who owe me a truthful read-out every time. Then I got a second opinion from another set of independent experts. The opinions were unanimous; these plans were sound, and if something went wrong, which

111

obviously it did, it wasn't due to any design defect, and it happened long after my client's efforts were complete."

Jake fixed his classic stare on Sean sensing that he hadn't fully come to grips with the nightmare of Jean's death and now had to reconcile Jake's representation of someone accused of criminally causing that death. "You know the rules I live by, Sean. Absolute integrity is demanded. I will not be compromised, and this includes my belief in a client's cause. I won't say I haven't taken guilty people to trial, but I prefer not to. Because of this I've gotten a reputation that if I turn down a case, the defendant must be guilty. That's bullshit, of course, but the public puts stock in rumors and this one keeps getting harder and harder to squelch."

Jake rolled his eyes and shrugged his shoulders as he said this. "And so I live with it. The truth is, I have a balance between totally innocent clients and other clients who are guilty of something but not necessarily the principal crime or crimes charged. In both instances, I win a fair share of acquittals. But I never take on a client who I think is lying or who I feel intends to perjure himself on the witness stand. I won't pander to fraud. I've been fooled a few times, I'm sure, but not knowingly. If a client can't tell the truth, then I'll suggest a negotiated plea. If he doesn't want to do that, then he has to go somewhere else. If I can't believe in a client's cause, I can't represent him. Every case has two clients, first the accused, and second, the system. I have to protect both with equal vigor. I let no client corrupt the system through me, and no one dictates tactics or strategy on a case to me."

Jake was on a roll and Sean wasn't missing any of his points. "I put my new client under a microscope, for your sake as well as mine. This included the detailed engineering reports. He has had to pay a bundle just to find out if I would even take the case. That's an indication of sincerity on his part. If the District Attorney had been this thorough, he would not have sought an indictment. But, as usual, it was round up the usual suspects and then shotgun the charges. I hate that mentality but so far I haven't been able to reform the system to open grand jury proceedings to all defense counsel and the presentation of defense evidence. Someday, maybe?" Jake then added, "Oh, yes, one more thing, I believe in my client's innocence in this case. I will take up his cause with a vengeance. I know you can understand that kind of determination. Crusade is stamped on your forehead."

He then closed gently, "I wanted to explain the reasons for my decision. Maybe I was preaching to the choir because you already knew these things, but I'd like to make an observation. I feel that Jean would understand, and from what I knew of that extraordinary woman, I am confident she would tell you she didn't die in vain. Out of that hellish tragedy a better Sean O'Ryan emerged. A Sean O'Ryan who wouldn't want an innocent man to be punished anymore than Jean would, even for her own death."

Jake had a way of touching the heart. Sean knew he was right, but it didn't make it any easier to relive the pain and to accept Jake's decision to become involved in that horrible experience by representing someone accused of its cause. It took more than a thoughtful lecture to come to terms with the truth of what Jake was saying. But eventually he did accept Jake's wisdom. When he did, the dark shadows in which pain had taken residence from the moment he saw Jean's eyes, loving and giving even in death, fell away and he acknowledged what had to be done.

That was six years ago but he never lost sight of the lessons Jake impressed on him. The scars have softened and the wounds slowly healed. After a long, bitterly fought trial, Jake's client was rightfully acquitted.

Jean understood.

CHAPTER 18

October 1964

Trial in the Johnson case was set for Monday, October 12th in the courtroom at Camp Pendleton. Sean drove down on Sunday and stayed at the *Miramar* in Oceanside so he wouldn't have to make a long drive before court convened. Over coffee in Jack's office Monday morning they spent a half hour with Lee Johnson who had been brought over early from the brig. Lee was scared but reluctant to admit it. With false bravado Sean assured him he needn't be worried because he was innocent and both Sean and Jack believed in him and the system. Sean wondered how many innocent men and women, who ultimately have been convicted, had heard that from their counsel just before trial.

The three of them moved to the courtroom at five minutes to nine. The presiding judge was already there; a refreshing change for Sean who was more accustomed to judges not only being late, but also making a grand entrance after all the rest of the participants had been cooling their heels for some time. The judge, technically known as the *Law Officer* in those days, was Colonel Tim Malone. This was a break for both sides. Judge Malone was considered to be the fairest in the military system. He weighed his rulings carefully, not favoring either side, and he wasn't afraid to make hard calls. He also granted defense counsel considerable latitude, which was welcome in this case since the key witness was still a stranger to the defense. At the same time he was also eminently fair to the government, and didn't flinch from ruling in the prosecution's favor, if it was the correct thing to do, simply because someone might claim error later on. Colonel Tim, as counsel referred to him informally, was the best. None of the counsel on either side had any complaints about the luck of the draw in this instance.

The spacious and ample courtroom, which covered an entire wing of the Base Legal buildings, ably accommodated the large assemblage on the first day of trial. Four separate tables were provided for the accused and defense counsel, with substantial working space in between each for privacy. The prosecutor, Major Bryant, was located across the room directly opposite and facing the Court-martial Board. The Board, which was the counterpart of *the jury* in civilian courts, sat in a straight row along the west wall; the most senior member being centered and the rest of the members flowing out alternatively by rank in descending order on either side from there. There were twenty-five members initially, which was more than the required quorum, but it was expected that peremptory challenges, along with various challenges for cause, would reduce the panel to the minimum number of jurors required by law when the trial on the merits began.

The judge's bench, which rose above the rest of the court, was located along the north wall. The spectator section provided sixty seats with standing room for twenty more. Some media reporters were present, while the rest of the audience consisted of interested civilian and military. Rape and murder are not a way of life with Marines aboard Camp Pendleton; this case was a rare exception.

Brendon Bryant read the preliminary jurisdictional matters into the record and all counsel were introduced. Sean advised that, although he was in civilian clothes, his affiliation with the Corps went back a long way, and that he was presently a major in the Marine Corps Reserve. This was important because military juries sometimes resent civilian counsel, viewing them as carpetbaggers. Sean wanted the jury to understand his status as a Marine officer. He was one of them and he appreciated the needs of the military for firm discipline.

After the introductions, Judge Malone formally convened the court-martial Board. Both the prosecution and each defense counsel took turns with voir dire of the board members and exercised various challenges. Several challenges for cause were made. Most were denied by Colonel Malone, but some were granted, such as in the case of one member who stated he could give each accused a fair trial through the findings of guilt or innocence, but if any were found guilty, the only appropriate sentence he would consider would be the maximum available under law. He was honest. So, of course, he had to go.

In this fashion the Board was ultimately reduced by challenges to twelve members consisting of Colonel Ted "Cold Steel" Orlowski, the senior member as President, two lieutenant colonels, three majors, four captains, one first lieutenant and one second lieutenant. The trial on the merits then got underway with Major Bryant calling Chrissy Long as the first witness.

Witnesses in a military case are usually excluded from the courtroom until called so this was defense counsels' first view of Chrissy Long and it was her first view of them. Because this would be a matter of initial impression, Sean asked for a brief pause before Miss Long entered the courtroom. He then sought the permission of Judge Malone to undertake a demonstration that would relate directly to identification of the accused by the victim. Major Bryant objected, but Colonel Malone heard Sean out. "What is it you want to do, Mr. O'Ryan?"

"A courtroom demonstration on what I believe to be the inability of the witness to identify my client, your honor."

"How do you propose to do that? This is somewhat unusual if not downright procedurally questionable."

"I believe I can demonstrate what I have suspected for a long time, Sir, and that is that the witness picks out the defendant only because he is sitting with his lawyer. I believe the witness, more often than not, doesn't remember the accused but claims she does only because of the structured setting of the courtroom." I genuinely believe this is very important because there has been no pretrial lineup conducted in this case.

"So what do you propose? That your client not sit at the table with you?"

"Well, yes, Sir, that is exactly what I want to do. He will be in the courtroom, but not next to Captain Coleman and me. He will be in the back of the room with a group of spectators, some of whom bear a strong resemblance to him. As you can see there are a number of Negro or black, if you prefer, Marines among the spectators, who I purposely assembled for this demonstration. They are all wearing the same uniform as the accused, the Green Service A uniform. All are clean shaven so that not even facial hair is a distinguishing feature."

"Even if I allow this, Mr. O'Ryan, wouldn't the absence of an accused next to you at counsel table be conspicuous?" Judge Malone asked.

"Yes, Sir, it would, but with your permission I would have a Negro Marine of similar build and features seated next to me at the table. I think the witness will pick out that man as the black accused in this case simply by virtue of his being at the table with counsel."

"Well, this is irregular, but I find the concept interesting, so I will overrule Major Bryant's continuing objection and allow you to proceed. After the identification process is complete, however, your client will have to return to counsel table. Is that understood?"

"Yes, Sir, perfectly, Sir." With that, Sean had a black Marine very close in appearance to Lee Johnson take his place at counsel table. Johnson was then seated among the spectators in the back row with eight other blacks of similar features. When this was accomplished, Chrissy Long was brought into the courtroom. Jack and Sean were stunned. Chrissy was beautiful. The blond hair and blue eyes they were prepared for, but they had not expected the extraordinary, delicate beauty of the young victim. She stood five feet two inches, and had the kind of features movie producers would kill for. Her figure was slim but wonderfully proportioned overall. She looked like she stepped out of a Madison Avenue ad. Sean realized they could not take this rape victim over the coals by attacking her character. This was no tramp. Chrissy was a lovely young woman upon whom they didn't dare heap abuse. She had been defiled enough.

After administering the oath and soliciting preliminary background information about the witness herself, Brendon Bryant asked Chrissy Long if she could identify any of the accused in this case, starting from her right as she faced the counsel tables. She pointed to the first white defendant, Thomas Panos, and said, "I recognize that man as one who was there on that night, but I don't know his name. I don't know any of their names, but I recognize him, and also the one at the second table." Chrissy had next identified Anthony Fennelli, who she said was also present on the night of the crimes.

"At the third table," Chrissy continued, "I recognize the Marine but don't know his name either." She had identified Rick Cox. "He was there that night too."

Chrissy then shifted her gaze to the fourth table and looked directly at the black Marine sitting next to Sean and Jack. She said nothing. Sean looked at the jury. They could see the pause and Sean could feel the suspense building. Chrissy still said nothing and Sean began to feel confident. She looked at him and then at Jack and then back to the Marine seated with them. Then she looked over at Major Bryant and at the Judge. She seemed out of sorts and turned to the spectators as if to find some relief in what had become an oppressive setting.

"Can you identify the fourth defendant, Miss Long?" Brendon asked.

"Chrissy looked back at Sean and at his bogus client, then once more stared long and hard. Not a word. *I've got her, she can't make the identification,* Sean thought. *She can't pick out Johnson as the fourth man.*

Then, in the middle of Sean's exultation, Chrissy lifted her eyes with what seemed like a far off, detached look. He didn't realize she was focusing on the back row of the spectators. She then gazed softly at Sean and he thought she was going to smile, but she didn't. She merely lifted her right arm and pointed to the back of the courtroom and said, "The fourth man who was there on that terrible night is sitting in the last row with several other Marines. He is the third from the left." She had picked out Lee Johnson. Every member of the jury fixed their eyes on Sean. Some glared, others looked like they wanted to laugh. His experiment was a dismal failure and it backfired on the client. Johnson resumed his seat at the counsel table, and the trial proceeded. Sean whispered rather sheepishly to Jack, "It's going to be a long week, partner. Rolled the dice and they came up snake eyes. I really fucked up on that one"

Brendon Bryant took Chrissy through direct examination skillfully and with great kindness. He knew how difficult this was for her, particularly in front of so many strange faces. It was obviously much harder testifying in person than it was in giving her affidavit, in private, to the ONI agent from her hospital bed many weeks ago. Being the complaining witness in a rape case is difficult anytime if the victim is truly a victim and not making unfounded accusations for motives of revenge or spite. Chrissy Long was the genuine victim of a most brutal sexual assault. There was no question this lovely woman was telling the truth. She made the best kind of witness. No badgering could revoke one word of her gospel statement as she recalled the details originally set forth in her affidavit that had been introduced at the Article 32 investigation, but that affidavit was not before the court and could be used only for impeachment purposes, or, when appropriate, as a prior consistent statement. It didn't seem likely either one of those circumstances would arise in presenting Sean's case for Johnson. He had to walk carefully and cautiously with this witness; the entire sympathy of every person in the courtroom was with her, including Sean's.

Some women you take to the brink and paint them as the aggressor with a past full of lustful experience and temptress attitudes. With those witnesses you lay bare their whole soul, and lawyers would continue to ride roughshod over victims, no matter how sordid their past - even if they are truth tellers - until rape shield laws are universally in place to protect them from such tactics. If the thought of implementing techniques of this nature against Chrissy Long ever entered Sean's consideration, however, it was dispelled from the moment she walked into the courtroom. This young woman was brutally raped and she hadn't invited a second of the evil attention inflicted on her. It matters not if she had slept with her boyfriend, David Hall, or was as virginal as she appeared prior to the attacks. She was a true rape victim and the only defense in this case was innocence.

The story of that dreadful night was ably developed by Brendon on direct, bringing Chrissy back time and again to the difficult but unmistakable details of the vicious assault upon her most intimate person by the three white Marines she identified in the courtroom. All of which took place after they had engaged in a deadly brawl with David Hall, who died trying to protect her. Testifying to the terror of that brutal attack was very difficult and Chrissy had to stop several times to compose herself and wait for tears to stop falling. She made a sympathetic witness but there was no question she was able to recall the events clearly and credibly. Without equivocation she identified Anthony Fennelli as the one who made the original sexual remarks to her and tried to grab her as she and David walked along Lake O'Neill.

She also identified Fennelli as the one who first struck David without warning. Chrissy was certain the other two white Marines, Thomas Panos and Rick Cox, had joined in the fray and delivered several blows and kicks to David as he was standing, and then as he lay on the ground. She could not remember seeing the black Marine do anything to David, but she acknowledged that she had been rendered unconscious by blows from the defendant, Fennelli, and Johnson could have been involved in the fight, but she didn't know. She was clear in her recall that it was Fennelli who not only punched and kicked her but also first attacked her sexually. She was positive Fennelli had penetrated her after manhandling her by tearing her clothes and roughly touching her breasts. He then brutally inflicted himself - first manually, then with his penis - into her genitalia. All of this occurred after he had placed a knife against her throat and cut her. The not fully healed scar from the cut was clearly visible across the room.

Chrissy was certain none of the other three defendants had punched or kicked her, and that Fennelli was the only one who cut her. But she was equally certain Thomas Panos was the second man who had intercourse with her, even though she begged him not to. He did not threaten her, but he did force himself on her, and ignored all of her tearful pleas. She was adamant that there was no doubt about penetration, and she believed that Panos, like Fennelli, had reached a climax while inside of her vagina. She then testified that the next defendant, Rick Cox, was the third man who violated her that night. She admitted to being in a state of shock, but she was certain he too penetrated her, even though she had begged him to get away from her, and she was certain that he also had reached a climax inside of her.

Chrissy was then directed by Brendon to relate what, if any, experience she had with Lee Johnson that night which he categorized as a night of terror. Sean objected to the inflammatory language and Colonel Malone sustained the objection but didn't feel it was necessary to instruct the Board members to disregard. Sean didn't press the point. It *was* a night of terror. To say anymore would merely emphasize the obvious.

Chrissy then related how she had not known that Johnson was at the scene until she had been dragged over behind the rise and thrown on top of him by Fennelli. She did remember how Johnson was dressed and obviously was able to recall what he looked like. Sean's earlier demonstration reinforced the competency of the witness on that point. Brendon asked what, if anything, happened during the time she was in proximity to Johnson after being left there by Fennelli. She repeated what Fennelli had said about the "Nigger" deserving her and when asked to be more specific, she most reluctantly, and with exceptional embarrassment, repeated the language Fennelli had used when he laughed and said, "Niggers deserve fucked up women and this bitch is about as fucked up as you can get."

Sean suspected that Chrissy had been assisted with this quote by the ONI agent at the time of making her affidavit. Now he was convinced of it. But he didn't give a damn what she said about Fennelli. Nothing good was going to be said about him and the worse he looked, the better Johnson looked, because Lee hadn't said anything to Chrissy as far as Sean knew.

Chrissy went on to say how she had fainted for a period and couldn't remember exactly how long, but she could remember that when she came to, she was naked from the waist down and Johnson was on top of her with his penis sticking out of his trousers and fully exposed. Sean silently thought, *so what? All this does is confirm what Johnson had been saying all along, that he didn't do the girl.* Then the bubble burst.

"What, if anything, do you recall as to the defendant, Johnson, having intercourse with you?" Major Bryant asked. Both Jack and Sean were on their feet. "Objection, your honor, leading and suggestive," they seemed to cry in unison.

"Hold everything, gentlemen. First of all, only one counsel need make objections, so you decide whose turn it is next time. Secondly, I realize there are some questions posed on direct examination that are patently leading, and some that are cleverly disguised with the - what, if anything - technique. This may be one of those times. Nonetheless, I feel this question goes right to the heart of an essential element of the crime and I am going to allow it. Miss Long you may now answer the question," Judge Malone said pleasantly.

"Would you repeat the question?" Chrissy asked.

"What, if anything, do you recall as to the defendant, Johnson, having intercourse with you on that night?" Brendon repeated.

"I am certain he had intercourse with me, the same as the others did."

"What, if any, permission did you give the defendant, Johnson, to do this?"

"None. None, whatsoever."

Sean saw every member of the court and Judge Malone look directly at Lee Johnson, something neither Sean nor Jack dared to do or they might have driven the nails in deeper than Chrissy Long had just done with a statement that far exceeded what she had said in her affidavit. The week just got longer.

CHAPTER 19

First Lieutenant Dan Richardson, tall, rugged, former all American football player from the University of Pennsylvania, rose to begin his cross examination of Chrissy Long on behalf of Anthony Fennelli. It was a calculated move and Sean couldn't imagine what Dan could possibly ask her that wouldn't hurt more than help. But every counsel has his own game plan and Sean sat back and watched with interest hoping that young Dan was aware that cross-examination is a lonely street and no one in the courtroom could help him if he made a mistake. The witness is usually unfriendly and the other counsel are not disposed to offer assistance. More than likely, anything other counsel would have to offer would be decidedly adverse to the impression the cross-examiner is trying to make anyway.

Dan was careful not to launch a frontal attack on the sympathetic witness, but he did test her ability to not only recall but to identify the participants in what he suggested was the dark of night. He erred. There was a bright moon on the night of the incident and the usual marine layer of low clouds had not reached inland as far as Lake O'Neill, some ten miles from the ocean. In addition, San Diego County was on the periphery of a Santa Ana condition that had been strong over Los Angeles. That had kept the skies clear and added to the excellent visibility created by the moonlight.

"The pathway leading back to the parking lot is lighted with lamp posts every fifty yards or so, Lieutenant, and that, along with the moonlight, really made it easy to see everyone and everything that was happening," Chrissy testified simply and without trying to be cute. Dan had been caught in a mistake. He then made a second mistake which was to ask a question he had prepared in the event he got a favorable answer to the first. He hadn't, but he went ahead anyway.

"Miss Long, I'm certain you understand the accusations you have made against Anthony Fennelli are very serious and how important it is to be accurate in these matters, so how can you be sure that he is the person who did the things you describe?" The question in its form was objectionable, but neither Sean nor Jack were about to say anything. The only counsel with an interest in objecting would be the prosecutor, but Brendon Bryant was wise enough to recognize the rope Dan Richardson had just handed Chrissy and he let her hang him.

"I was violated by that Marine," Chrissy said, pointing to Fennelli. "He did terrible things to me and he did them for what seemed like a long time. He could not have been closer to me throughout it all, and I can tell you, Lieutenant, there is no mistake about my memory of that vicious man and what he did to me."

Dan realizing he had run out of hope for a mistaken identification, and understandably chagrined, announced, "No further questions, your honor." He sat down soundly defeated by the delicate victim and Fennelli was dead in the water. It was well deserved. But it did cause Sean concern. Fennelli might get on the witness stand during the defense case in reply and try to hang the rest of the defendants.

He was the kind of scum who wasn't disposed to go down alone.

Captain Dusty Burns, Notre Dame undergrad and law school, was next. Dusty was a delightful character who found humor in almost every situation, except the deadly serious business involving his client, Rick Cox.

"Miss Long, I realize you could see rather well that night and have identified my client as being on the scene, but isn't it true you were badly hurt by Anthony Fennelli and you were in a state of shock by the time you say another man violated you?" The question was reasonable and Lieutenant Richardson's objection that the question assumed a fact not in evidence was summarily shot down by Judge Malone with one word, "Overruled." While the question did reinforce the evidence of an attack by a second Marine, Dusty was on the mark about whether Chrissy was able to recall with accuracy the necessary element of forcible rape, that is, penetration of her vagina - or at a minimum beyond her labia—without her consent, which gives meaning to the legal expression "penetration against the will, however slight, constitutes an offense." It is a risk, of course, because it allows the witness to confirm her certainty of the offense. It is the kind of question defense counsel don't like to ask, but in this instance Dusty had no alternative. His defense of Cox, like Sean's defense of Johnson, had to be innocence.

"I was very shocked by what happened Captain, and I was crying and frightened, but I did know what was happening. I begged that Marine - pointing to Rick Cox - not to do this to me. But he did anyway and he forced himself inside of me. In a little while he reached a climax. I am sure of it."

Dusty was stuck with the answer and tried to test Chrissy's ability to know that someone had a climax inside of her. The question was objected to by Major Bryant immediately, and Colonel Malone, being light years ahead of the law on that point, ruled it irrelevant. "I haven't heard one word about consent as a defense Captain Burns. I find any question of prior sexual experience of the witness immaterial at this time. The objection is sustained. You do not have to answer that question, Miss Long, and the Board is instructed to disregard the question and any inferences that might be drawn from it," Judge Malone announced with authority.

"Did you see Rick Cox hit David Hall anytime on the night in question?" Dusty asked.

"I truly believe I did, Captain. It was happening very fast, but I remember more than one of the three men dressed in Marine uniforms fighting with David. I ran over and tried to stop them and I was punched and kicked myself."

"Move to strike as unresponsive, your Honor," Dusty said loudly.

"I would be inclined to agree counselor except you opened the door. Any gratuity offered is relevant to the witness' ability to recall. Objection denied."

"Miss Long, my question was did you see Rick Cox hit David Hall? Not whether you believe you did," Dusty pressed.

"Yes, Sir, I did see him strike David at least once and maybe more than once," Chrissy said firmly but politely.

"Move to strike the last part of the answer as unresponsive, your Honor," Dusty jumped in almost before Chrissy had finished.

"Denied." Judge Malone gave Dusty a stern look that said no more unreasonable objections. Dusty got the message. "Miss, Long, did you see - and I ask what you saw not what you believe - Rick Cox kick David Hall anytime on the night in question?" Dusty wasn't giving any extra room this time.

"I don't know. I saw David lying on the ground, and I saw him being kicked in the head several times. But I have to be honest, I cannot say for certain that it was your client who kicked him. I do remember seeing that Marine - pointing to Anthony Fennelli - kick him at least twice."

Dan Richardson leaped to his feet. "Objection, your honor, outside of the scope."

"Outside of the scope of what counselor?" Judge Malone asked with mock surprise. "Certainly not direct examination. Do you mean outside of the scope of Captain Burn's cross?"

"Ah...Yes, Sir, of course, sir. The witness wasn't asked about Anthony Fennelli," Dan replied clutching at anything he could at that moment.

"Well, it's not, Lieutenant. The witness may answer questions that go to her competency and ability to recall. That includes saying what she saw even if not asked precisely by Captain Burns. Objection overruled."

"Nice touch," Sean said softly to Jack. "Might as well hold a little school while we go, and besides it continues the assault on Fennelli and any pressure will help Johnson unless Chrissy kills him on cross. We'll have to tread very carefully here. We don't know what she has to say and we don't need any more surprises."

Dusty knew he had gotten as much mileage as he was going to for Rick Cox. He had the witness concede that Cox may not have kicked the deceased midshipman. Since David Hall had died from a laryngeal hemorrhage, this was a plus because it was more likely to have happened from a kick than from a punch. It was not totally exonerating, however, but it was helpful because this affair did not arise out of a conspiracy, but rather spontaneous, stupid participation. The law of principals and accessories would control and Dusty had something to argue about, even though there was no doubt the Board was going to believe that Cox had thrown at least one punch. Dusty wisely had no more questions, and Captain Frank Chase took over cross-examining Chrissy. Frank was the most experienced of the other three counsel. Not very tall, but a first rate trial attorney. A graduate of Yale Law School, he mixed a Yankee twang with his Midwest accent and used his well modulated voice as an excellent trial tool.

"Miss Long, I know this has been very difficult for you and I will try to be brief," Frank Chase said solicitously. It was a nice ploy and it gets the jury a little less angry with your client. It also lowers the guard of the witness.

"I really only have a couple of questions. First, isn't it true that you claim three Marines forced themselves on you the night in question?"

Chrissy paused for a moment, and then said with conviction, "I said there were three men at first, Captain, and then later a fourth."

"That's my point, Miss Long. Isn't it true that only three men had intercourse with you that night against your will?"

"When you say, only three, that would exclude any other number. I cannot say that Captain. But I can say that three white men were the first to attack me that night, and one of them was your client," she replied pointing to Thomas Panos. Frank proceeded unfazed by the response. "Isn't it possible that one of the other two white Marines violated you a second time that night and your recall of the events is confused, making you believe it was three separate white males?"

Chrissy paused while reviewing the terrible trauma in her mind. Sean wondered for a second where Frank was going with this line of questioning and then the answer occurred simultaneously to both him and Jack who leaned over and whispered, "Frank doesn't care what the answer is, he's just trying to set up some reasonable doubt. It looks like we are going to see Panos called as a witness for himself and he's going to deny it all." Jack was right.

"It's possible, Captain, but not likely. I am certain that Marine - *pointing to Panos once again* - forced himself on me."

"Did he threaten you?"

"No, Sir."

"Were you crying and pleading, and mostly keeping your eyes shut?"

"Yes, Sir."

"So it is possible that the third time you were violated, it could have been by one of the first two white Marines."

"I admitted it was possible, Captain, but it's not the way I remember."

"No further questions, your Honor."

Frank had done a good job but he had walked a dangerous line with a highly sympathetic witness. Trial lawyers constantly have to weigh the potential risks of tactics employed. Too many lawyers think they can ride roughshod over witnesses. The fact finders let you know whether they approve of such conduct. Watch their eyes and body language. They reveal a lot, particularly when the jury is on the witness' side and is getting turned off by counsel's tactics.

Then it was Sean's turn. He got the feeling the whole courtroom was expecting some Perry Mason activity from the hot shot Los Angeles mouthpiece. They were going to be disappointed. No one was going to jump up from the back of the courtroom and shout out, "Lee Johnson is innocent. I was there the whole time and saw everything and he didn't do anything." Secondly, Sean wasn't ready to question Chrissy because he and Jack still didn't have all the facts. They needed to know more before developing a precise strategy for approaching the beautiful victim.

Sean stood and asked Judge Malone if the Board members could be excused while the court held in Article 39a, UCMJ, session which is a session before the judge, recorded on the record, but outside of the hearing of the jury. In response to that request, Colonel Malone indicated he wanted to see all counsel at a sidebar, which is a conference conducted quietly from the bench with counsel and the reporter crowded around so the jury cannot hear. All counsel approached and Judge Malone asked, "What is it you want to do Mr. O'Ryan?"

"The defense team for Corporal Johnson wishes to present a Motion for Finding of Not Guilty with respect to the homicide charge, your Honor. Also we wish to defer the cross-examination of Miss Long until after all evidence is presented on both sides since we never had an opportunity to talk to her prior to coming to court. Our preparation for cross-examination hinges directly on the presentation of further evidence by the government and on cross," Sean said respectfully.

"I have no problem with the motion hearing, but I am not convinced you have a right to defer cross-examination in this instance," Colonel Malone replied.

"I don't suggest I have a right to defer, Sir, but it is discretionary with the court and to grant the request would not be an abuse of discretion."

"Major Bryant, what's your position on this?" Judge Malone asked.

"Naturally, I'm opposed to any delay. If you allow this, Colonel, Miss Long will have to come back another day and she already has been traumatized throughout all of this. The Government opposes the request," Brendon responded.

Sean jumped in, "I realize this will inconvenience Miss Long, Colonel, but convicting our client because we were denied an adequate opportunity to prepare would be an injustice far worse than any inconvenience to Miss Long who only has to come back another day. Corporal Johnson, if wrongly convicted, could be making little ones out of big ones in Leavenworth prison for many years to come. That's a greater inconvenience for an innocent man."

"I read you, Mr. O'Ryan. I still have serious reservations about this, but in light of the fact that you have not been able to talk to Miss Long before coming here today, I am going to allow you to defer cross-examination until all other evidence has been produced by both sides. I will give the Government and the other counsel the opportunity to redirect or re-cross, as appropriate, at the end of your cross-exam, if they feel it is necessary. Is that agreeable? It is an absolute condition of my permission in this instance."

"Yes, Sir. And we thank you for that. May we now turn to the Motion for Finding of Not Guilty as to the homicide charge?" Sean asked.

"Yes. I will dismiss the Board members until tomorrow morning, as well as all witnesses. It is getting close to seventeen hundred and there won't be time for any more testimony today. When do you anticipate Miss Long will be needed again?"

"I would say not for at least two or three days. How do the other counsel feel about this?" Sean asked. Everyone agreed that was a reasonable estimate, and it told Sean - by implication - that not only did the Government have more witnesses, but that some or all of the other accused would be called by the defense as witnesses for themselves. No one else could call a defendant and force him to testify, but if they voluntarily take the stand, they are fair game for such purposes as they testify to on direct examination.

As all of the counsel returned to the tables, Colonel Malone advised the President, Colonel Ted "Cold Steel" Orlowski, that the members and all witnesses were excused until 0900 in the morning, with the exception of Miss Long who was not required to be back in court until 0900 three days from now unless otherwise notified by Major Bryant. The members left, along with Chrissy Long. The spectators were allowed to remain since none would be a witness. Judge Malone then turned to Sean and said, "Proceed with your motion, Mr. O'Ryan."

"For the record, your honor, this is a motion for a finding of not guilty with respect to Charge I alleging the commission of murder while in the act of committing a felony. We are not addressing Charge II, the rape charge at this time. The evidence before the court, which is the only evidence we believe the Government is able to present in this matter, the eye witness testimony of Miss Long, negates any participation by Corporal Johnson in the assault and subsequent death resulting from the attack on Midshipman David Hall. The record being devoid of any possible connection between the elements of the crime of felony murder and our client, we respectfully submit that a finding of not guilty is appropriate at this time."

"Major Bryant, response?" Colonel Malone asked.

"Yes, Sir. I don't agree with counsel for Corporal Johnson. The case isn't over, and the Government has not rested. We may well be producing additional evidence over and above that submitted by Miss Long."

"I don't know how the Government could, your honor. There are no witnesses on the list furnished to us by trial counsel who would have information that could provide proof of the elements of that charge," Sean shot back.

"There's always the possibility of rebuttal testimony, your honor," Brendon reclamored.

"Rebuttal to what?" Sean challenged. "Is the court to presume any or all of the defendants will testify? I realize this motion is usually made at the time the

Government rests, and the Government has not yet rested. But the only witnesses Major Bryant could call cannot add anything to the essential elements. He shouldn't be allowed to oppose the motion merely on the chance that he might be able to cross-examine one or more of the defendants," Sean urged.

"I don't agree that the Government has nothing more to offer on the elements of this charge, your honor," Brendon countered. "One of my witnesses, an ONI agent, will testify about certain admissions made by one of the defendants which will affect Corporal Johnson." Brendon was referring to Thomas Panos, and seemed to be suggesting that he could somehow use Panos's statement made to the ONI agent against Johnson. This was incorrect and Sean made his feelings known.

"If the good Major is suggesting he can introduce a statement made by one of the defendants which is adverse to Corporal Johnson, he is just plain wrong. First of all there is no evidence of a conspiracy here, and secondly the use of a defendant's confession or admissions that incriminates another defendant, even if interlocking, violates the rights of that defendant to confrontation. No instruction by the court could cure that error. I think Major Bryant knows this as well as I do, and is grasping for straws," Sean said a bit sarcastically.

"I am not, your Honor. I am only suggesting that the motion is premature," Brendon fired back heatedly.

"I've heard enough, gentlemen," Colonel Malone said. "I think Mr. O'Ryan's point is well taken, but I share Major Bryant's concern that the motion is premature. There is still the possibility of the introduction of evidence that will run to the elements of this charge. To grant the motion at this time would forever foreclose resurrecting the charge under the principle of double jeopardy."

"May I ask the court not to deny the motion at this time then, Colonel, and instead take it under advisement pending the receipt of additional evidence, if any?" Sean asked.

"I was disposed to deny outright, Mr. O'Ryan, but I will give you some leeway and take the motion under advisement and defer a ruling until such time as I deem appropriate."

"Thank you, Sir." Sean answered grateful for this much concession.

"Exception to the ruling for the record, your honor," Brendon added, even though it wasn't necessary to preserve his objection.

"Exception noted, Major. Anything else for today, gentlemen? If not, we will adjourn until 0900 in the morning."

When they had gone off the record, counsel invited Colonel Malone for a drink at the O'Club but he wisely declined. He assured them there was nothing he would like more than to drink with a bunch of wild Irishmen, but it would have to wait. Sean and Jack said good night to Lee Johnson who was shackled by the guards, along with the other three defendants, and returned to the brig. Sean assured Johnson that things were going all right and not to worry. It was bullshit,

127

of course, but clients need to be reassured even when counsel can only hope things are not too screwed up. As they were leaving, Jack said, "Nice work on the motion, Sean. You knew Colonel Malone wouldn't grant it but you handcuffed Brendon from trying to slip in Panos's statement into evidence. Brendon knew the statement wasn't admissible but our objection to the attempt in open court would create an impression on the jury that we are trying to hide something. Pretty slick," Jack said smiling broadly.

"Not slick, Jack, just careful. I sensed a problem when it became obvious Brendon had more than one witness left. I was certain he would call the ONI agent and try to introduce Panos's statement, which could only hurt the other defendants since it is fully exculpatory as to Panos. Brendon sure as hell wasn't going to offer it to exonerate."

There wasn't anything Jack and Sean could do on the case that evening, and they were both too wound up to think about going to bed early so they headed for the Officers Club. In spite of the evidence so far, they still had confidence that Johnson was telling the truth when he once again swore just before being returned to the brig, "I didn't do the woman" and she was "ab-so-fucking-lute-ly mistaken" when she testified he had intercourse with her. Right now the rest of the case was reduced to playing it by ear so Sean and Jack could relax a bit at the O'Club.

Brendon Bryant and some of the other lawyers from Base Legal accepted their invitation to catch a beer, but only on the condition that no one would talk about the case. That was easy because there usually were a number of nurses from the Naval Hospital at happy hour on Mondays. There wasn't much else to do the first day of the week in the Oceanside area. Besides, who wanted to talk about trials when there were single, pretty, female officers around.

As for the nurses, Sean decided he needed to socialize with a woman who wasn't angry with him, and there was this really cute blond from Kansas City who helped the time pass pleasantly. She accepted an invitation to dinner and joined the lawyers along with what seemed like a battalion of her friends. "Big city lawyers have lots of money," Sean heard someone suggest when he advised he would take the check. *What the hell*, Sean thought, *I can write off some of it, they can't.*

The group visited and danced to a juke box for a couple of hours after dinner, and then Sean and Jack bailed out about ten after kissing a host of appealing faces, especially the very lovely Kansas City nurse who Sean decided to kiss more than once. He promised to see her, and the rest of the nurses, very soon. Sean then said good night to Jack and headed for the *Miramar*.

There was a phone message to call Susan Sullivan at home whenever he got back. He dialed her number and Susan answered. He was hoping she had calmed down a little and they could talk about what was bothering her without further stress. He was wrong.

"I hear you got egg on your face today counselor. Serves you right."

"Oh fuck, Susan, is this why you asked me to call? To gloat?"

"Not to gloat, but to ask you if you had come to your senses."

"I did that a long time ago when I was first attracted to you and decided to do something about it. But tell me, how do you know what went on today?"

"Chrissy's mother was at the trial. She called and told me what had happened. Your client - bastard client I should say, or is that a redundancy - is getting his ass kicked. Well I'm glad. He should get his balls cut off for what he did to Chrissy," Susan said angrily.

"What the hell do you think I was talking about the other day? Did any of it get through? I'm representing a man I genuinely believe is innocent and doing what I have to do, and what he has a right to expect," Sean snapped.

"Oh, Sean, are you still hung up on this good guy routine? Can't you just let it go before it's too late?"

"No, I can't. Do you really think I could abandon Johnson just because you think he's guilty? I won't even mention the fact that this case is getting in the way of the delightful affair we had going," Sean answered sarcastically. "I don't suggest you would want me to give it up for that reason."

"Oh, shit. You are even more hopeless than I thought. God, Sean, they ought to institutionalize fanatics like you. Your client is guilty and you know it. You talk like you were attending a different trial than the one reported to me today. All four of those animals are guilty and you refuse to admit it."

"Gosh, Susan, you are full of compliments tonight. By the way how did you know I was at the *Miramar*?"

"You always stay there, Sean. I didn't have to be a psychic to figure that out. You're so damn predictable at times. How about adding a little serendipity to your life and do something less goddamn, melodramatic, Irish for a change."

"I can't. Not just won't, but can't. You know what I'm saying. I've got to see this case through to a proper conclusion. It doesn't matter if that takes a toll on my personal life. It's what I am all about and what I have to do, not just want to do. If you can't understand this, then you have a lot to learn about me."

"I know, Sean, the law is your mistress, and a jealous mistress at that. Everything else is second. You are the most moral, immoral lawyer I know. There's no way to understand you. I shouldn't have called. There's no hope for you, Quixote. I'm sorry it turned out like this."

Susan hung up before Sean could tell her he could separate his professional life from his personal, but she wouldn't have believed him. He cradled the receiver, more disappointed than angry. He figured he had lost one of the better sexual relationships he had known for many years, and maybe a friendship as well. Either way he knew that even if they remained friends, the affair probably would have ended in a natural course in time. But, still, there was no question he would miss their lovemaking. A whole lot.

CHAPTER 20

Tuesday, October 13, 1964

Morning broke with a flood of colors and painted the beaches along Oceanside a brilliant orange and gold. Sean was on the beach at the foot of Mission Avenue when the first fiery fingers reached for the Western horizon. Wet and chilly from his swim, the sight warmed him and he felt alive, ready to take on the world of military justice and the challenges waiting in the courtroom at Camp Pendleton. He reflected on the artificial setting of any trial, but notwithstanding that synthetic environment, Sean understood how a trial, when properly conducted, re-creates the essence of the events when they were first played out. The happenings, places and persons are brought to life through the evidence to expose the vitality present at another time and place.

A good trial, particularly a criminal trial, vividly transports all of the color of the events into the sterile environment of the courtroom. In the process it enriches their re-creation with the excitement of the street so that the judge and jury and all other participants in the trial are part of the drama as it unfolds. Some lawyers fail to understand this and their trials are deadly dull. Others, like Jake Rogers, who shares a last name with the late, great Earl Rogers, appreciate the magic that transforms mere words and objects into living theater. Sean had learned well from Jake and he looked forward to his own staging of life and death scenarios in the courtroom today as he felt stimulated from a mile swim. His only regret was that Susan wasn't with him. He would have loved to adjourn to the *Miramar* for a romp through a *disneysque sex-adventure land* before he had to be off to court. But unfortunately, for the very reason he was there, she wasn't, although he preferred to believe she wanted to be. His desire for Susan reminded him that life can be strangely contradictory, and his unrequited longing at this inappropriate time was akin to the rhythm method for birth control. Papal roulette is the only method openly sanctioned by the Catholic Church. But, unfortunately, this draconian procedure only works, if it works at all, when it denies normal sexual responses at a time of greatest desire. So much for masochistic methods that mandate leaving one's sexual urges dangling when you need to satisfy them most.

Sean showered under cold water at the lifeguard tower and then jogged back to the *Miramar*. He felt invigorated, much like his first day in Korea, but he reminded himself that he'd best be careful because the other side was still not shooting at a crowd, it was still gunning for him personally.

He met Jack at 0830. Over coffee they discussed tactics for the day acknowledging that all of their planning was subject to sudden shifts when the unanticipated occurs during trial. The prosecution still had witnesses to present, and it didn't appear the Government would rest before afternoon, at the earliest.

As for the order of defense presentations, Sean had worked their position into last in the order since he had won the concession to defer cross-examination of Chrissy Long until all other evidence was presented.

The prosecution opened the morning session with the emergency room physician who had examined Chrissy Long on the night of the rape. Douglas Adams, M.D., Lieutenant, Medical Corps, United States Navy Reserve, looked like a young Doctor Kildare. "If he doesn't make it in medicine, he'll be a natural for television, except maybe on *Gunsmoke*, which already has a Doc Adams," Sean suggested to Jack.

After reviewing his impressive credentials, Dr. Adams explained how he had examined Chrissy on the night of her terrible ordeal, a description gratuitously offered but no one dared to object. He further advised that his examination revealed, among other things, substantial trauma to her limbs and genitalia, as well as clear evidence of substantial violence to her face and skull, including a significant fracture and an elongated cut along her throat, which fortunately had not severed major blood vessels.

The witness also testified that he had taken smears from the victim's vagina, which specimens he ordered tested at the lab. He felt he could say without equivocation that the young woman had been brutally assaulted and the physical evidence indicated that her violations could not have been consensual. After once again reviewing his notes and refreshing his recollection, Dr. Adams was able to state that samples of smears taken from Chrissy Long on that night revealed the presence of three separate strains of semen with three distinct blood types, A-negative, O-positive, and O-negative.

For purposes of this trial he had been designated custodian of the health records of the defendants and was able to advise that Anthony Fennelli has A-negative blood, Thomas Panos has O-positive, and Rick Cox has O-negative. He also noted that Lee Johnson, like Thomas Panos, has O-positive blood. Doctor Adams explained that the physical evidence clearly indicated that at least three separate persons had engaged in sexual intercourse with Miss Long and that each had completed the act with ejaculation. Then Doctor Adams, rendering an opinion as an expert, testified that it was not possible for three different sperm samples to be present in Miss Long if less than three persons had sexually known her that night.

Major Bryant anticipated cross-examination on David Hall's death and asked Doctor Adams if he had examined David Hall on the night in question. He said he did and he pronounced Midshipman Hall dead on arrival at the United States Naval Hospital. He was asked what blood type David Hall was known to have from the records and Doctor Adams advised it was type AB-positive, which is rather rare. No semen of this blood type was found in Chrissy Long's body cavity. Because of the substantial trauma to Miss Long on that evening, which was manifestly inflicted both manually as well as by male organ penetration, Dr. Adams could not speculate as to whether she had been a virgin prior to the violations of her at the Lake O'Neill site.

"Clever move on Brendon's part," Sean whispered to Jack. "Takes away some of the guessing game as to whose calling card is whose." There could be no question that three out four of the defendants were in deep trouble. Which three and what the evidence portended with respect to the fourth remained to be seen. Sean hoped that Lee Johnson had been playing it straight with him since the re-creation of the trauma inflicted on the fragile image of Chrissy was damning all four defendants. None of the other counsel wanted to cross-examine Doctor Adams, so Jack stepped forward and asked him if he had examined any of the defendants that evening. Doctor Adams said he did after he had examined Miss Long, but it was solely for the purpose of pre-confinement physicals before they were taken to the brig, and admittedly they were somewhat cursory. Jack then asked him if he had examined Lee Johnson to determine if he had been involved in any sexual activity that night, or any of the other defendants for that matter. Doctor Adams said he had not. This was strictly routine pre-confinement, and the examination was deliberately limited. Jack then asked, "Did you for any reason draw blood from Corporal Johnson, Doctor?"

Doctor Adams replied, "Now that you mention it, I do recall ordering a blood sample because I had been told by one of the military policemen that this man apparently had been unconscious for a while. I wanted to be certain he had no injuries that were not obvious in my somewhat perfunctory physical examination."

"What was the result of that blood sample. Was it tested? If so, for what?"

"I was looking for the results in Johnson's health record as you asked the question, Captain, but I don't find them here. If for no other reason I would have checked the blood alcohol level since I was told he might have passed out from too much to drink. For some reason none of that information has found its way into his records, so I cannot answer the question," Doctor Adams replied.

"Would the hospital lab have a record of any tests in its log for that evening," Jack followed up.

"As a matter of standard procedure, it should. I can check it if you'd like," Doctor Adams volunteered.

"Yes, we would, Doctor, and I would appreciate your giving me a call during the lunch recess," Jack said kindly.

Something was raising a warning flag, but Sean didn't grasp it just yet. *We will just have to look into it further,* he thought. Sean believed they knew all about that night but Jack mentioned he had a hunch that something might be missing from Johnson's health record, and he was right.

"Just one more question. Do your notes reflect that Corporal Johnson had a broken right hand on the night you examined him?" Jack added.

"Yes, they do, Captain. But his health record doesn't indicate the circumstances. His record does show that he reported to sickbay a few days earlier and an x-ray revealed a break of three carpal bones in his right hand. This is the kind of break sometimes seen in boxers who fail to wrap their hands properly before a fight. I don't know why the record doesn't contain some explanation as to the cause, but with Marines we often see them cover up their fighting and brawling with a myriad of excuses. Not the least of which is 'I fell over a locker box someone had left in the aisle in the barracks.' I call it the meandering locker box; it always seems to be getting under Marines' feet," Doctor Adams said smiling. The court members also smiled at that classic lie.

"By the way," Doctor Adams continued, "Corporal Johnson's record indicates his hand was placed in a cast. I recall, however, that he wasn't wearing the cast the night I examined him. I see he is now, but I am certain he was not at the time I examined him on the night he was confined in the brig."

"Thank you. No further questions."

The next witness for the prosecution was the pathologist who conducted the post-mortem on Midshipman David Hall. He was a slight individual whose appearance seem to fit the impressions of someone who worked with the dead. The pathologist had an almost ghoulish look and it lent credence to his testimony as he reiterated the information already contained in the autopsy report, which was then proffered into evidence with no objection. David Hall had died from a laryngeal hemorrhage caused by a blow or blows to the larynx and would have died even without that hemorrhage unless he had received immediate attention as a result of a subarachnoid hemorrhage caused from a blow or blows to the back of the skull. In the pathologist's opinion David would have died within a matter of hours if he had been left unattended.

Sean rose to cross-exam the pathologist. "I have only a couple of questions, Doctor, one of which is a follow-up on an earlier question addressed to Doctor Adams. In your opinion were any of the fatal or potentially fatal blows administered to David Hall done with the hands as opposed to the feet?"

"In my opinion, unless the blows to the larynx were administered with the knife edge of a hand by someone quite powerful, they most likely came from one or more shoe clod feet," the pathologist answered.

"In your opinion, Doctor, would someone with a broken hand be able to administer the kind of blow which you described as capable of producing fatal results?" Sean inquired.

"It would depend on the extent of the break, but in my opinion if the break was substantial, it is most unlikely," the pathologist replied.

"In your opinion is the break of three carpal bones in the hand a substantial break?" Sean followed up.

"It certainly is in my opinion."

"Thank you. No further questions."

Brendon Bryant called his next witness Agent Corbin Wright of the Office of Naval Intelligence who testified to the geography of the crime scene and identified photographs he had personally taken on the night of the rape and murder. He also introduced a graphic display of the area over which the locations of Chrissy Long and Lee Johnson were superimposed showing their respective positions when police authorities first arrived on the scene. Chrissy was less than five feet away from Johnson, which was consistent with her testimony that she had been able to roll away from him when she came to after losing consciousness for an indeterminateperiod of time. The pictures and graphic revealed that Johnson could not be seen by the other participants at the place where he had been found if he had been lying on the ground. He could be seen only by going up a slight rise since he was on the other side. How it was that Fennelli knew Johnson was there was not yet explained by any testimony, but obviously he did at some point because he had dragged Chrissy over to Johnson and threw her on him.

Major Bryant asked if Agent Wright had taken any statements from the defendants, and every defense counsel rose as if a bolt of lightning had lifted them off their chairs as they shouted "objection." Colonel Malone called for a sidebar, and with all counsel crowded around, said to Brendon, "You'd better have a good reason for that question counselor or you and I are going to have a long talk in my chambers about legal ethics."

"I do your honor, but I don't want to give away my tactics with all counsel assembled. If I could speak to you alone, perhaps," Brendon countered.

"When pigs fly, Colonel," Sean said with undisguised anger.

"I'll decide when pigs will fly, Mr. O'Ryan, but right now the answer to that request is not only no, but absolutely no, Major Bryant," Colonel Malone admonished.

"In that event, Colonel, I can only say that Agent Wright has substantial evidence to offer which forms the basis for fair comment in closing argument," Brendon submitted.

"Like what?" Colonel Malone asked.

"I'd rather not to say at this time, Sir."

"Then you may not ask the question," Colonel Malone advised.

"But, Sir."

"But, nothing, Major. I've made my ruling, and just in case you aren't convinced, let me suggest that I suspect you want the agent to testify that when he gave the defendants the Article 31, Fifth Amendment type warnings, some of them talked and some didn't. If any statements are self-incriminating by the speaker, I'll entertain them. If, however, they are self serving and exculpate the speaker but incriminate any of the other defendants, I will not admit them,"

Colonel Malone admonished. He then continued, "And above all, although the law is not definitive in this area as yet, it is with me. I will not allow you to comment on the failure of any of the accused to deny complicity in the crimes through the exercise of their right not to incriminate themselves. The right to remain silent includes the right not to proclaim one's innocence. I will not allow you to comment on any alleged failure to assert a lack of guilt to the agent or the whole world for that matter. Is that clear?"

"Yes, Sir," Brendon replied unenthusiastically, but politely.

Counsel returned to their tables, and Frank Chase, Panos's counsel, seized the moment along with Sean. On cross-examination they each asked the agent if their clients had made any statement to him denying any and all guilt. The agent advised that both Panos and Johnson definitely had adamantly denied any personal complicity. Brendon was visibly upset by this tactic but his hands figuratively were tied. There was no way he could ask if Panos or Johnson, while denying personal guilt, had said anything about Fennelli and Cox. Nor could he ask if Fennelli or Cox said anything exculpatory about themselves or had refused to make a statement. Thus, Sean would be able to comment in his closing argument, as would Thomas Panos through Frank Chase, that his client had persisted in his proclamations of innocence from the inception of the investigation of the crimes, but Brendon could not comment about the other two about refusing to make a statement. Nor could he use Panos's indictment of Fennelli and Cox in his statement to the agent. It was a ploy consistent with the variables of evidentiary rules which sometimes help and at other times hinder the pursuit of truth and justice. In Johnson's case, Sean was convinced the rules were working for these elusive twins and not against them. As for Panos, Sean had some doubt, but that was Frank Chase's problem.

When all counsel had finished cross-examination of Agent Wright, Judge Malone suggested this would be a good point to break for lunch. The President of the Board, "Cold Steel" Orlowski, agreed. Sean and Jack rushed back to Jack's office to give Doctor Adams a call and see if he had discovered anything from the lab about Lee Johnson's blood test.

"I was about to call your office, Captain. I just got the results. Nothing significant with respect to any diseases, but I think you'll find the blood/alcohol reading interesting. It registered .18 percent; considering that this was a falling blood/alcohol, he must have been sloshed a few hours earlier."

"Damn, Doctor, that's quite a discovery. Could we ask you to be available in the next day or two if we need to put you on the stand as our witness. You're not going anywhere are you?" Jack asked.

"No, I'll be here at the hospital. I'm working days this month. Long days most of the time. Feel free to give me a call whenever you need," Doctor Adams replied.

"Thank you, Doctor. Really appreciate your help."

"Point .18," Jack repeated. "Sloshed is an understatement."

"You're right, but can it turn out to be a two edged sword?" Sean wondered aloud. "I can see Brendon arguing that this simply meant Johnson couldn't recall clearly the dastardly deed he did when he did Chrissy, which Johnson keeps adamantly denying. Naturally, that will be in response to our suggestion that he was too drunk to participate. I recall something Shakespeare said about booze enhancing sexual desire but diminishing the ability."

"Hell, every male has made the mistake of using alcohol as a sexual stimulant only to find out it is a central nervous system depressant. Too much spirit means too little flesh. Hard to keep it up when the rest is falling down," Jack quipped.

"Well considering that every member of the jury, good Marines that they are, will probably be able to recall the effects of too much happy hour on their own sexual adventures, we've got to use it in the hope that they will conclude Johnson was too out of it to partake. I'm curious as to why the results didn't get into Johnson's health record, although sometimes these things fall between the cracks. I wonder if someone didn't want it to, but I don't have a clue as to why that would be," Sean commented.

They went outside and caught a sandwich and coffee from the mobile food wagon that stopped in the 24 area. Marines affectionately referred to it as the "roach coach" but they were always glad to see those familiar trucks, especially on the rifle range when they had been out there since O'dark thirty busting the first cap before the mist had cleared from the target area.

"God bless Johnny Miller, Jack. I would have starved many times without his food wagons coming to my rescue. Especially when I had to rush back to the base just in time for morning formation after a night of debauchery and didn't have time for breakfast - well, at least the kind you can digest. Eating one's cupcake is not quite the same and besides she couldn't come along," Sean said with a big grin.

"Know what you mean," Jack said smiling. "Not that I ever was in that situation, of course. You know I never go anywhere on liberty except to the library and the chapel. I'll just have to guess what you ass bandits must have been doing in the *ville* while we saintly types walked the straight and narrow."

"What a crock, you Ivy League fraud," Sean laughed. "But speaking of the straight and narrow, that's where we are headed. Obviously we have to put Johnson on the stand, and I hope he is ready for some credible explanations. Cold Steel Orlowski and company are going to see through any attitude he serves up, so we've got to impress on him how important it is that he play it cool and avoid jive talking bullshit. I hear Orlowski is as mean as he looks with his high and tight haircut and face like a mad dog. But I also hear he is fair as hell so we want to work our case in a no nonsense manner. I believe he will influence any member who is on the line to come over to our point of view, at least I'm hoping he will, if he thinks we are being straight with him. If I didn't believe this, I would have peremptorily removed him with a no-cause challenge."

"I still think our client is innocent," Sean continued, "in spite of some nagging questions, like what was he doing with his pecker out, and did he avail himself of the opportunity to get to Chrissy. Couple that with motive up the *ying yang*, like getting even for Jan Thompson the ex-girlfriend who recently dumped him, plus the village whore who started him down the path of hate and distrust when he was a juvenile. We've got to walk very carefully with our client as a witness."

Sean recited this with more apprehension than he preferred, but there was no denying the problems they had to overcome to make Johnson sound convincing. Technically the burden of proof doesn't change in a criminal trial, but the burden of persuasion often does. Brendon Bryant had carefully made a prima facie case for the Government as to Johnson and his alleged participation in the rape of Chrissy Long. There still was no prima facie case on the homicide, however, other than Johnson might have participated while Chrissy was unconscious and she didn't see him strike or kick David Hall. But this wasn't about to raise the evidence to the level of proof beyond a reasonable doubt on the murder charge. Thus Sean's primary focus was on the rape charge and on making efforts to meet the burden of persuading the jury that Johnson did not have intercourse with Chrissy against her will, or in any other manner.

CHAPTER 21

The afternoon session opened promptly at 1300 hours with Judge Malone calling the court to order. Sean's focus on the rape charge was sharpened immediately as Major Brendon Bryant unexpectedly announced that the prosecution rested. This came as a surprise. Sean had anticipated that the prosecution would be calling one or two additional investigators as witnesses, but Brendon apparently felt he had made enough headway in his case in chief and would rely on cross-examination and rebuttal evidence, if necessary, to fill in any gaps.

Since Dan Richardson was the junior counsel, the rest of defense counsel agreed he had to start the defense case in reply whether he liked it or not. It didn't matter because Dan stood up - tall and dashing in his Marine Officer greens - and said "no witnesses at this time your Honor," which was a smart move but a little amazing since Sean would have bet that Fennelli would lower the boom on everyone else considering the case against him was solid for conviction on both charges. Dan probably made this move because he had to go first and he wasn't about to give the other defendants a shot at his client until he had a better handle on where the others were going. Sean whispered to Jack, "Don't bet this is the last we see of Fennelli. I suspect Dan will use him in rebuttal if he needs to. I think he's sandbagging to see what everyone else does to him."

Frank Chase and Dusty Burns flipped to see who would go next. Frank lost. It wasn't important because Frank was clever and would finesse his position no matter when he launched. He realized he had to put Thomas Panos on the witness stand, and he did. "Lance Corporal Panos, were you in the company of Lance Corporal Fennelli and Private First Class Cox on Thursday evening, September 3, 1964?"

"Yes, Sir. We met at the enlisted club after chow and had a few 3.2 beers. At least that's what we would buy from the bartender, but actually any number of guys who are older would buy pitchers of beer and we shared quite a bit of regular beer as well as the 3.2."

"What time did you get to the E-Club and how long were you there?"

"About 1930 hours. We stayed there until maybe 2130."

"Do you know Corporal Lee Johnson?"

"Yes, Sir. I know him from the 5th Marines. He was in the same company and battalion as Anthony Fennelli."

"Did you see Corporal Johnson at the E-Club on the night of September 3d?"

"Yes, Sir, but I didn't talk to him because he was getting drunk and we don't like each other."

"Why not?"

"Because he and Fennelli are always at each other. The week before that night, I stepped between them outside of the club and Johnson punched me. I was only trying to help and he decked me. He thinks he's a bad ass."

"Objection, calls for a conclusion and is immaterial," Sean recited jumping to his feet.

"Sustained," Colonel Malone responded. "The members will disregard the opinion stated by the witness in the last portion of his answer."

"Did you see Corporal Johnson anywhere else that night other than at the enlisted club?" Frank Chase asked.

"Yes, Sir, at Lake O'Neill. It was after 2200 or so."

"What were the circumstances?"

"Fennelli, Cox and I left the club and started driving around. We didn't go anywhere in particular but ended up at Lake O'Neill because we heard the nurses sometimes walk around out there and we thought we might be able to talk to 'em. We parked and walked for a while, and then started back to the parking lot. That's when we came across a girl and a midshipman. The girl was the one who was here yesterday. I didn't know who the midshipman was, but I guess his name was David Hall."

"Where were you when you saw this couple?"

"We were maybe a couple of hundred yards from the parking lot, along the path. There were only a couple of cars in the lot. I think we had sat down and were throwing stones in the lake. We might have just stood up to leave. I thought we were the only ones around, but then they came by and Fennelli said something to them."

"What did he say?"

"I don't remember exactly, something like 'what's a good looking broad like you doing with a squid or swabbie?' or something like that."

"What happened?"

"The middie said something and jerked Fennelli up short. We were all in uniform so it was plain he outranked us being a midshipman. Fennelli told him to fuck off and walked towards them. The girl said something like 'let it go David and let's just leave.' Then Fennelli said something like 'too bad you won't listen to your pussy, sailor,' and then he grabbed for the girl. The midshipman yelled and Fennelli punched him."

"Did the midshipman defend himself?"

"Yes, he might of hit Fennelli at least once or maybe twice, but then Private Cox jumped in and starting hitting the middie too. Pretty soon the Navy guy went down and Fennelli and Cox started kicking him."

"Then what happened?"

"I think that's when the girl ran over and started screaming at Fennelli and tried to push him away. Fennelli hit her a couple of times and she went down. Then he kicked her more than once and I think she got knocked out."

"What was happening to the midshipman at this time?"

"He started to get up. And it was then that I saw Corporal Johnson. He seemed to come out of nowhere and he ran over and cold cocked the middie saying something like 'Fennelli you couldn't punch your way out of a wet paper bag.' The middie went down and just laid there. No movement at all. Then he seemed to disappear, but I guess he went over a little rise 'cause that's where I saw him a little later lying on the ground."

"What happened to Miss Long?"

"Just what she said happened, except I didn't touch her. Fennelli did and Cox did, then Fennelli did again. Three times they screwed her. Fennelli really roughed her up, and he cut her because she was screaming and begging him to leave her alone. He said she was attracting too much attention, and that's when he cut her. Then he ripped her clothes and fucked around with her - oh, excuse me Colonel - I mean he touched her all over and then got on top of her and it was obvious he was dorking her. When he got done, Cox dorked her too, and then Fennelli went back for seconds."

"Where was the midshipman during this time?"

"He was just lying there, not moving. He was out of it."

"Where was Johnson?"

"Over the little rise, I guess, because I next saw him was when Fennelli climbed off after humping the girl twice and dragged her over behind the rise. Then he threw her down on Johnson."

"What happened then?"

"I don't know, we all left after I heard Fennelli say something like, 'This fucked up bitch is for you, nigger'."

"How did the investigators find you?"

"I heard they found Cox's piss cover. It had his name and serial number stamped in it. They picked him up at the barracks and he led them to Fennelli and me a little while later. We were all taken into custody and confined in the brig after getting physicals."

"Did you at anytime on the night of September 3, 1964, at Lake O'Neill or anywhere else in Camp Pendleton have sexual relations with Miss Chrissy Long, the young woman who testified here yesterday?"

"No, Sir, I didn't."

"Did you strike or kick the midshipman who was with Miss Long that night?"

"No, Sir, I didn't."

"Who, if anyone, did you see strike or kick Midshipman David Hall on that night?"

"I saw Fennelli and Cox punch and kick him several times. I saw Johnson punch him once."

"No further questions, your Honor. Cross-examine counsel?"

Frank Chase sat down. He appeared weary and Sean wasn't sure why. But he wasn't feeling sorry for him. Sean could have killed him because Frank had to know what Panos was going to say about Lee Johnson. Sean stood and asked for a sidebar conference. When all counsel and the reporter were assembled, Sean asked Judge Malone if they could adjourn for the day so defense counsel could better prepare for cross-examination of Thomas Panos. Frank Chase objected, but it was purely pro-forma. Judge Malone saw the devastating effect Panos's testimony was having. Since none of the defense counsel knew before trial if Panos was going to testify nor what the extent of his testimony would be even if he did testify, it was only fair to give the other counsel, including the prosecution, the rest of the afternoon to prepare the task of meeting Panos's damning testimony.

Colonel Malone, without stating anything specific, merely advised, "For procedural reasons it is necessary to adjourn for the day." Colonel "Cold Steel" Orlowski didn't like it, but he wasn't in a position to argue the point. Trial was ordered to resume at 0900 on Wednesday morning.

Sean directed the prison chaser to take Lee Johnson to Captain Coleman's office. After the guard left Jack's office and closed the door with Jack's assurance that they would take full responsibility for Johnson's safekeeping, Sean turned to Johnson and said, "Somebody's lying and it damn well better not be you."

CHAPTER 22

Wednesday, October 14, 1964

The third day of trial opened at 0901 hours. Sean and Jack had spent Tuesday afternoon going over possible lines of questioning to attack Panos's testimony. They hammered away at Lee Johnson about what was true and wasn't true in the damning scenario that had him striking the deceased midshipman at least once. Convinced that Panos was lying, they speculated as to motives and concluded that Panos implicated Johnson in the fight in order to persuade the jury that the blood type he shared with Johnson could only have shown up among the strains of semen found in Chrissy Long's body because Johnson, and not Panos, had raped her. Lee was a convenient scapegoat for Panos's mendacity. Although confident of their client's version of the events, Sean had to be careful not to dismiss the possibility that Johnson did have nonconsensual intercourse with Chrissy. This way there would only be three semen strains found in the victim even if all four accused had raped her.

Sean thought back about the demeanor of Panos as he testified the day before. While he attempted to appear straight forward, Panos avoided looking at Johnson when he said anything damaging about him, although he demonstrated no reluctance to do so when he spoke of Fennelli and Cox. Sean also wondered about Frank Chase's weariness when he sat down after finishing his direct examination of Panos. He got the feeling that Frank realized his client had perjured himself, although Sean was certain Frank would not have allowed Panos to commit perjury. Unfortunately, from the beginning, Frank was trapped by the consistency of Panos's story, false though it might be, and he had no choice if his client wanted to testify in his own defense. Having made a major concession to the rest of defense counsel yesterday, Judge Malone granted Major Bryant the right to defer his cross-examination of Panos until after the three remaining defense counsel had completed theirs.

As the court convened, Panos was directed to resume his place on the witness stand. Dan Richardson rose to his full imposing height and approached the witness as closely as the judge would allow to commence his cross-examination. He looked at Panos with an amused expression and asked how long the fight and sexual assault had lasted. Panos seemed surprised by the question and paused for a moment. Then he said, "Maybe about a half hour."

"Well, Corporal, maybe and about, are not precise words. Could you be more specific? Let's start with the time you first saw the young woman and young man. What time was that?"

"I think somewhere between 2200 and 2215."

"O.K., between ten and ten fifteen p.m.," Dan said translating military time into its civilian counterpart.

"What time did you and Fennelli and Cox leave the scene?"

"Maybe 2230 or 2245."

"O.K. about ten thirty or ten forty five," Dan translated. He then added, "As I understand you then, in a space of time fairly close to thirty minutes, give or take a few, Corporal Fennelli was supposed to have gotten into a knocked down, dragged out fight with a midshipman and then, not only assaulted and battered a young woman, but sexually ravished her and then had sexual intercourse with her, not once but twice. Is that correct?"

"Yes, Sir."

Dan Richardson depersonalized both victims by deliberately not referring to them by name. This is a common technique when the victims are genuinely sympathetic and counsel has no desire to remind the jury of their personae. Victim is general enough to blur intimate identification in an attempt to desensitize.

"Have you ever had sexual intercourse, Corporal Panos?"

"Objection, irrelevant," Frank Chase cried.

"Overruled," Judge Malone responded, "it's both relevant and material."

"Yes, Sir," Panos answered.

"Have you ever had intercourse twice in one night in which you ejaculated?" Dan asked.

"Objection," Frank Chase interposed.

"Overruled."

"Yes, Sir?" Panos answered.

"And how long was the interval between the first act and the second?"

"Your honor, this is totally immaterial," Frank shouted. "Thomas Panos's sexual qualifications are not an issue in this case."

"Really, counsel?" Colonel Malone asked amused. "I thought the sexual ability of all the defendants was in issue. Overruled."

"I don't remember, Sir, maybe an hour," Panos said softly.

"Seems about normal, Corporal, at your age, but you say Corporal Fennelli was able to engage in lethal combat with a man fighting for his life and accomplish two completed acts of intercourse with a young woman against her will and over her substantial struggles, along with cutting her throat, all in the space of thirty minutes? Is that your testimony?"

"Yes, Sir. I just said what I saw that's all."

"Sure," Dan replied sarcastically.

"Objection," Frank said, but without enthusiasm. The feeling that Panos was lying grew stronger. Not only had Dan punctured Panos's facade, but it was increasingly clear that no one was buying Panos's self serving denials, including

Frank Chase by this time. But that didn't change the implications made against Johnson. Sean couldn't rely on the jury disbelieving Panos on that point.

"Sustained. No gratuitous remarks, counsel," Colonel Malone said for appearances sake. Which in itself was a gratuitous gesture since every member of the jury was probably saying the same "sure" that Dan Richardson had just uttered contemptuously.

Dusty Burns was next. He had a tough job. Even if Panos was a liar, there was nothing before the court to suggest that Panos had reason to lie about Dusty's client and he probably was telling the truth. Cox had joined in the fray against David Hall and helped to kill him even if he didn't intend to do so. The rape was the problem. If Cox took part in the rape and the fight, it didn't matter if he lacked specific intent to kill when he struck and kicked David Hall. Cox was in the particularly bad spot of being a principal to the homicide of David, which arose out the felony rape of Chrissy.

"How long have you known Private Cox, Corporal Panos?" Dusty asked.

"I don't know, at least a year. He used to hang around with Fennelli before I knew him. We met at the E-Club and I'd see him around the base or at the gym, but mostly at the club. We weren't friends."

"Was Cox with you the night you got into an altercation with Corporal Johnson a week or so earlier?"

"Yes, Sir. He was there, but he didn't do anything. I asked him why he didn't help me against Johnson, and he said it was over too quick. I called him chicken but he said he wasn't afraid of no nigger, and he would have helped but there wasn't anything left after Johnson hit me once. I think he was chicken."

"To your knowledge, were Fennelli and Cox good friends?"

"Yes, Sir, it seemed that way to me."

"Was it natural for Private Cox to come to the aid of his friend when he saw him fighting?" Dusty asked.

"Objection," Sean said, "calls for a conclusion."

"I see your point, Mr. O'Ryan, but in this instance I am going to allow the question," Colonel Malone advised.

"Yes, Sir," Panos replied, "I suppose it would be natural for Cox to help Fennelli. It wasn't the same with me. Cox wasn't my friend, and neither was Fennelli for that matter. I can see where Cox would help Fennelli and not me. That's why I didn't jump in when Fennelli got into it with the midshipman. It's not my style."

"I would move to strike, your honor, but I guess I opened the door," Dusty commented.

"You sure did, Captain, but the point was made," Colonel Malone said.

The point was well made. Panos was a coward as well as a liar. No Marine in the room missed it. Dusty had gone about as far as he could. He was wise not to risk going over the details of the fight and rape again because Panos wasn't going to change his story and there was no point in letting him reinforce the damage. There comes a time in cross-examination when you just plain stop. Too many lawyers go well beyond that point and destroy the good work they did before they got there. It is a natural tendency to want to rip the witness up, but cross-examination is often better accomplished by doing less rather than more. It is a matter of instinct. The lawyer must recognize that the final question you ask a witness must never be one to which you *do not want to know* the answer. This is substantially different than the old, overused, and dangerous maxim *never ask a question that you don't know the answer to.*" There are many questions that a trial attorney will not know the answer to, but he has to ask anyway. Thus the refined point *is to never ask question* to which you *don't want to know the answer.* But every trial lawyer has gone too far at times, much to his or her regret, and has asked one or more fatal questions, rather than stopping before asking them. Dusty wisely said, "No more questions at this time, your Honor, but I respectfully reserve additional cross-examination following Mr. O'Ryan's if need be."

"You may, if necessary, Captain Burns," Judge Malone announced. "Your witness, Mr. O'Ryan." Sean approached Panos with considerable distaste, but he tried to conceal his feelings and present as easy and friendly a presence as he could summon.

"Corporal Panos, we have heard that the light was more than sufficient so one could see all of the activities on that fateful night fairly well. Is this true?"

"Oh, yes, Sir. The moon was very bright and there were lights along the path leading to the parking lot. I could see everything real good," Panos answered.

"You had no trouble identifying all of the Marines you say were there and the activity they were engaged in?"

"No, Sir, no trouble at all."

"What were you wearing at the time?"

"Summer Service 'C' uniform, Sir. Khaki short sleeve shirt and trousers, and piss cutter."

"By piss cutter, you mean the soft cover. What we used to call the fore and aft cap?"

"Yes, Sir."

"Were Fennelli and Cox wearing the same type uniform?"

"Yes, Sir."

"What was Corporal Johnson wearing?"

"I am not sure, Sir, but I think he was wearing Summer Service 'C' too."

"Why aren't you sure?"

"I don't know, Sir. I'm just not."

"Didn't you see Corporal Johnson that night?"

"Yes, Sir, I saw him at Lake O'Neill."

"How many times?"

"Twice, Sir, once when he came running out and then later when Fennelli threw the girl on him."

"Is that the only time you saw him that night?"

"Yes, Sir."

"Didn't you testify yesterday afternoon that you saw Johnson at the Enlisted Club but wanted to avoid him because you didn't like him?"

"Oh, yes, Sir. I remember. I did see him there and he looked drunk."

"What was he wearing when you saw him in the well lighted Enlisted Club?"

"I remember now Sir, he was wearing Summer Service 'C' uniform, without his cover 'cause you can't wear that in the club."

"When you said Johnson ran out at Lake O'Neill, was that the first time you knew he was present at the scene?"

"Yes, Sir."

"Did he attempt to strike Corporal Fennelli at the time you say you saw him run out?"

"No, Sir, only the midshipman."

"Did he attempt to strike Private Cox?"

"No, Sir."

"Did he make any advances toward the young woman, Miss Long?"

"No, Sir."

"Why would Corporal Johnson run out and strike a total stranger, and do nothing to Fennelli and Cox who he didn't like?"

"Objection," Major Bryant cried. "Calls for a conclusion which this witness is not qualified to give."

"Sustained," Judge Malone said somewhat reluctantly.

Sean knew the question would be objected to and the objection would be sustained, but his only purpose was to reinforce the same question that was already present in the jury's mind. Sean was confident the jurors were asking themselves why Johnson would do this. It didn't make sense. If anything, he would have come out to help the midshipman if he intended to get involved, but certainly not to help Fennelli who was demonstrably prejudiced against blacks. Also there had been a long-standing antagonism between Johnson and Fennelli. The asking of the question was sufficient to make the point. Sean not only didn't need Panos's answer, he got more effect by not having Panos's answer.

"Is it your testimony that Corporal Johnson simply ran out sometime during the altercation between Fennelli and the midshipman and for no discernable reason struck the midshipman?"

"Objection," Brendon said. "Mischaracterizes the witness' testimony."

"Overruled," Judge Malone replied. "It is comment but technically phrased in the form of a question, so I will allow it. I would caution you Mr. O'Ryan, to save your comments for closing argument."

"Yes, Sir," Sean replied, having made his point which Brendon reinforced by his objection. There's a time to stand up and there's a time to shut up. The hardest part is figuring out which is which.

"Please answer the question, Corporal Panos."

"Yes, Sir, Johnson just came running out, and that's the first I knew he was there. He punched the middie in the jaw and he went down and that was the end of it. Johnson then sort of disappeared. I guess behind that little rise."

"One punch in the jaw. You are certain of that?"

"Oh, yes, Sir. I saw it clearly."

"In the jaw?"

"Objection," Brendon shouted, "asked and answered." Brendon saw what was developing and wanted to stop Sean from emphasizing that Johnson did not strike David Hall in the throat where the laryngeal hemorrhage occurred.

"Sustained," Colonel Malone said. "The point is established, the witness claims he saw only one punch and that was to the jaw of the midshipman."Good old Judge Malone," Sean thought. "He must have said this on purpose in order to reinforce the answer." The Judge didn't believe Panos either, and he was jerking him up because of his obvious perjury. This gave Johnson a boost with his defense of no culpability for the deathblows rendered to David Hall. If Johnson could get by the rape charge, there was no tie in to the felony murder charge. Furthermore, since there was no conspiracy, Johnson could only be liable for the midshipman's death if he rendered a fatal blow to the victim, even though technically he could be found guilty of battery. Sean had made his points. Time to shut up. "No further questions at this time, your honor."

Dusty Burns decided he had no need for additional cross-examination, and Dan Richardson followed suit. Sean expected Brendon Bryant to engage in some lengthy cross-examination of Panos for the Government, but he had only one question as to whether it was possible that Corporal Johnson had struck the deceased victim more than once and possibly in the throat. Panos replied, "It was possible," but "I only saw one punch."

Panos wasn't swift enough to see where Brendon wanted to go with this, but it was obvious Brendon was fully aware of the direction Sean's questioning was leading in founding a defense for Johnson just in case he actually had hit David Hall. As for the rest of Panos's testimony, Brendon seemed content to let the blame fall on Fennelli, Cox and Johnson and not attack Panos's disclaimers just yet. No doubt he thought he'd get what he needed from Cox and maybe Fennelli, if their counsel let them testify.

Frank Chase declined any additional direct examination, and Panos was excused from the witness stand. When he resumed his seat next to his counsel, Frank Chase shifted his weight away from his client in an exhibition of body language which Sean hoped the Board members caught. Nowhere is it written that a lawyer has to like his client, but when the feeling turns to loathsome contempt, it is hard to maintain objectivity. Unfortunately, unless the judge allows it, defense counsel cannot quit in the middle of a criminal trial no matter how much he comes to despise the client. The attorney's oath has to carry the attorney through in those situations. Sean was confident Frank Chase would continue to meet his sworn obligations notwithstanding his growing disgust for Panos.

Dusty Burns called his client, Private First Class Rick Cox, as a witness for his own defense. After Cox was sworn and the preliminary identification matters were fully accomplished, Dusty lowered the boom.

"On Thursday, September 3, 1964, did you engage in a fight with a Midshipman David Hall at Lake O'Neill at approximately 2200 hours?"

"Yes, Sir."

"Why?"

"The midshipman gave me, Fennelli and Panos some static about military courtesy, and asked us for our I.D. cards to put us on report. How dumb can you be?"

"Then what happened?"

"I wasn't going to give him my I.D. card, but before I could tell him that, Fennelli made a grab for the girl. He told me just before this that he was going to get some ass off of her whether she liked it or not. The middie yelled and Fennelli hit him. I was pissed at the middie and so I hit him too, a couple of times, but when he went down, I didn't kick him. Panos is a fucking liar...oh shit...I apologize Sir, it just slipped out."

"We've all heard it before, Private, just keep a lid on the colorful expressions," Colonel Malone smiled.

"Well, that's all I can say, Sir. I hit the guy; maybe twice, but Panos is lying when he says I kicked the middie, 'cause I didn't. No way."

"Was Panos involved in the fight?"

"Yes, Sir, but only after the middie was on the ground. He ran over and kicked him a couple of times after Fennelli had knocked the guy down. Panos wouldn't get into it when the middie was on his feet and able to fight back. He's the one who's chicken, and he calls me chicken. What a crock."

"Did you see Corporal Johnson hit the midshipman at any time?"

"I don't know. I can't even remember Johnson being there until I saw Fenelli drag the girl over behind a hill. I followed him to see what the hell he was doing and I saw him throw her down on Johnson, but that's the first I remember Johnson being there. He might have hit the middie but I didn't see it. I think Panos is wrong. And one thing for sure, I never called Johnson a nigger."

"When you hit the midshipman, where did your punches land?"

"I remember hitting him twice, once in the face and once on the shoulder."

"Did you hit him in the throat?"

"No, Sir. No way. He was in a boxer's stance, and his chin was down mostly, so there was no way I could have hit him in the throat even if I had tried."

"Did you see where any of the kicks administered by Fennelli and Panos landed on the midshipman?"

"Mostly they were kicking him in the head and face as far as I can remember. Maybe a couple of times in the body, but mostly in the head and neck."

"Had anyone said anything about getting in a fight with the midshipman when you first saw the girl and David Hall?"

"No, Sir, it just sort of happened when Fennelli said something about the girl and then he hit the sailor. It went from there. Nobody said anything like let's get him or nothin', but Fennelli said he was going to get some ass off the girl."

"About Miss Long. Did you engage in sexual intercourse with her on that night?"

"Yes, Sir, but she didn't say I couldn't."

"Was this after Corporal Fennelli did?"

"Yes, Sir. He really roughed her up, and then he screwed her."

"Did you hear Miss Long consent to any of Fennelli's conduct towards her that night?"

"No, Sir. She was crying and screaming. She got hurt pretty bad I guess, first when she came over to try and stop the fight, and then when Fennelli was dorking her."

"Why did you have intercourse with Miss Long that night?"

"Well, I was watching Fennelli and Panos get her and I just sort of got excited. I thought it couldn't hurt if I got some too. She didn't resist, she didn't scream. I don't think she even said leave me alone. I just figured she didn't care by that time, and I didn't hurt her or nothin'. I just sort of got a piece and then let her alone."

"Did Fennelli have intercourse with Miss Long twice on that evening?"

"No, Sir, just once. We all only did it once, the three of us, Fennelli, Panos and me."

"At anytime on that night did Miss Long say you could have intercourse with her?"

"No, Sir. But she didn't say I couldn't, and I just sort of thought it was all right. I was the third guy. It didn't look like it was wrong by that time."

"No further questions, your Honor."

Dusty showed a lot of integrity in his line of questioning. Cox was dead in the water through Chrissy's testimony. There was no point in trying to hide in the weeds and hope for a miracle. Cox had a shot at skating on the murder charge, slim but some. On the rape charge, however, he had none unless he could slide through on a technicality. The law is complex in this area. This is particularly true with respect to the doctrine of mens rea, which means a guilty state of mind necessary to commit a specific intent crime. Forcible rape - as opposed to statutory rape, which cannot be consented to due to age limitations - is the type of crime that requires a mens rea. The criminality doesn't arise out of the act of intercourse, per se, but rather whether or not the act was nonconsensual and the perpetrator knew or should have known that. It is a delicate line that has to be walked and the defense fails more often than it succeeds, but lack of mens rea, that is, lacking a guilty mind, is a valid defense. In Cox's case it was obvious that Dusty was relying on Cox's room temperature I.Q. and the simple fact that Cox was too stupid to know that lack of resistance by the victim after being brutalized to the point of shock and despair is not consensual acquiescence. Cox may have believed this was just one more sex act in the woman's life, and when she didn't resist or say anything, it was acceptable to use her. He was wrong, of course, but the issue is not what a reasonable man might think, but what the particular individual involved was thinking at the time.

Lack of mens rea is not an insanity defense, but rather a defense of mistake, which mistaken perception negates the necessary guilty mind. For example, if one gets into his own bed thinking the woman there is his wife, and he has intercourse with her while she is asleep or in a drunken state, it is technically tantamount to nonconsensual rape if the woman is not his wife and has not consented to the sexual act. But the essential guilty mind - the mens rea - is missing and the offense might be excused. Dusty had to travel a long road in order to convince the jury of that requisite state of mind or more accurately, lack of state of mind in the case of Private Cox, but it was all he had and he took it to the wall. In the process he did a good job, win or lose.

Brendon had a few questions for Cox, but nothing new came out of them. Basically, Brendon was glad to have Cox admit his participation and Sean suspected that Brendon was going to rely on the inferences to be drawn and the emphasis he could make in closing argument to negate Cox's defenses both as to the rape and homicide charges. Sean could see no point in belaboring Cox's testimony about the absence of Johnson from the fight, so he left well enough alone. He had a question, however, and it went right to the heart of the rape.

"Private Cox, after you saw Corporal Fennelli throw Miss Long on Corporal Johnson who was lying on the ground, did you see Corporal Johnson do anything to Miss Long?"

"No, Sir, I didn't. He just laid there with her on top of him, and we got to hell out of there. If I hadn't dropped my cover, maybe none of us would be here today."

"Just one more question. What was Corporal Johnson wearing when you saw him?"

"I think it was civies, Sir."

The other three counsel announced no further witnesses. Sean thought a character witness would have been in order for each of the other three defendants, but apparently they couldn't find anyone willing to come forward in a case of this offensive nature to say anything good about the accused. Not even a mother or two, who usually show up to say what a good boy their son always was.

After a pause that added to the building of the suspense, Colonel Malone looked at Sean and he could see the question in the judge's eyes. The same question was reflected in the look of every member of the jury. *Are we going to hear from Johnson? And will Johnson's team be cross-examining Chrissy Long?* They wanted Sean to close the loop. The unknown factor was yet to be heard from, and it seemed like they were looking for some magic revelation that could only be imparted by Sean's client.

Before Sean could say anything, Colonel Malone noted the hour and suggested that this would be an appropriate time to break for lunch. "I think it would be best to break now Colonel Orlowski so as not to interrupt the next stage of the proceedings."

Colonel Orlowski agreed and the trial was adjourned until 1300 hours. Sean had Johnson taken to Jack's office rather than return to the brig for lunch. One of the enlisted men in Base Legal volunteered to go out and pick up a few sandwiches for them so they could go over Johnson's upcoming testimony.

"Lee, I've got to ask one more time, have you been straight with us?"

"Shit, Major, I told you a hundred times I didn't even know the sailor was there and I didn't do the broad. For Christ sake," Johnson said highly annoyed.

"I understand your feelings, but you've heard the testimony and you've got to realize that you are the best witness we have," Sean admonished. "If you've left anything out, you'd better remember it right now. We don't need any surprises this afternoon. If you've been holding back you could kill your own case."

"Fuck, Mr. O'Ryan, you got a thick skin. I told you what I know."

"It's not my skin that's at stake, Lee, it's yours, and don't forget that. I'm going to take you through every minute of that eventful day. When I'm done, Major Bryant will have at you and will do his best to discredit you. If you aren't believable, your ass is grass."

"I ain't afraid of Major Bryant or any of those other assholes," Johnson said with unconvincing bravado.

"O.K., eat your sandwich and relax. We'll be going back into court in about twenty minutes."

CHAPTER 23

The afternoon session was called to order at 1305 hours. Judge Malone asked, "Are you ready for the defense, Mr. O'Ryan?"

"Yes, Sir," Sean replied and thought there's no point in keeping them waiting, the moment of truth has arrived. "We call Corporal Lee Johnson."

Johnson was sworn as a witness and responded to the preliminary identification questions. Then he turned to Sean and looked like he was going to pass out. Gone was the surly, jive talking individual they first met in the brig and who was still putting on a show of bravado in Jack's office a few minutes ago. In an effort to calm Johnson, Sean took him through the entire day of September 3, 1964, exactly as he had told it to them the first day they met, as well as several times thereafter.

Lee was consistent in his responses to questions, and his denials of involvement in the fight were convincing. His drunken state at the time aided his denials. Further, his ill will towards Fennelli, Panos and Cox was credible and understandable. He denied coming to the aid of Fennelli and was adamant that it was the last thing he would have done. If anything, Johnson assured that he would have helped the midshipman, but he didn't even know the fight was going down. He added that fights are common in the Corps. Since he was passed out, semi-conscious at best, he said he wouldn't have given a damn about the fight as long as it wasn't directed at him. The jury seemed to accept these statements. Coupled with their impression of Panos as a liar, Sean believed they would be inclined to acquit on the murder charge. Just in case, however, he still would argue that even if they thought Johnson had thrown one punch, it was not in furtherance of any design, plan or execution of the rape of Chrissy Long. Thus, Johnson could not be guilty of felony murder. Johnson was doing a good job as Sean brought him to the delicate point where Fennelli had thrown Chrissy on him as he lay in his drunken stupor.

"Were you ever aware that Miss Long had been thrown on top of you?" Sean asked, expecting Johnson to say he never realized it until the military police rousted him and he found out for the first time that Chrissy was even in the area. But his expectations exploded when Johnson replied, "I knew she was there from the time she landed on me. It woke me up I guess, and I could feel her and smell her. I opened my eyes and I realized I was with a woman."

Sean was taken aback but he had to stay calm so he wouldn't shout, *Why the fuck didn't you ever say so before this?*

"How long," Sean asked trying to appear unfazed, "did Miss Long stay on top of you?"

"I don't know, but it was a little while. She wasn't moving and I was pretty drunk, so I didn't push her off or nothin'."

Sean was more than reluctant to ask the next question because he didn't know what Johnson would say. But he had to ask and he couldn't request a recess since it would look like Sean needed to coach his witness. This would be fatally damning in the jury's eyes. Besides, Judge Malone would most likely turn him down, and this would look worse. He could only hope Johnson had not been lying to him. If he had, he just invited his own destruction. "Then what happened?" Sean asked calmly hoping the jury hadn't sensed anything unusual about this turn of events.

"I saw she was messed up, but she still looked like a pretty woman with her blond hair and good smell, so I rolled over on top of her."

Where is he getting this from? Sean wondered silently trying to maintain an even expression. He was trapped by this alarming admission, but he had to continue as if this were a natural evolution in the questioning process.

"And then?"

"And then to be honest, Mr. O'Ryan, I took out my cock and thought about sticking it in her."

An audible gasp came from the spectator section. Sean would have joined them if he could, but he had no choice. He moved to the next potentially fatal question, to which he had no answer.

"And did you?"

"No, Sir, I didn't. I wasn't in the best shape to be trying that kind of stuff anyway, but more than that, I decided it was wrong. I could see the girl had been hurt enough. She had blood caked on her chest and she had been beaten up for sure. So I didn't."

Something prompted Sean to take a serious risk at this point and he decided to gamble on Johnson coming through. The question would surprise Lee, but sometimes that evokes the sincerest answer. "Did seeing a blond, blue eyed, white girl influence you in any way?"

The question was leading but Sean was counting on the prosecutor to be more interested in the story than the legal niceties. He was right, no objection was made.

"Yes, Sir. It made me think of another blue eyed, blond, white girl who falsely accused me of rape when I was in high school. This was right after she screwed four white guys right in front of me. It also made me think of a white girl with blond hair and blue eyes I used to date here in Oceanside. She shafted me too."

"Did you want to get even with blond, blue eyed, white girls under the circumstances?" Sean asked, realizing it was once again leading but he was sure the Judge would allow it. Brendon didn't object, so the point was moot.

"Yes, Sir, at the time I took my cock out I was thinkin' that very thing. But then I couldn't do it, and I just kind of fell on the girl and she seemed to come to."

"Was anything said by either of you?"

"Yes, Sir. She looked at me and said, 'no, please, no,' and I said 'it's O.K.' Then she pushed me with her arms and I rolled over and she rolled away. I think I fell asleep or passed out, but that's the last I remember until the M.P.s were kicking and beating on me."

"Did you have sexual intercourse with Miss Chrissy Long on that night or any other time?" Sean asked softly.

"No, Sir. I thought about it, but I didn't. I couldn't. I think she thinks I did, but I swear to Jesus, I didn't."

"No further questions."

On cross-examination, Brendon Bryant took Johnson over the coals. He went over every line of his testimony starting with breakfast that morning. He challenged him at every turn and hammered away on the vengeance theme against white, blond, blue eyed, young women. He made him reveal every aspect of the juvenile rape matter. He had a right to do so. Sean had opened the door with his questions. But in the end, Brendon wasn't able to change one word of it, and Johnson hung tough, sounding convincing as far as Sean was concerned. Unfortunately, defense counsel are notoriously bad judges of how convincing a client appears. They get too close to the story and after a while persuade themselves. But in this instance the other half of the story had never been revealed to Sean. Perhaps Johnson was ashamed to admit he had given serious consideration to using Chrissy Long, which would have been without consent and for all the wrong reasons. Whatever Johnson's motive, Sean was as surprised as the rest of the souls assembled in the courtroom, although they didn't know it. But he felt Johnson had done better than expected in his strong stand against a blistering cross-examination. The other defense counsel wisely chose not to cross-examine Johnson.

Colonel Malone, noting the lateness of hour, concluded it would be a good time to adjourn for the day. This was fine with Sean and Jack because they had homework to do to prepare for the final aspects of their case. They had supper at the Officers Club and later contacted the two remaining witnesses they would call in the morning. Then they went to work on Chrissy's cross-examination. It was close to eleven by the time they closed up shop and Sean drove back to *The Miramar*. The clerk at the front desk said Sean had a message and handed him the form. It read:

> Miss Sullivan called and said she
> had heard about the session today,
> and wanted to extend congratulations.
> Your crusade for truth and justice
> turned those elusive twins into martyrs
> for an unworthy cause. How sad.

******

Thursday, October 15, 1964

Colonel Malone called the court-martial into its fourth day session at 0900, Thursday morning. Jack and Sean were ready.

"You may call your next witness, Mr. O'Ryan."

"Thank you, Sir. We call Hospitalman Second Class Nathan Andrews, United States Navy."

HM2 Andrews was sworn as a witness and then looked around the courtroom as if he had been thrust into a strange environment that was making him more than a little uncomfortable. He was a shy little man, and rather homely. His glasses were typical Navy issue, gray colored frames, and ugly. He looked at Sean as just another hostile object in that strange setting. Sean wasn't hostile but he had some questions the witness would prefer not to be asked, particularly because much had been learned about HM2 Andrews from Sergeant Major Ed Tabor who had done quiet detective work through his many contacts at the Base.

The witness could not identify any of the defendants, but he did say that in accordance with Sean's request he had been designated custodian of the records of the laboratory at the Naval Hospital, Camp Pendleton, for the night of September 3, 1964, and the early morning of September 4, 1964. He testified that a blood sample, ostensibly belonging to a Corporal Lee Johnson, was submitted by the emergency room and he, Andrews, had personally conducted a test of that sample. Andrews advised that the test reflected nothing unusual with respect to abnormalities, nor the presence of any drug except alcohol. He further advised that his records reflected a blood alcohol at the time of testing of .18 grams of alcohol for each cubic centimeter of blood. In his opinion this measurement would be a falling blood alcohol reading if the donor had not ingested any alcohol for at least three hours. Although he had to admit he did not know if Corporal Johnson had ingested any alcohol during a three hour time period prior to the test.

Sean asked the witness the one question Andrews wished wouldn't be asked, but it was necessary because Sean was armed with information Ed had already dug up and he gave Andrews no choice.

"Did you forward a report of your testing to the records office so a formal notation of it would find it's way into Corporal Johnson's health record?"

"No, Sir. But I did call the doctor on duty, Doctor Adams, and told him of the results, but I didn't forward a written copy of the report at that time."

"Why not?"

Andrews paused and looked at Sean realizing that the question reflected squarely on the performance of his duties. "As I look back on it, I guess it was foolish of me, but to tell the truth, Sir, it was because I was afraid," he answered.

"Afraid of what?"

"A rather large military policeman named Sergeant Stanley Williams, to be honest with you, Sir."

"What did Sergeant Williams do to make you afraid?"

"He came down to the lab and told me I shouldn't send the report to the records office, and, if I did, it wouldn't be healthy."

"What did you believe that meant?"

"I took it to mean that I could be harassed by this M.P. or his buddies if I didn't do what he said. I asked him why I shouldn't send the report up. He said because it involves a 'nigger' - yes, he used the word 'nigger' - which I found surprising because Sergeant Williams is a Negro. But he did."

"What, if anything, was said then?" Sean asked.

"I asked what the person he called a 'nigger' did, and he said that 'he had killed somebody and raped a white girl,' and he, Sergeant Williams, 'wasn't going to let that 'nigger' get away with rape and murder just because he was drunk.' He repeated his threat, and I held on to the report."

"Did you ever forward the report to the records office?"

"No, Sir, I still have it. In fact, I brought it with me this morning, along with the lab log. The log shows the blood alcohol reading the same as the report; it was .18."

"May I have the original report, please?"

After Andrews had handed it over, Sean showed it to Brendon Bryant and the other counsel. He then moved that it to be admitted as Johnson defense exhibit next in order. Judge Malone accepted the report in evidence, and Sean had no further questions of Andrews.

Brendon had one question. "HM2 Andrews, would a .18 blood alcohol prevent someone from committing a violent crime in your experience?"

"Objection your honor," Sean interjected. "HM2 Andrews has not been qualified as an expert in this regard, but I can save Major Bryant time by advising that I am presenting such an expert as our next witness. I'm sure Major Bryant will be able to fully explore this area if he feels it is necessary."

"I tend to agree with Mr. O'Ryan," Judge Malone replied. "HM2 Andrews may be an expert in lab procedures, but he hasn't been qualified on the effects of any intoxication in this case to this time. The objection is sustained. If you can't get what you need from the next witness as promised by Mr. O'Ryan, I'll let you call your own in rebuttal.

HM2 Andrews was excused with an admonishment from Judge Malone to do his duty in the future and to report any threats or intimidations to his superiors. "In short do your job, threats or no threats." Andrews was embarrassed, but replied respectfully, "Yes, Sir," and stepped down. The Colonel then directed Major Bryant to report this matter to the Provost Marshal for appropriate action.

Sean stood and announced his next witness. "We call Doctor Douglas Adams. Doctor Adams has previously testified in this matter for the Government, your Honor."

"Doctor Adams, since you are to be a witness for the defense you will be re-sworn," Judge Malone advised. After Doctor Adams was sworn and re-identified Lee Johnson, Sean went over his credentials and his extensive experience which qualified him as an expert with respect to blood alcohol. He then asked what a reading of .18 blood alcohol meant.

"Blood alcohol is measured in grams of alcohol per each cubic centimeter of blood," Doctor Adams advised. "This reflects the concentration of alcohol in the blood of the donor. One drink will cause an average increase in the blood level of .02% at the end of each half hour. For the average person a .02% level has little effect, but at .04%, most persons will suffer a measurable effect on their concentration and comprehension. At .06%, the individual will exhibit impaired judgment, indecisiveness and some impairment of motor performance. At .08%, there is a discernable loss of fine muscle coordination, impaired depth perception, and gross impairment of judgment. At .10% this worsens considerably, and the person is substantially under the influence, but to the untrained eye the person surprisingly could appear to be in good control. You see this in social settings, at the club, and other places in our society where alcohol and a good time are tied together all too often. At a .16 level, there is loss of large muscle coordination and partial anesthesia of the senses, that is, touch, vision and hearing. Judgment is grossly impaired, and yet an individual can surprisingly not exhibit outward signs of drunkenness, particularly an experienced drinker. A reading of .18 will further impair coordination and worsen judgment. By the time the level reaches .20%, the person is sleepy, has lost some sense of equilibrium, and his mind records little of what is going on around him, but, surprisingly, he can still make some judgment calls and can remember some things that occurred. All of this loss of ability, judgment, muscle and motor control, exacerbates as the levels go up. By .30% the person is patently intoxicated and all mental and physical functions are grossly impaired. At .40% the person would be comatose, and by .50% he would be near death if not already dead."

"Doctor Adams, Corporal Johnson's blood alcohol level was tested at your direction on the night of September 3rd or the early morning of September 4th, isn't that correct?" Sean asked.

"Yes, it is."

"HM2 Andrews from the hospital lab staff testified that he ran the test personally and immediately reported the results to you by telephone in the early morning of September 4th as .18% blood alcohol.

"That's correct."

"In terms of your experience and expertise, I ask for your opinion, Doctor, as to what, if any, effect an .18% blood alcohol would have on Corporal Johnson's ability to form and maintain an erection?"

"That would depend on the physical condition of the individual and whether he had no other impairments to such endeavor. Assuming he is otherwise normal in all respects, his sexual ability would be lessened or diminished by the amount of alcohol in his blood. But in the case of .18% it would still be possible for a healthy, young man to obtain an erect state and maintain it if he didn't fall asleep during the act," Doctor Adams said smiling. Most of the males in the courtroom smiled with him.

"Would a person be able to make judgment decisions with a blood alcohol of .18%, Doctor?" Sean followed up.

"Once again, the answer is yes, but judgment definitely is impaired with that high a reading. But not totally, and certain judgment calls can be made."

"Would someone with that high a reading be able to recognize that a young woman had been hurt and be able to feel sympathy towards her in spite of his drunken condition?"

"In my opinion, he could. It would depend on prior disposition to such feelings of empathy. Some people are kinder than others either by nature or conditioning. But a blood alcohol of .18 would not necessarily deprive someone of the ability to recognize another person's plight and respond in a sympathetic and empathetic manner."

"Thank you, no further questions."

Brendon was on his feet before Sean sat down. "Doctor, if someone had developed a serious distrust of white women with long, blond hair and blue eyes, would it be likely that he would demonstrate a response of sympathy and empathy towards someone of that description when his judgment was grossly impaired through a concentration of blood alcohol in the .18 range?"

"Objection, Colonel, the question assumes a fact not in evidence." Sean shouted.

"That's a close question, Mr. O'Ryan, but you did open the door with that description earlier in the trial. Counsel has a right to phrase his hypothetical questions in terms of the testimony adduced at trial. I find it is sufficiently part of the record so that the question is proper. You may answer, Doctor," Judge Malone replied.

"That probably is a better question for a psychiatrist, but in my opinion as an expert in blood alcohol concentrations, I feel that the person would act consistent with his prior learned responses, and if distrust is part of the scenario before he was drunk, it isn't likely he is going to become trusting when his judgment is grossly impaired. He might become incautious, of course, since that often is a natural concomitant of drunkenness. But as to whether or not a distrustful person would feel sympathy for someone he didn't trust before he got drunk, that is rather unlikely in my opinion," Doctor Adams submitted.

Brendon had made a telling point and wisely sat down. "No further questions, your honor."

Sean stood and advised he had one more question. "You said it might be unlikely, but you didn't say impossible. It could be possible couldn't it?"

"Oh, yes. It could be possible. There are so many psychological variations at play here that I wouldn't be able to exclude such response from the realm of possibility."

"Thank you, Doctor. No further questions."

The other three defense counsel took turns at Doctor Adams trying to relate a state of intoxication to their individual client's conduct on the night in question, but it was to no avail. None of the other three accused had his blood drawn on that night or early morning. After they were apprehended they were presented only for pre-confinement physical examinations, and not for fluid testing. Thus, questions as to degree of drunkenness of the other defendants were purely speculative. Brendon didn't bother addressing the point when the defense counsel finished and Doctor Adams was excused.

"Do you have another witness, Mr. O'Ryan, or any other proffers of evidence?" Colonel Malone asked.

"Yes, Sir, at this time we would ask that Miss Chrissy Long be recalled for purposes of cross-examination."

Another audible gasp came from the spectator section. Many had forgotten that Sean had been allowed to reserve cross-examination of Chrissy. The critical moment had finally come, that moment that can be the most difficult in a trial lawyer's life, the instant when everything may turn on the testimony of the final witness. It usually is more comfortable to fire broadsides early in the trial and only use a final witness to reinforce earlier testimony. This case had taken several strange turns, however, and Sean had to close the circle even though the risk was substantial. He had alerted Brendon Bryant that he would need Chrissy in court today, and she was in Brendon's office waiting to be called.

CHAPTER 24

Chrissy entered the courtroom looking more beautiful than the last time and every bit as fragile and delicate. Sean had to walk gently around this image of innocence and purity who had been outrageously violated. "You are reminded you are still under oath, Miss Long," Judge Malone advised politely.

When she was seated, Sean approached Chrissy slowly, stopping a few feet from her to avoid any suggestion of intimidation. He didn't want her to view him as some kind of ogre whose only purpose was to degrade her or brand her unworthy of belief. Chrissy had been humiliated enough by the brutality to which she had been subjected and Sean felt deeply about her pain. He admired the courage that brought her to this room full of strangers seeking justice for David Hall and herself. "I apologize for having to ask you to return today, Miss Long, but it is important. I promise I will not dwell any longer than necessary on the events I must ask you to recall," Sean said with genuine kindness. Preliminary remarks are commonly employed on cross-examination to place the witness more at ease and to humanize the confrontation. Lawyers who immediately go for the juggler lose not only the cooperation of witnesses, but often lose credibility as well. There is a time to go for the kill, but coming on like a raging bull as an opening gambit usually is not effective. This approach turns cross-examination into a contest of wills rather than adherence to the witness's oath to tell the truth.

"I will keep my questions brief," Sean reassured, "and with that, I would ask you to recall your testimony of a few days ago with respect to Corporal Lee Johnson."

"I think I remember what I said," Chrissy responded.

"I'm sure you do, but if at anytime you aren't certain, I have a copy of the transcript of that testimony and you may refer to it as often as you like," Sean added.

"Turning to your previous testimony, you said you did not see Corporal Johnson strike or kick David Hall at anytime on the night of September 3, 1964, is that correct?"

"Yes, that's correct. I didn't see him do anything to David."

"As a matter of fact, isn't it true you first became aware of the presence of Corporal Johnson when you were dragged behind a slight rise by the defendant you identified as Anthony Fennelli, and were thrown on top of the Corporal?"

"Yes, that's correct?"

"I ask you, then, to recall the exact sequence of events as best you can from that moment on. What do you remember?"

Chrissy hesitated for a moment, and took a deep breath before answering. "I remember that man - pointing to Fennelli - said something crude about 'niggers' deserving...deserving...please excuse me, it is difficult to use his exact language. But I'll try...again. He said 'deserving a...fucked up bitch,' meaning me, I guess. Then he left me on top of that man," the fragile witness replied, while pointing to Lee Johnson. "I'm sorry about having to use this kind of language, but that's what he said. This is not easy for me." Chrissy paused for a moment, and everyone could see she was embarrassed. Sean assured her that they all understood this was not her normal speech pattern. She thanked him and then added, "At that time I think I fainted, but I don't know for how long."

"What do you recall after that?"

"I came to sometime later. I was naked from the waist down and the black man was on top of me. I know his penis was fully exposed because I could feel it against me, and later, as I rolled away from him, I could see it sticking out."

"What happened after you came to the first time?"

"I said something like no, please, no."

"Why did you say that?"

"Because I thought he was going to do to me what the others had done."

"Did Corporal Johnson say anything in response to what you said?"

"I didn't remember this at first, but I have thought about it for several days and I am certain he did say something."

"And what was that?"

"I think he said it's O.K., or it's all right."

"What did you take that to mean?"

"I thought he meant it was all right to do to me what the others had done, and I got so scared I fainted again."

"I can appreciate your being afraid, Miss Long, you had been through a terrible ordeal. But I must ask you to recall that ordeal so the court can have a complete picture of the night," Sean said as kindly as possible without patronizing.

"You said you could feel Corporal Johnson's exposed penis against you. What part of your body were you referring to in that context?"

"I could feel it against my stomach kind of, maybe a little lower. Against my pubic area."

"Was his penis touching your vagina?"

"Not exactly. It was higher up. Maybe not much, but not against my privates."

"Was his penis erect?"

"I think it was?"

"I apologize for having to ask you this, Miss Long, but were you familiar with an erect penis prior to that night?"

"Objection," Brendon Bryant shouted.

"Overruled. Since it goes to competency and not prior acts, I will allow the question but only insofar as it calls for a yes or no answer," Judge Malone replied. "But I am going to hold your feet to the fire on this Mr. O'Ryan. No questions about prior acts."

"Yes, Sir," Sean replied.

"Do you mean other than the men who raped me?" Chrissy asked.

"Yes, other than your unfortunate experience of that night and the other men involved on that terrible occasion. But I wish to assure you that you do not have to relate any specific acts which might have given rise to your ability to answer the question."

"Yes, Sir, I have had experience with such condition. It was with David. He and I were very close and intimate. He was a kind and gentle lover. I am not ashamed that he was the first and only man in my life," Chrissy replied with tears filling her eyes. Sean paused for a moment as the reporter handed a box of tissue to the witness, who then dabbed at her eyes.

"We can take a recess if you need, Miss Long," Judge Malone said with genuine concern.

"No, it's all right," Chrissy said thanking him.

Sean then continued gently, "At the point when you think you recall Corporal Johnson saying it's O.K. or it's all right, I understand your testimony to be that his penis, although probably erect, was not touching your genitalia, and you could feel it more in the area of your mons veneris. Is that correct?"

"Yes, that's correct."

"And then you fainted?"

"Yes."

"And you don't know how long you were unconscious that time either?"

"No I don't"

"When you came to, was Corporal Johnson still on top of you?"

"Yes, he was."

"Did he say anything at that time?"

"No"

"Why not, if you know?"

"I think he was asleep."

"What did you do then?"

"I pushed at him and he didn't resist, and I was able to roll him over and roll away for a few feet. I fainted again after seeing his penis still sticking out of his trousers."

"Was it erect?"

"No."

"Miss Long, I ask you to recall your testimony of a few days ago. You answered a question from Major Bryant as to 'what, if anything, do you recall with respect to the defendant, Johnson, having intercourse with you?' Do you remember that?"

"Yes, I do."

"And do you recall your answer which was 'I am certain he had intercourse with me, the same as the others did'?"

"Yes, I do."

"In what way were you certain?"

"Well, his sex organ was out and hard and pressing against my body. Then he said it was all right, and I was sure he was going to take me even though I said no, please, no."

"You thought he intended to have you and then did have intercourse with you from the circumstances as you recall them?"

"Yes, that's right. Everything was the same. He was on top of me before I fainted and he was pressing his hard sex organ against me. A little bit after that I woke up. He was no longer erect but he was still on top of me."

"You had been terribly hurt and brutalized that night, isn't that true?"

"Why yes, of course, I was beaten and punched and kicked and cut and given a skull fracture. I was brutalized and then raped repeatedly," Chrissy shouted.

"I know, Miss Long, and I am terribly saddened that this happened. But I must ask you to be precise about Corporal Johnson. I'm sure you understand." Sean said this demonstrably sympathetic. "You *think* Corporal Johnson had sexual intercourse with you, isn't that true?" Sean emphasized.

"Yes, I said that."

"Please forgive my pedantic persistence, Miss Long, but thinking and knowing are poles apart. Some of us think there is a God, but we don't know it. It's based on belief."

"Objection," Brendon said, just to rattle Sean's cage.

"Sustained. Don't sermonize, Mr. O'Ryan." Judge Malone admonished.

"My question is simply in that context, Miss Long. Do you *know* without any doubt that Corporal Johnson had sexual intercourse with you that night?"

"Well, yes. I mean well, I am sure he did."

"That wasn't my question. Let me put it more definitively. Isn't it true that you only *think* he did from the circumstances as you recall them, but you don't *know* that he did?"

Chrissy's eyes filled with tears again. She looked at Sean and then at her mother in the spectator section.

"I think he did. I believe he did."

"Miss Long, isn't it true that you cannot say here today, under an oath to tell the truth, that you *know* Corporal Johnson's penis penetrated your vaginal area, at least beyond the labia?"

"I think it did."

"The question is: can you swear that it did as matter of unequivocal fact?"

"Objection" Brendon said, but without much conviction. "The question has been asked and answered."

"Overruled," Judge Malone responded.

"Miss Long, please answer my question. Can you swear that Corporal Johnson's penis penetrated your vaginal area on that night?"

Chrissy stated to cry and said something inaudible. The reporter asked that she repeat her answer. Through her tears, she sobbed, "No, no, I can't. But I think he did."

"But you don't know?"

"No, I don't know. I don't know," Chrissy shouted and then broke down completely.

"No further questions, your Honor," Sean said softly.

Major Bryant looked at Sean and shook his head. Sean didn't know if Brendon was disgusted with him or the turn of events, but he realized there was no way Brendon could rehabilitate the witness. Brendon knew it too and wisely said, "No re-direct your Honor."

None of the other three defense counsel wanted any further cross-examination of Chrissy, and she was excused as a witness. As she passed Sean, she hesitated for a moment and looked deep into his eyes as if to say *I know you did what you had to do, but I don't think I will ever understand or forgive any of this.* Sean knew what she felt and believed. He also knew what he believed and how he felt about Lee Johnson. They could never reconcile the differences. Sean stood and said, "The defense for Corporal Johnson rests, your Honor."

Each of the other three defense counsel made a similar announcement for their clients.

"Do you have any rebuttal witnesses or other evidence, Major Bryant?" Colonel Malone asked.

"Yes, Sir. The Government has one rebuttal witness."

This announcement took Sean and Jack by surprise. Neither had expected a rebuttal witness for the prosecution since they thought everything had been fully covered in the Government's case in chief. Generally, rebuttal is confined to matters raised by the defense and is not designed to restate matters that already were demonstrated in the prosecution's earlier presentation. Sean asked for a sidebar conference which Judge Malone granted. At the sidebar Sean challenged the calling of a rebuttal witness, and asked to voir dire the witness before he or she testified. Judge Malone turned to Major Bryant and asked softly, "What is the nature of the expected testimony of your proffered rebuttal witness?"

Brendon replied, "Sir, the witness will testify as to admissions made by the defendant, Lee Johnson, which admissions directly rebut his trial testimony."

"I object to this procedure, Colonel. Once again the defense is having to wing it in the dark and confront a witness we have had no opportunity to interview outside of court," Sean reclamored.

"That's the nature of the beast, Mr. O'Ryan. The prosecution has to furnish you a list of witnesses intended to be called in its case in chief, but not witnesses who might be called in its case on rebuttal. Furthermore the witnesses don't have to talk to you if they don't want to. And, of course, any newly discovered witnesses, whose testimony arises out of matters testified to by defense witnesses do not have to be disclosed in advance since it is not known if they will be called prior to the defense putting on its case in reply," Colonel Malone admonished.

"I appreciate that, Sir, but the prejudicial effect of a surprise witness may well outweigh the witness's probative value," Sean pleaded.

"Once again, that is the nature of the beast, counselor. The impact of a rebuttal witness is often far greater than if the witness appeared at other stages of the trial, but it doesn't disqualify his competency even though it may prejudice the defendant's case. This is an adversarial proceeding as you are well aware. Producing a witness for dramatic effect on rebuttal is a time honored trail tactic, Mr. O'Ryan. I am confident you have done this many times yourself." Judge Malone said this as if he were lecturing rather than ruling. Sean, although feeling chastised, had to admit the judge was right.

"I appreciate that, Sir, however…"

"However doesn't apply in this instance Mr. O'Ryan. I will allow the witness and, anticipating a renewal of your request to voir dire the witness before he testifies, I will deny that request for the record before you even ask. That's all gentlemen. Major Bryant you may call your witness." *This is bullshit,* Sean thought angrily. *Once again the fucking rules allow for sabotaging the truth we ought to be seeking in every trial. This is fucking bullshit.*

Counsel returned to their tables, and Major Bryant called Private Richie Bernard to the stand. After preliminary identification questions, Brendon asked, "Private Bernard, are you currently confined to the Base Brig at Camp Pendleton."

"Yes, Sir. I am serving a Summary Court-Martial sentence."

"When were you sentenced?"

"Two weeks ago, Sir."

"What for?"

"Twenty days unauthorized absence, Sir."

"Prior to your court-martial were you confined to the Base Brig awaiting trial?"

"Yes, Sir."

"And as a pretrial detainee did you share a cell with Corporal Lee Johnson who you identified in this courtroom a moment ago?"

"Yes, Sir, for a few weeks."

"At anytime during the period in which you shared a cell with Corporal Johnson did he discuss the criminal matters involved in these present proceedings?"

"I'm not sure what that fancy language means, but if you want to know did he tell me why he was in the brig, my answer is, yes Sir, he did."

"What, if anything, did Corporal Johnson say to you about the charges pending against him?"

"I asked him what he was in the brig for, and he said 'some...' should I use the exact words he did, Sir?"

"Yes, you may and you should."

"He said, 'some fuckin' broad got fucked and now she says she didn't ask for it.'"

"Did he say anything else?"

"Yes, Sir. I asked him if he had fucked her, and he said, 'sure that's what white bitches are for homeboy. Ain't good for nothin' else.'"

CHAPTER 25

Private Bernard had dropped a bomb on Johnson. Major Bryant considered it best not to expose Bernard to any great challenges to his credibility and decided to be satisfied with his crushing testimony. With a smirk, which the jury could not see, he turned to Sean and said, "Your witness."

When Brendon first asked Private Bernard if he had shared a cell with Lee Johnson, Sean considered objecting on relevancy grounds but decided not to since Judge Malone would probably overrule the objection. Objecting would only lend credence to anything said thereafter, and it would look like Sean was trying to hide something from the jury. He concluded it would be better to attack the witness after he testified on direct. As soon as Private Bernard finished the damning testimony about Johnson, Sean asked Jack to get hold of Ed Tabor to see what Ed could find out about all this. He also asked Jack to rush over to the brig to see what he could discover about Bernard. Sean would extend cross-examination as long as possible to give Jack some time, but it couldn't be much.

Sean rose to his full six feet one inch and, in a departure from his usual technique, he approached the witness with obvious contempt, firing his opening salvos with no intention of low keying his cross-examination.

"Private Bernard, how long have you been in the Marine Corps?"

"Almost three years, Sir."

"Almost three years, *Private*," Sean repeated, sounding deliberately incredulous while emphasizing the word, private.

"Objection," Brendon shouted. "Defense counsel is harassing the witness through ridicule."

"That's not possible, your Honor, Private Bernard is ridiculous enough without my help," Sean retorted.

"That'll be quite enough, Mr. O'Ryan. These asides between counsel are unprofessional and will not be tolerated. The members are instructed to disregard any inferences to be drawn by the fact that Private Bernard has almost three years active duty and is still a private."

Thank you judge, Sean thought, *for driving home the point I was making. No way the jury is going to disregard it now.*

"Private Bernard, you say you are presently serving a sentence of a Summary Court-martial for unauthorized absence. Is this the first time you have ever served time in the brig?"

"Objection, irrelevant," Brendon said softly not wanted the jury to think he was trying to hide Bernard's past. "Overruled," Judge Malone replied. "Normally evidence of specific instances of conduct for the purpose of attacking or supporting a witness' credibility are not admissible, but there is an exception when the witness has been the subject of a felony conviction that is not too distant, or any conviction for a crime of moral turpitude. Under the circumstances, I am going to let you explore this area, subject to a motion to strike."

"Thank you, Sir. Private Bernard, I will rephrase the question to make it more specific. Have you ever been convicted of a crime other than unauthorized absence?"

"Do you mean in the Marine Corps or in civilian life," Bernard asked.

"In either status," Sean replied.

"Yes, Sir, I was convicted of grand theft auto when I was seventeen in Detroit, Michigan."

"This was before you joined the Marine Corps?" Sean asked.

"Yes, Sir."

"You were seventeen. Were you tried as an adult?"

"Yes, Sir."

"Did you serve any time?"

"No, Sir."

"Why not?"

"I used my brother's name, and he had a clean record, so the judge gave me probation. They never found out I wasn't who I said I was."

"Is that how you were able to join the Marine Corps even though you had a conviction?"

"Yes, Sir. When I enlisted I used my real name. The Corps never knew about the conviction. I guess they didn't match the fingerprints that really went with my brother's rap sheet if they ran a check. I was wondering how you knew about it."

Sean repressed a smile at this question, not wanting Bernard to know that Sean didn't know a thing about the conviction and that the whole line of questioning was a fishing expedition to stall for time, and maybe learn that Barnard had a record in civilian courts as well as military. "I'll tell you sometime how I knew, Private Bernard, but right now I am asking the questions. Did you have any other convictions in civilian life or in the Marine Corps?"

"Yes, Sir, another court-martial, a special-court for disobedience of orders and possession of a false identification card. I served three months brig time, but no discharge."

"Your record in the Corps is pretty shoddy, Private, have you been put in for an administrative discharge?"

"Objection," Brendon shouted. "Improper impeachment."

"Sustained," Judge Malone replied. "The members will disregard the question and any inferences to be drawn from it."

Sean mentally noted, *Sure, Colonel, right after brain surgery.*

"Did you know Corporal Lee Johnson prior to meeting him in the brig?"

"No, Sir."

"You were not friends? Not confidants?"

"I don't know what confidants means, Sir, but I can tell you we were not friends."

"Since you were not close, isn't it true there would be no reason for Corporal Johnson to confide in you, especially something serious like sexual assault?"

"I don't know, Sir."

"You don't know, or there isn't any reason why he would ever confide in you?"

"I don't know, Sir, you are confusing me."

"Did anyone ask you to engage in a conversation with Corporal Johnson about the reasons why he was in the brig?"

"No, Sir, it's just natural to ask a guy why he's there. We all do that."

"And no one told you to specifically speak to Johnson about these things?"

"No, Sir."

"You are a Caucasian, Private Bernard. Corporal Johnson is a Negro who has a history of not trusting white people. Why would he admit something as serious as this to you?"

"Objection, calls for a conclusion," Brendon said.

"Sustained," Judge Malone replied, knowing that it didn't make a bit of difference since Sean had made his point for the jury and he could reinforce it later in argument. Sean glanced at his watch and wondered how much longer he could drag out his cross-examination of the witness. He decided to wing it a bit longer with the hostile witness, and if Jack hadn't returned when he ran out of questions, he would ask for a brief recess.

After continuing for a few more minutes with some additional, but mostly desultory questions directed to Private Bernard's background which might affect the witness' credibility, Jack appeared in the back of the courtroom and headed towards counsel table. Sean asked for a minute to talk to his co-counsel.

"Find out anything?" Sean asked with some urgency.

"I sure did," Jack replied enthusiastically. "First off, Ed found out that Bernard has been visited several times by Staff Sergeant Williams, the big M.P. who kicked the hell out of Johnson at Lake O'Neill the night he was apprehended. Secondly, I nosed around the brig and the visitor's log shows Williams visited Bernard six times in the last month, each time getting him alone in an interrogation room. Don't know what he was after, but obviously he has been able to convince him of something. That's all I could get other than Bernard's record with the Corps is really fucked up. He's facing an undesirable discharge when he clears the brig."

"This may be just enough, Jack. Let's give it a try." Sean said this as he turned to Judge Malone advising he was ready to resume his cross-examination.

"Private Bernard, do you know a Staff Sergeant Williams, a military policeman?"

"I don't recognize the name, Sir."

"That's amazing, Private, since Staff Sergeant Williams visited you six times in the brig over the past month. Does this refresh your recollection. I have him standing by to testify if that will help."

Brendon's head jerked up when Sean said this and he was about to object figuring Sean was bluffing when Bernard answered, "Oh yeah, that Sergeant Williams.

Yeah, I remember now."

"Then you do remember that Sergeant Williams visited you six times in the brig over the past month?"

"Yes, Sir."

"Why did he do that?"

"Objection," Brendon interjected, "this is irrelevant. Anything that may have transpired is hearsay."

"Not true your Honor, this goes to the bias and prejudice of the witness. Anything that transpired would not be offered for the truth of the matter, but to show the state of mind of the witness, past and present," Sean retorted.

"I will overrule the objection at this time, but tread carefully, counselor, you are on dangerous ground," Judge Malone cautioned.

"Yes, Sir. Private Bernard why did Sergeant Williams visit you six times in the brig?"

"We were friends, that's all. Nothing special, just wanted to talk?"

"Do you expect this court to believe a military policeman was a friend of a Marine with a record like yours?"

"Objection, argumentative," Brendon asserted.

"Sustained," Judge Malone replied. "Your point is made, Mr. O'Ryan."

Sean knew that his point was well made, but to ice it he took a gamble with the next question. "Private Bernard isn't it true that Sergeant Williams put you up to testifying against Corporal Johnson, and told you to concoct a story about a so-called admission that he had intercourse with Miss Long?"

"Objection," Brendon screamed.

"Overruled," Judge Malone said waiving off Major Bryant's insistence.

"Answer the question, Private," Sean admonished.

"No. No. We were just friends, and he was just visiting. I didn't have to make anything up. We were just visiting, that's all. Just visiting, honest."

The point was reinforced. Bernard was a liar. Sean knew it, and hoped everyone else in the courtroom knew it as well. "No further questions," he said with disgust in his voice for emphasis.

Brendon Bryant rose and said, "Just on more question on re-direct. Private Bernard, when did Corporal Johnson say these things to you about having had sex with Miss Long?"

"I don't remember exactly, Sir, but it was while we were in the same cell. Maybe that was six seven weeks ago."

"Nothing further, your Honor," Brendon announced.

Sean had made his point and decided not to give Private Bernard room to rehabilitate himself. If he was lying about Johnson, it would be consistent to extend the lie as he just did by implication that the alleged damning admissions were made early on rather than as a result of any recent prodding by Sergeant Williams. Sean weighed the potential for calling Williams as a witness, but concluded that the cloud hanging over Private Bernard's testimony, and its patent falsity would not be dispelled by more lies by Sergeant Williams. Also Judge Malone probably would not allow surrebuttal. Sean simply announced, "No re-cross, Sir," and sat down.

"Any other rebuttal evidence, Major Bryant?" Colonel Malone asked.

"No, Sir, the Government rests."

"I will not entertain surrebuttal by the defense. Both sides have rested, and I think this is the best time to take care of some matters that must be conducted outside of the presence of the members. Colonel Orlowski, I will please ask the members to break for lunch at this point and not return until 1300 this afternoon."

Colonel Malone was the model of courtesy even though he didn't have to be, since "Cold Steel" Orlowski couldn't object anyway. But the judge was that kind of gentleman. It made Sean think of old *Judge Numbnuts* in the L.A. Municipal Court who could take serious lessons from Judge Malone on how to be a real judge. It also made him wonder if *Numbnuts* had moved his truck as yet or if he was still double-parked. After the members left, Sean said, "I have a motion pending, Colonel, and I wish to make an additional motion. But I would first ask if you have made a decision on my pending motion you took under advisement. This was the motion to dismiss Charge II, the homicide charge?"

"I have, Mr. O'Ryan, and although I have serious reservation about the testimony of Thomas Panos, I have no choice except to deny your motion. The testimony, no matter how questionable it may be, does furnish sufficient evidence on the element of Corporal Johnson's possible participation in the fight that occurred on that night. Thus, it is for the court-martial members acting as a jury of fact finders to decide whether or not they are convinced beyond a reasonable doubt that Johnson did take part, and, if so, to what extent," Colonel Malone advised.

"Do you find a lesser included offense in this instance, that is, the offense of battery, your Honor?" Sean inquired.

"I suspect that will depend on the next motion I anticipate you now will be offering, which undoubtedly is for a finding of not guilty as to the rape offense. If Johnson prevails on that charge, then he cannot be an accomplice to felony murder. Furthermore, if the jury believes he actually only struck David Hall in the jaw and delivered no lethal blows to the deceased, then the only possible offense he could be guilty of would be simple battery," Judge Malone replied. "I do not see a sufficient basis for a finding of murder, or any lesser degree of homicide arising out of that one punch to the jaw if that's all there was. This is up to the Board, however, and thus unless the Board finds that Corporal Johnson delivered a lethal blow, or was also involved in the rape, which is the felony out of which the homicide flowed, there isn't sufficient evidence of homicide. To cover the possible offenses, however, I will instruct the Board as to the rape homicide connection, also as to the lethal blow requirement even without a rape connection, and finally simple battery."

"In that event, Sir, I will present my second motion. As you predicted, it is a motion for a finding of not guilty as to the rape charge," Sean advised. He then added, "There is no evidence of penetration in this instance, and that is an indispensable element to the crime of forcible rape. By the alleged victim's own testimony, no penetration was established. I realize the Government will contend that the circumstantial evidence is sufficient to send the matter to the jury to determine if the offense occurred and if Johnson was the perpetrator. I could understand that argument in a murder case where, even though the body is not found, the reasonable inference to be drawn from the direct evidence is that the missing person has been done in. In this case, however, there is no such reasonable inference to be drawn out of an act of rape in spite of opportunity. The circumstances were concurred in by both witnesses, but Corporal Johnson negated any inferences to be drawn of a consummation of the act. Mere opportunity and even potential inclination are not evidence of consummation," Sean argued.

"Major Bryant, your views?" Judge Malone asked.

"I think there is enough evidence to give this to the jury, Sir. Corporal Johnson freely admitted he thought about penetrating Miss Long, but then alleges he changed his mind. Contrary to Mr. O'Ryan,'s opinion, I think reasonable inferences can be drawn from the direct evidence of opportunity and inclination," Bryant reclamored. "In addition there is the admission that Johnson made to Private Bernard that he actually had intercourse with Miss Long, with no suggestion that this was consensual. I admit Private Bernard's credibility was sorely tested by Mr. O'Ryan, but that still leaves a fact question for the jury."

"I would agree with Major Bryant," Sean replied, "but for the fact that there is no evidence, direct or circumstantial, other than Private Bernard's patent lie, to support the suggestion that because Johnson may have thought about it, he actually did penetrate Miss Long. In truth, there is not one shred of direct evidence to show that a penetration of Chrissy Long was ever accomplished by Lee Johnson. I submit that the missing element cannot be provided by circumstantial inferences. This is not an issue to be presented for the jury to determine beyond a reasonable doubt."

Judge Malone paused for a full minute and then said, "I can see the reasonableness of your argument, Mr. O'Ryan, but I can also see a reasonable argument by the Government in this instance. I am not persuaded as a matter of law that reasonable inferences cannot be drawn from the facts surrounding the confrontation between Miss Long and Corporal Johnson which would allow the Board members to conclude that penetration by Corporal Johnson was accomplished that night. Also, of course, there is the testimony of Private Bernard. While his credibility was attacked, and is suspect at best, it is still up to the members to determine if they believe him or not. I am inclined to view the evidence as going either way and although there is an admitted lack of knowledge by the victim as to penetration, this is not compelling. Thus, the circumstantial evidence and the reasonable inferences to be drawn by the fact of opportunity and perhaps inclination, are for the jury to determine."

Judge Malone paused and rubbed his eyes, as if trying to see the whole picture better. He then stated, "Under the circumstances I find as a matter of law that the Government has produced sufficient circumstantial evidence on the indispensable element of penetration with respect to Charge I as laid against Corporal Johnson. Your motion for a finding of not guilty on Charge I is denied."

"Is there anything else, gentlemen? I intend to give specific instructions along with the usual ones in these cases, including reasonable doubt, the elements of the offenses, on the lesser included offenses, the credibility of witnesses, discussion and voting procedures on the findings, and the like. If there are any additional ones you desire, or if you think I have missed any, please let me know."

The judge then closed, "If there is nothing else, we will reconvene at 1300 for closing arguments and instructions. I commend all counsel for the fine manner in which you have deported yourselves to this point, and I expect you will continue to do the same to the end of trial. That's all gentlemen."

The intended instructions were acceptable but Sean had lost what he hoped would be a victory on the rape charge without going to the jury. With that defeat he had a tough road to travel in closing argument to convince the jury that Johnson did not consummate an act of intercourse with Chrissy Long on that fateful night. He only had one crack at it, while the Government had two, in both opening and closing arguments. Sean was convinced that Johnson did not rape the vulnerable young woman. He realized he might never know with absolute certainty if Johnson was innocent, but he felt he could argue his innocence in good conscience.

Chrissy Long would never know either. Everything now was up to the jury. Whatever the result, Sean hoped that, in spite of the terrible ordeal this fragile young woman was subjected to on the night in question and then having to relive the terror in the courtroom, some day she would understand that the criminal justice system is designed to protect and not merely to accuse and convict.

CHAPTER 26

Thursday afternoon, October 15, 1964

The trial reconvened at 1305 hours and the members of the Board turned their attention to counsel. No one smiled. Every face reflected deliberate reserve. A poker game was being played for mortal stakes. Sean had seen this calculated lack of expression on the face of military juries before, as though some display of warmth or compassion was against regulations. He attributed this to the regimented military bearing drummed into Marines since 1775, and noted how it contrasted with civilian juries who are more free with facial expression and body language, sometimes favorable, sometimes not. True to form, the members of "Cold Steel" Orlowski's court-martial board were not reflecting friendly dispositions.

Major Brendon Bryant delivered his summation and opening argument, doing a fine job. He went over the case of each defendant in complete detail, fleshing out the testimony and drawing inferences from all of the evidence to demonstrate that Anthony Fennelli, Thomas Panos and Rick Cox had raped Chrissy Long. He further illustrated how each of them in the course of committing that outrageous felony, had participated in a brutal beating of her fiancé resulting in his death, which conduct constituted felony murder.

Brendon then also hammered home the guilt of Anthony Fennelli on the two additional charges of assault with a deadly weapon and assault with intent to inflict grievous bodily harm that had been lodged against him alone and not the other three defendants.

Brendon had to walk a finer liner with Lee Johnson on the rape and murder charges, however, since he only had circumstantial evidence on the rape charge and couldn't directly tie Johnson to a rape connection with the murder. But he pounded hard on the one punch Panos claimed he saw Johnson deliver. Brendon suggested this was a lethal blow that, among others, had contributed to David Hall's death. It was a good try, but Sean didn't believe the members were going to buy the suggestion that Johnson - with a broken hand - had administered a lethal blow, even if they believed Panos's testimony that Johnson had struck David Hall once in the jaw. Brendon had to persuade the jury that Lee had raped Chrissy and therefore his striking of David Hall, even if not lethal, was in concert with the other rapists and was the natural concomitant of the vicious sexual assault which would make Johnson guilty of felony murder as well as rape. A form of guilt by association in the law.

Brendon argued, "The Government concedes that Miss Long cannot recall at this time the precise penetration of her vagina, but the members, nonetheless, may draw the logical inferences from all of the circumstances that clearly reflect not only opportunity but inclination on the part of Corporal Johnson to violate this young woman victim. I submit that his denials defy credulity. Each member of the Board can reasonably conclude, in good conscience, that there had to be a nonconsensual penetration of Miss Long by Corporal Johnson, and he is guilty of rape along with the other three defendants. By his own admission, he had been victimized by two other blond, blue eyed, white women. Is it likely that this drunken Marine, filled with rancor and distrust of someone of that description and sexually aroused by the proximity of this beautiful, vulnerable victim, would refrain from the ultimate act of revenge and violation?"

Brendon paused and then added, "Furthermore, we have the testimony of Private Bernard concerning Corporal Johnson's admission that penetration occurred. In the law such voluntary statement is admissible into evidence as an admission against penal interest. Defense counsel will no doubt suggest that Private Bernard constructed his testimony out of whole cloth for some ulterior motive. But that is pure speculation. What is more likely is that Corporal Johnson, like most other individuals who are confined in the brig, was more than willing to discuss, and yes, even brag about his conduct never considering that such assertions could be used against him."

Brendon paused again for effect letting the jury digest these considerations, and then continued, "I ask you, which person has more reason to fabricate in this instance? Private Bernard? Or Corporal Johnson? Was Corporal Johnson lying when he admitted to Private Bernard that he had intercourse with Miss Long? Was this just some sort of macho braggadocio, or was it the truth being spewed out by a vengeful man who had been allegedly wronged by two other blond, blue eyed, young women? Or was Private Bernard lying for reasons defense counsel wants you to infer? I ask you, who has the greater stake in the outcome of this trial, and therefore, a greater motive to deceive the court? Rape is a terrible crime, and most of us are not able to put ourselves into the minds of rapists because we don't live with their anger and hate. It is hard to visualize how any man can commit this kind of violation. The act of sexual intercourse is designed in its essence to be an inherently beautiful mode of intimate and loving communication. So why do rapists resort to it as an expression of violence? We cannot reduce the outrage of the act through mitigating terms like date rape and suggest that the act is merely a logical extension of a sexual relationship that, deep down, is wanted by women and is expected by men. We also cannot excuse the violence of the act by pretending that women are no longer vulnerable and that they actually invite sexual advances by provocative dress and conduct. Rape is more than a strong sexual response to stimuli. It is predicated not only on passion, but also on hate and anger. These two words categorize Corporal Lee Johnson."

Brendon looked firmly at each member of the jury before continuing. "Rapists have been found to have a high degree of anger, resentment, and an abysmally low tolerance for frustration. More often than not they are hostile towards women and are particularly hostile against those who trigger their malevolence through appearance or status. With Jack the Ripper it was prostitutes. With Corporal Johnson, I submit, it was young, white, blond, blue eyed women. Whether the rapist violates out of anger, or because he is on a power trip, or because he is sadistic and not only rapes, but tortures and kills, the act is clearly not sexual passion, but rather springs out of hate. In fact, the more vulnerable the victim, the more likely the victimization. Corporal Johnson is a man admittedly filled with hate and frustration. Chrissy Long is as vulnerable a victim as one could find. Is it likely that a violation of this vulnerable victim by Corporal Johnson did not occur? I submit, gentlemen, that Corporal Johnson's disclaimers ring hollow. A finding of penetration is justified from the reasonable inferences to be drawn from all of the evidence before you. Corporal Johnson is guilty of both the rape of Miss Long and of the murder of her fiancé, David Hall, and I ask that you so find."

Brendon had gone into great detail in his opening summation just in case any or all of the defense counsel chose to waive argument. That would have foreclosed further closing argument on the Government's part, so Brendon took no chances. None of the defense counsel waived argument, however, and each of the other three counsel who preceded Sean in presenting closing argument made a valiant stab at convincing the jury of lesser responsibility, or even no culpability on the part of their respective clients.

Frank Chase started his summation and gagged on his words as he argued for acquittal of Thomas Panos. Nevertheless, he made a moral effort to argue the evidence as presented and not make personal judgments about which he had no proof. He thought his client was a liar, but he couldn't say so. It was up to the jury to decide if that were the case. Frank exhibited great integrity in his summation.

Dan Richards went next but he faced an impossible task in trying to present anything exculpatory on behalf of Anthony Fennelli who sat arrogantly and contemptuously throughout Dan's argument as if realizing there was no hope, and not giving a damn. He was a hard case and nothing about this trial was going to change that. The Marine Corps, like any other service, takes its members where it finds them. Some youngsters can be helped, some can't, but either way they bring with them what they learned at home and on the street. If they are amoral inside, it usually doesn't always surface during the highly structured environment of boot camp, but later with less restrictions they revert to character. Others, conversely, benefit from the rigors of Marine Corps discipline and turn their lives around while rejecting street lessons. Not everyone makes it, but the Corps is made up of some one hundred ninety thousand members and the vast majority are fine men and women. Unfortunately, Fennelli was one of the exceptions and sooner or later he was bound to return to form and follow his criminal patterns. That time arrived at a tragic moment for Chrissy and David. Thomas Panos, on the other hand, was an insecure manipulator and a pathological liar. While it is unlikely he would have orchestrated a vicious rape and fatal beating on his own, he was easily moved to take advantage of the situation instigated by Fennelli, particularly when the victims were rendered helpless.

On the flip side Rick Cox was a follower with limited intelligence, and Dusty Burns emphasized this in his argument to the jury, noting that over considerable protest by the service chiefs, the military services had been required to recruit a number of individuals who would not ordinarily qualify. It is one of the problems associated with using the military as a social agency. A disproportionate number of major offenses, particularly crimes of violence, were committed by members of this lesser qualified group. Dusty closed with a solid statement on a lack of mens rea, that is, a lack of a guilty mind on behalf of his client, Private Cox. In spite of Dusty's fine efforts, Sean didn't think he would succeed, but it was all Dusty had going for his client and he flashed brilliantly in the struggle.

When Sean's turn came, he wasn't going to leave Thomas Panos's status as a lying son of a bitch to chance, and he launched a full broadside against Panos in his closing argument. Sean rose and, rather than use the lectern, he moved directly in front of the jury and addressed them without notes. "Isn't it amazing, gentlemen, that Corporal Panos was the only one who uttered even one syllable in this courtroom about Corporal Johnson supposedly running out and striking David Hall. If anyone believes that, I respectfully suggest he has been watching and hearing a different Thomas Panos than appeared in this hall of justice."

Sean was hoping to see some change of expression on the members as he said this, but they remained impassive as he continued. "Not only does such allegation of misconduct on Lee Johnson's part defy belief, but it is totally illogical. Why would he run out from his place of repose - in a drunken condition - and help an avowed enemy? The answer to that is obvious. He wouldn't. And there is another question that also can be answered, and that is why would Thomas Panos make such a grossly false and illogical statement? I submit it was because he too had an axe to grind with my client because he got knocked on his backside a few days earlier by that very man. He admitted his long standing dislike of Corporal Johnson, which dislike was exacerbated by a physical confrontation in which Panos was the loser."

"Furthermore," Sean added, "Corporal Johnson had a seriously broken hand on the night of September 3rd, which incidentally came from punching Panos at their earlier confrontation. The question then is not only why would he run out and hit David Hall with that hand, but how could he? It challenges both logic and belief. I respectfully submit that Thomas Panos is falsely accusing Lee Johnson and is strongly motivated to do so to cover his own tail. This testimony was orchestrated entirely to make Corporal Johnson an accomplice to the assault and ultimate death of Midshipman Hall and then segue that absurd allegation into the rape of Miss Long in order to convince you that the blood type found in the third sample of semen, which blood type Panos and Johnson share in common, could only have come from Johnson."

Sean rested for a moment and looked each member of the jury in the eyes, and then said firmly, "The patent attempt by Thomas Panos to brand Corporal Johnson as an aggressor in this instance is reprehensible. I respectfully ask the members to pierce Thomas Panos's veil of fiction and acquit Corporal Johnson of any involvement with Midshipman Hall on that tragic night." Sean saw a slight shift in body language of three jurors as he pressed on.

"I turn now, gentlemen, to the charge of rape as it has been alleged against Corporal Johnson. I do not make light of this charge, and I am genuinely saddened by the terrible and brutal crimes that were committed against Miss Long who is a true victim. There is no question that she was totally innocent of anything on that night of terror and was caught up in a vicious assault against her person and the death of her loved one simply because she was in the wrong place at the wrong time. A place, incidentally, she had every right to be and had every right to expect not to be dangerous. There is no excusing the conduct visited upon her and David Hall." Sean said this as sincerely as he could because it was what he felt. He hoped the jury understood he was not just giving lip service to these feelings.

"The question then is whether or not Corporal Johnson was a participant in any of that conduct. I assure you, he was not. I don't deny he thought about having intercourse with Miss Long when he found her on top of him. I admit he had been nursing frustration arising out of bitter experiences with a pair of blond, blue eyed, white women. The prosecutor proposes that this was motive for rape. That's his opinion, but it is not a hard fact, and it should be viewed in that light. I ask each of you to consider this. Do you act out every frustration in a pattern of violent revenge? When you make judgments about the conduct and credibility of Corporal Johnson, I ask that you make them on the sound basis of your own life experience.

You do not leave the sum of your experience in the courtroom when you retire to deliberate in this case. You take everything you are and everything you know with you."

Sean paused for a moment and then resumed, "I urge you as a matter of common sense to address the question of whether or not Corporal Johnson imposed himself on Chrissy Long. Corporal Johnson may have been disappointed by a brace of women who happen to bear common physical characteristics, but does that mean he would respond violently against each and every woman who shared those same features?"

Sean paused to let that thought germinate with the jury. He then continued, "In addition, you heard from two principal witnesses on the charge of rape as levied against Corporal Johnson. You heard from Chrissy Long, and you heard from Lee Johnson. I ask you to recall carefully that neither witness testified to an actual act of penetration, an essential element of rape. Without penetration, however slight, there is no rape; there is no forcible taking of this young woman against her will. Miss Long says she thinks it happened from the circumstances. That's what Major Bryant wants you to believe. But Miss Long admits she has no knowledge that it did. And not one word was ever produced in this courtroom by anyone that it had occurred other than Private Bernard whose credibility is so lacking he is completely unworthy of belief. But Major Bryant wants you to believe Private Bernard, and he asks who is more likely to lie in this instance. Well, we all saw Private Bernard as he testified. We all were able to observe his demeanor when he said his so-called friend, Staff Sergeant Williams, paid him six friendly visits in the brig," Sean said with undisguised satire.

He then delayed for a moment and looked squarely at each member of the jury before going on. "This is the very same Staff Sergeant Williams who threatened HM2 Andrews so that he would not put Corporal Johnson's blood alcohol readings into his health record. The same Staff Sergeant Williams who took it upon himself to beat the hell out of Corporal Johnson on the night of his arrest and is now dating Corporal Johnson's ex-girlfriend. I ask you, gentlemen, who has a self-serving stake in the outcome of this case if it isn't Staff Sergeant Williams and his stooge, Private Bernard, who is willing to sell his soul to save his hide?"

Sean paused for dramatic effect and paced slowly before the jury. Then he turned gesturing with his right hand extended, palm upward. "Conversely, compare the demeanor of Corporal Johnson as he made a sincere statement in this courtroom, under oath, that there had been no penetration. Now you might think what would you expect someone accused of rape to say? In answer to that I suggest that if he had something to hide, he would have hidden behind circumstances far more favorable than simple denial. Corporal Johnson was obviously drunk and had been sleeping or passed out. How easy it would have been to just deny any awareness of the activity of that night, not only the fatal beating of Midshipman Hall, but even the very presence of Miss Long. His blood alcohol, taken several hours after his last drink, was .18%. That was a falling blood alcohol. How easy it would have been to hide behind his drunken stupor. But he didn't. He was forthright. He recalled the events, even though drunk. We all know this can be, at least those of us who have been there."

Sean said this watching for reaction from the members. He was not disappointed as he noticed a sign of recognition of a shared experience. No one smiled, but four members came close to a change in their poker expressions. Sean pressed the point. "Corporal Johnson made no pretense about his initial reaction when the beautiful, sweet smelling victim was thrust upon him. He thought about sex. What man wouldn't? But Lee Johnson set aside that thought when he realized the young women had been badly hurt. This is a reflection of his humanity. Other than being falsely accused of sexual misconduct as a juvenile by a girl of outrageous reputation for group sex, there is not one thing in Lee Johnson's record that reflects a propensity for violence towards women. Or men either for that matter."

Sean once again looked squarely at each member of the jury as he said this for effect. He knew that each of those Marines knew that young Marines mix it up with regularity, and he added, "Certainly Marines getting into fights now and then is not to suggest that somehow Corporal Johnson is violence disposed, particularly against helpless women. Corporal Johnson isn't that kind of man, but he is an honest man. He didn't hide behind any convenient facade of drunkenness and unawareness. He came before you and admitted his recall of the evening and his genuine concern for Chrissy Long when he realized she had been brutalized. He may be a tough kid, whose toughness has been honed by the loss of his father as young boy and his being disappointed in some relationships, but he is a feeling and caring person, and his true character manifested itself when he realized the abuse Chrissy had already suffered.

"You have heard from this man, the only witness to testify directly, and I respectfully submit, truthfully, as to the essential element of penetration. Major Bryant asks you to take Corporal Johnson's own testimony - that he thought about sticking his erect penis into Miss Long - as an admission worthy of belief, but at the same time reject anything else he says. In short, the prosecutor asks you to believe Johnson when he damns himself, but then doubt him when he denies any ultimate, wrongful, conduct. How convenient. I respectfully submit, gentlemen, that Lee Johnson is a consistent truth teller, particularly because he didn't have to tell you anything. He could have ducked behind a claim of unawareness. He didn't have to damn himself with admissions of a natural inclination to avail himself of Chrissy Long. That speaks volumes. He isn't being just half truthful. It wouldn't make sense."

Sean paused once more, and fixed his eyes on Colonel Orlowski as if to cue the entire jury, "I ask you to assess the testimony from a common sense perspective. Why would Lee Johnson say one thing that could hurt him and then have to lie about the rest to exculpate himself from his own words? He honestly admitted what he knew. That is the only direct evidence of record on the very critical and essential element of penetration. All the rest is circumstantial. Such evidence does not outweigh the direct. Lee Johnson has been a good Marine. He is worthy of belief. Chrissy Long is a beautiful woman who was terribly harmed. She too is worthy of belief, particularly when she says she doesn't know what happened. This lovely woman was violently abused on that night of terror and I feel deeply for her. But convicting a man who is innocent of the violence inflicted on her doesn't cure anything. Gentlemen, I respectfully ask, and even more, because he has told you the truth, I beg you to confirm that Lee Johnson is that innocent man. Thank you."

Brendon closed with a restatement of the Government's position as to each defendant and their complicity. He pounded away once again on the circumstantial evidence he felt justified a finding of rape against Lee Johnson, but he had to walk a finer line on the homicide charge because the evidence was not credible. He did make a run at it, however, and suggested that the jury could believe Thomas Panos in one instance, that is, as to what he said about Johnson, but at the same time reject any notion that Panos is a consistent truth-teller in the rest of this matter. And he urged the jury to believe Panos about Johnson even though refusing to believe him when Panos denied personal participation in the assault and death of David Hall and the rape of Chrissy.

Thank you Brendon, Sean thought, *I couldn't have said it better. There is no way the jury is going to bifurcate their acceptance or rejection of the stories of an obvious loser like Panos. Either he is a consistent truth-teller or a consistent liar. No way he is a little of each.*

After Brendon finished, Judge Malone instructed the members as to their duties, the elements of the offenses, and a host of other matters usual to criminal trial, and then he requested the members to withdraw to the jury room and commence deliberations. Time: 1735 hours. Date: Thursday, October 15, 1964. It was all over except the waiting. The members deliberated for four hours, and then adjourned for the night to return the next morning for further deliberation.

Sean spent a restless night at the *Miramar*. The only thing harder than trying a criminal case is the agonizing wait for the jury's verdict. Gratefully there were no maudlin messages from Susan to make his life more miserable and he managed to get a little sleep. Very little.

CHAPTER 27

Friday, October 16, 1964

The jury resumed deliberations at 0800, and finished at 1235 hours at which time they sent for the judge and counsel announcing they had reached their findings. Colonel Malone, all counsel, and the four defendants were assembled in the courtroom at 1300 hours. The court was called to order.

"For the record," Judge Malone asked, "has the Board arrived at findings in accordance with my instructions, Colonel Orlowski?"

"Yes, we have," Cold Steel announced as somber as ever.

"Would you please hand them to the bailiff so I can review them for proper order before you read them for the record." After reviewing the findings, Judge Malone returned them to Colonel Orlowski and announced, "The defendants will rise and face the Court-martial members."

The wonderful old courtroom seemed terribly grim at that moment. Sean could see the packed spectator section filled with eager faces. None of the Board members appeared any different than they did when the trial first started. Usually, when there is only one defendant, the attorneys get a feel for the verdict by reading the expressions and body language of the jurors. But not in this case. There were four defendants and the military presence was overwhelming. And the usual brief interim between Judge Malone ordering the defendants to stand at attention and face the members as the President of the Court-martial prepared to announce the verdicts seemed like a lifetime. "Cold Steel" Orlowski stood up, looking every inch the coldness his nickname suggested. The other members of the jury remained impassive. Sean didn't want to believe this had anything to do with Johnson, but rather was directed at the other three defendants, but then he had to admit that, as the jury is about to report its verdict, wishful thinking is common in a trial lawyer's life. As Colonel Orlowski began the litany of the jury's findings, Sean glanced at Jack Coleman and Lee Johnson and saw the same expressions of serious concern he was feeling. *Had I done enough? What more could I have done?* Sean silently asked.

"With respect to Lance Corporal Anthony Fennelli," Colonel Orlowski intoned, "the Board finds as to Charge I and the specification thereunder alleging the crime of forcible rape, Guilty. As to Charge II and the specification thereunder alleging the crime of felony murder, Guilty."

Colonel Orlowski then addressed the additional two charges of aggravated battery lodged *solely* against Fennelli. "As to Charge III and the specification hereunder alleging the crime of assault with a deadly weapon, Guilty. As to

Charge IV and the specification there under alleging the crime of assault with intent to inflict grievous bodily harm, Guilty."

The President of the Court then turned to Lance Corporal Thomas Panos and Private First Class Rick Cox, each in order, pronouncing findings of guilty as to each with respect to the charges of forcible rape and felony murder.

He then turned to Johnson and Sean's heart was pounding so hard he thought it could be heard by the entire assembly. Without changing expression, even the slightest, Colonel Orlowski looking very somber and stern advised in a strong voice, "Corporal Lee Johnson, with respect to Charge I and the specification there under alleging the crime of forcible rape, the Board finds you, Not Guilty. As to Charge II and the specification there under alleging the crime of felony murder, the Board finds you, Not Guilty, and Not Guilty of any lesser included offenses."

A murmur could be heard from the spectators. Sean wasn't certain whether it expressed *atta boys* or disappointment. But he didn't care. Lee Johnson let out a long sigh as if he had been holding his breath from the time he rose to hear the verdict. It was a sigh of relief, and it looked as though Johnson was going to break down, but he stood tall. He had been acquitted of all charges. Sean felt a sense of genuine satisfaction although this victory had cost him a great relationship with Susan Sullivan. It made a big difference in his personal exultation. But he had done his job and there was joy in fighting the good fight.

Colonel Malone thanked the members and advised that the court would break for lunch, and upon reconvening move into the sentencing phase of the trial, but Lee Johnson was excused from further participation. He had been found not guilty and the sentencing aspects had no bearing on him. He was a free man. They took Johnson directly to Jack's office to say goodbye, and wish him well. He would have to go back to the brig to be formally released, but that would be accomplished by this afternoon so he could be on liberty by tonight, but staying sober.

Lee thanked Jack with a firm handshake as he apologized for any lack of military courtesy towards the Captain. He then turned to Sean. With a genuine smile he said, "I don't know how to also thank you, Major O'Ryan. I'm not real good at this, but I hope you know I appreciate everything you did for me." He then extended his hand and Sean got the feeling that for the first time in a long time, Lee Johnson trusted a white man. Sean should have simply said "You're welcome" and left it there but he couldn't resist that last unanswered question. "Just one thing, Lee. Were we right about you? The reason I ask this, now that it's all over, is because what I did for you, I did because I believed in you. I know Captain Coleman did too."

Johnson looked at Sean and stopped smiling. Repressing a rising anger he stared at Sean for a long moment and then said, "You'll never know for sure, will you, chuck dude? You *want to believe* I didn't do the broad. You want to believe I don't think that's what white bitches are for. The problem is there's a big difference between believing and *wanting to believe*. So I'll let you figure it out. Do you believe me as you say you do? Or do you just *want to believe*." With that Johnson turned to walk away.

"Fair enough, Lee. Fair enough," Sean answered softly. "Only one thing you ought to know, and that is: I went to the wall in this case because I do believe you are innocent, and not just that I wanted to believe in you. But this wasn't only for you alone. It was also for a little guy named Willie Earle."

Johnson stopped and with a quizzical look asked, "Willie Earle? Who the fuck is Willie Earle?"

"Someone you never knew, but he died for you in South Carolina back in 1947. Don't ever forget that."

"Shit, Major, sometimes I don't think I understand you at all. Shit, Major," Johnson said, smiling on his way out the door.

"Don't sweat it," Sean called, "you aren't alone."

After Johnson left, Sean paid his respects to Colonel Hanley and thanked him for his hospitality. The Colonel said he looked forward to seeing Sean again; a compliment not extended to every civilian counsel. Then Sean and Jack drove over to the O'Club for lunch and chatted about everything except the case. Trial post-mortems are not high on the list of priorities of litigators. Around three, Sean dropped Jack at Base Legal and shook his hand thanking him for all his fine help. "Hope we can do it again, Jack. It is a genuine privilege to work with you," Sean said warmly. "And by the way, I not only believed in our client, but I am convinced he was innocent in every respect."

"I'm with you on that Sean, and it's been a real pleasure going to the wall for Johnson with you. Look forward to seeing you again one of these days."

Sean waved as he drove off and then went straight over to Sergeant Major Ed Tabor's regiment. Ed said he wasn't surprised at the outcome. "How come you didn't say anything before this?" Sean asked.

"I didn't want to jinx your case," Ed answered, "but I felt confident you would win. I know your determination."

"I appreciate the confidence, Ed, but frankly if I exude any of my own, I learned it from you at the Chosin Reservoir a long time ago. You taught me the will to win and the will to survive." Sean paused for a moment, then asked, "So what's the plan for the weekend? I've been out of the social scene for a while. It's been long time for a lot of things. I'm way overdue."

"Bobby Stein called this morning," Ed replied. "He hasn't been able to reach you, so he asked me to pass along an invitation to spend the weekend on his boat. He suggested cruising over to Catalina tonight and thought we might want to bring along a couple of guests. Female types, of course. His boat sleeps eight quite comfortably, and we would only number six. What do you say?"

"Sounds great," Sean replied enthusiastically, "only one question. Who do you suggest our guests should be at this eleventh hour?"

"I anticipated that, old buddy, and took the liberty of calling Gerry and Joy, who happily accepted the invitation."

"Damn, Ed, you are a piece of work. Better be careful, you know what they call guys who procure women."

"I'll risk it," Ed said laughing. "How about if I meet you at Gerry and Joy's at eight. Bobby is expecting us around nine."

"You're on. See you at eight," Sean replied, happy to note he wouldn't be spending a lonely weekend in his apartment. The let down that follows the high after a big win hadn't set in, but Sean knew it would by the time he hit L.A. He didn't want to dwell on what this case cost him emotionally. The evening traffic was a nightmare and it took over three hours to make it to the Marina. He felt tired and his emotional high had crashed an hour earlier. Gratefully the Santa Ana condition had hung around and the sunset promised to be magnificent. He lugged his bags off the elevator and fumbled for the key to his apartment. He got the fit and pushed the door open when the phone rang. Sean caught it on the fourth ring. "Sean? It's Susan. I called to say I'd heard about the outcome. I'm not calling to start an argument or be cute. I wasn't surprised you had won."

"I didn't win, Susan. Justice won," Sean said softly.

"I know you believe that," Susan answered evenly. "But I don't know how much was due to your skill, and how much was because of your client's innocence as you claim. I'll always have doubts." Susan paused and Sean said nothing. Then she continued, "I don't think I will ever understand you, especially that part that puts dedication to an ideal above everything else in life. It's difficult to be second to a dream."

Sean started to speak but Susan asked to let her finish. "I probably will set a date to marry Stan, but surprisingly not because of you. I think it is in spite of you, because the worst thing I could do would be to make that decision for any reason other than it is something I must do of my own accord. Maybe it's something I should have done a long time ago instead of losing myself in a lovely affair with you. But I have no regrets about our loving and I am grateful for your help with my decision-making. As for the rest I must admit I don't understand you. And I'll always harbor resentment against your client for what happened to Chrissy, even if he is totally innocent. I can't help it. I suspect you'll understand that part of me better than I can understand that part of you that causes you to march off to your personal wars be they in a strange land or in a courtroom."

"I respect your feelings, Susan. I'm sorry it turned out like this. We had something terrific going, but it couldn't sustain itself on the loving alone. Sooner or later we were going to fall in love or fall apart. The sooner just came before the later, that's all. I hope we can remain friends, okay?"

"I think we can," Susan said a little too sadly, "but I think we need some time apart right now. Then I'll give you a call and we can get together socially with Stan and the gang. Maybe we can get our lives back where they were before that special night at the *Hilton* last May. Which I will never forget."

"Sounds fair enough," Sean answered. "Just one thing I've got to be honest about before you hang up."

"Sure. Okay, what's that?" Susan replied a bit apprehensive.

"I think you are making a very serious mistake marrying Stan. That's all. I just wanted you to know what I thought."

"Thank you, I won't comment on that. But I have a question of my own," Susan replied. "Do you really think we would have fallen in love if we had stayed the way we were?"

"Tough question, Miss Sullivan, but I'll be candid. I think so. In time. I was getting very used to you and missed you terribly when you weren't around. Who knows for sure, but given time, it was more likely than not."

Susan didn't say anything for a moment and Sean remained silent realizing she was weighing his last statement carefully. He wasn't sure if he said it only to test the waters for a possible reunion, but he was certain he meant it as a genuine possibility. The future might hold something for them, but right now it was too indefinite.

"Thank you, Mr. O'Ryan," Susan responded after the pause. "I don't think you would say that just to make me feel good. I appreciate your feelings. I'll keep in touch as best I can. It'll probably be a while. I'm involved in a lot of things right now and, of course, there is the lingering disappointment about your representation of Johnson. It's going to take time. Take care, Quixote."

Susan hung up and Sean went out on the balcony to look at the sea and ships. Surprisingly he didn't feel sad. Maybe he should have, but he thought about other lovely women who had been in his life and he felt comfortable knowing that the time he had with them, however limited, was a precious gift. He recalled Jean with particular clarity and felt the love he would always have for her. "Jean, my dearest, we had such little time together, but it was worth every heartbeat. Better one day with you, than a thousand without," he said softly.

His thoughts then shifted to present reality and he pictured the cruise to Catalina they would be making tonight. Looking forward to the companionship of Ed and Bobby and their beautiful guests gave rise new feelings. He stood on the balcony a few minutes longer savoring the soft beauty of the approaching twilight. The high that winning produces had returned and the prospect of other challenging adventures added to the warm glow as he watched the sun begin its slow descent into the blue-gray waters of the Pacific bringing a new dawn to distant islands.

About the Author

In a long and distinguished career, Michael Patrick Murray has been a trial attorney, both as a prosecutor and defense counsel, as well as a trial judge and appellate judge. In addition, he has enjoyed extensive teaching experience as a law professor at four different law schools.

A Marine Corps veteran of the Korean and Vietnam wars, he knows the military as well as he does the law. Asked what aspect of his experience he enjoys most, Mr. Murray advises, "Added to the genuine pleasure as well as the challenge of writing about the law, it is a close call between studying law, teaching law, and fighting the good fight for truly worthy causes be it in war, or in the courtroom."